The
HIDDEN PLACES

B

of
Lancashire & Cheshire

Including The Isle of Man

Front Cover: The Bridgewater Canal
by
Graham Lewis

Acknowledgements

The Publishers would like to thank the following for their assistance in the production of this book: Elaine, Deborah and Kelly for Administration. Graham and Joanne for Production. Bob, Rick and Sam for Research. Joanna, Gerald and Graham for Writing. Sarah, Les and Graham for Artwork. Julian and Clare. Last, but not least, Simon at Scorpio for the maps.

Printed & Bound By Guernsey Press, Channel Islands.

Copyright M & M Publishing Ltd. 118 Ashley Rd .Cheshire. U.K. WA14 2UN

Foreword

The Hidden Places Series

is an established collection of travel guides which cover the U.K and Ireland in 16 titles.

The aim of the books is to introduce readers to some of the less well known attractions of each area whilst not ignoring the more established ones.

We have included in this book a number of hotels, inns, restaurants, various types of accommodation, historic houses, museums, and general attractions which are to be found in this part of the country, together with historical background information.

There is a map at the beginning of each chapter with line drawings of the places featured, along with a description of the services offered.

We hope that the book prompts you to discover some of the fascinating "Hidden Places" which we found on our journey, and we are sure the places featured would be pleased if you mentioned that our book prompted your visit.

We wish you an enjoyable and safe journey.

THE HIDDEN PLACES
of
LANCASHIRE AND CHESHIRE

CONTENTS

CHAPTER ONE

Greater Manchester

Bramhall Hall

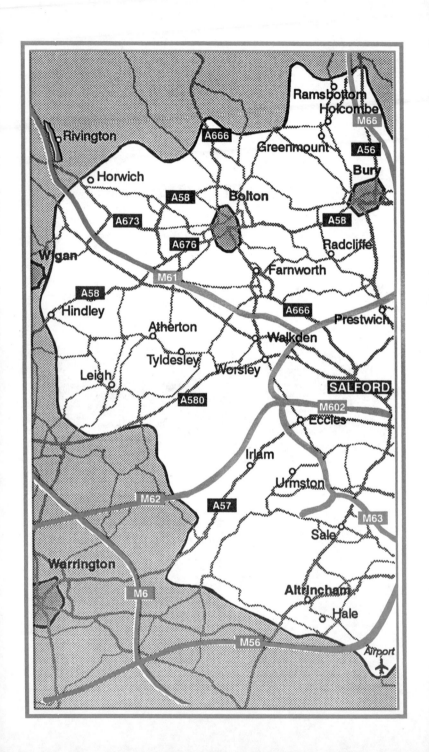

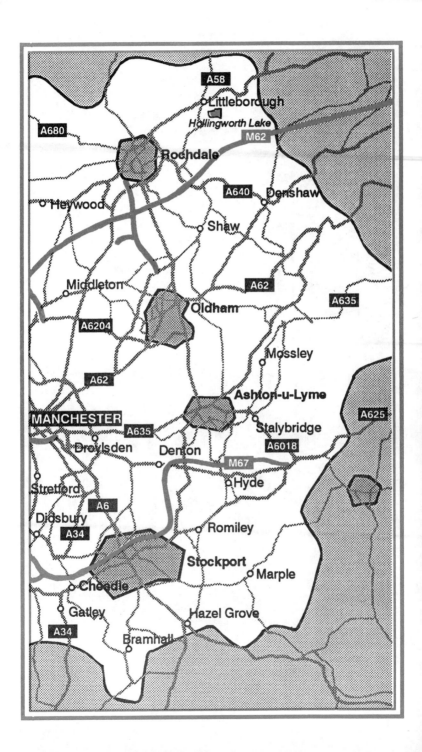

The Cental Library

CHAPTER ONE

Greater Manchester

MANCHESTER. Only a very short time ago, if anyone had suggested taking a short holiday here, they would have been regarded, to say the least, as eccentric. These days, however, Manchester has a thriving tourist industry and is a popular destination.

What has changed? Put simply, Manchester has. The city is cleaner, brighter than it ever was in the past, with purer air, cleaner buildings, green spaces and parks where once was dereliction. It also has a new regard for its extraordinary civic and industrial heritage.

Manchester's history begins in Roman times when a small but important fort was built on the River Irwell, a tributary of the Mersey, where the road between Chester and York began its long ascent through the Pennine hills. During medieval times the town of Manchester grew in the area where the cathedral now stands and the ruined fort, Castle-in-the-field, stood abandoned in what had become a deer park.

The development of **CASTLEFIELD** began in the late 18th century when James Brindley constructed the Bridgewater Canal for the Duke of Bridgewater, to bring coal from his mines at Worsley. Later, in 1804, the Rochdale Canal was opened, connecting Manchester with Yorkshire, and the Castlefield Canal basin developed as the junction of the two.

When trains began to take over from canals, Castlefield was the site for the World's first passenger railway station. Liverpool Road Station was the terminus of the Liverpool and Manchester Railway. It was designed by rail pioneers George Stephenson and his son Robert and was opened by the Duke of Wellington.

Castlefield, just behind Deansgate, close to both Deansgate Station and the G-MEX exhibition centre, is an ideal place to start a visit to the city. The area has been redeveloped in recent years to create an urban heritage park. The trains do not run from Liverpool Street station any more, and the canals are not used for transporting coal, but there is still plenty to see and do. You can step back in time and visit the reconstructed Roman Fort on the site of the ancient fort of Mancunium or simply stroll along the renovated canal paths, perhaps pausing for a drink or a meal at one of the many canalside pubs, cafes and hotels.

Castlefield Information Line 0161 832 4244.

Manchester's most important period of history was the Industrial Revolution of the late 18th century.

It was the mild, moist climate of Lancashire, together with the abundant water of fast flowing Pennine streams that created an ideal environment for the spinning and weaving of cotton. As far back as the

13th century they were weaving cloth around Manchester - mainly wool. The mechanisation of the industry following the invention of Crompton's Mule and Arkwright's Spinning Jenny in the 18th century, led to rapid growth of the industry, not so much in Manchester but in the rapidly growing towns and villages nearby - Bolton, Oldham, Ashton, Bury and Rochdale. Vast imports of raw cotton from the United States which came through the port of Liverpool along the Bridgewater and Leeds-Liverpool canals were balanced by equally significant exports of fabrics to the expanding British Empire.

Manchester became the region's great trading centre, affectionately called Cottonopolis, with its Exchange fixing the price of raw cotton worldwide.

You can still visit the **ROYAL EXCHANGE** where much of this trading took place in the late 19th and early 20th century, a vast handsome building between Corporation Street and St. Anne's Square. When it was no longer needed for this purpose, rather than being demolished or altered beyond recognition, it became the home of a remarkable theatre which was constructed inside the original great hall.

The building still keeps its flavour and character and the prices from its last day of trading remain to this day! The Royal Exchange Theatre is now a leading centre for arts in the North West.

Royal Exchange Box Office 0161 833 9833.

Manchester's emergence into what historians describe as the world's first industrialised city was not just based on cotton. Good communications and easy access to nearby coalfields enabled it to grow rapidly as a major centre of engineering, initially forging mill engines to service the new mills, followed by steam locomotives and, as the 19th century progressed, a wide variety of heavy engineering equipment and machinery, from power stations and ship engines to aeronautics, much of it for export.

Trade was given a considerable boost in 1894 with the opening of the Manchester Ship Canal. Manchester had been under the stranglehold of the Port of Liverpool for years, having to pay heavy dues for any imports and exports passing through. This was the main reason for the decision to build the Manchester Ship Canal, an amazing feat of engineering which, at the substantial sum of £15m, turned an industrial city forty miles from the sea into a major inland port.

Coming into the twentieth century, Manchester was still at the forefront of modern technology. In the nearby suburb of Hulme, in the years after the first world war, Charles Rolls and Henry Royce manufactured their first motorcars, before moving South to Crewe and greater things.

The world's first modern electronic computer was developed in the city - at the University of Manchester Institute of Science and Technology, or UMIST for short. Built in the 1950's, and in use until quite recently, it had a slower 'brain' than most of todays pocket calculators and filled a large room, weighing tons rather than ounces.

Much of the region's past can be understood from a visit to the remarkable **MUSEUM OF SCIENCE AND INDUSTRY** in Manchester, which is situated in Castlefield. The museum is located in the buildings of Liverpool Road Station. In this site of international importance, the museum charts the history of the world's first industrial city.

You can see the wheels of industry turning in the Power Hall, with the largest collection of working steam mill engines in the world.

The gallery also houses some of the finest locomotives ever made in Manchester, including a massive Beyer Garrett steam locomotive from South Africa Railways, made at Beyer Peacock's works in Gorton. Huge exhibits also feature in the Air and Space Gallery, which is packed with the planes that made flying history, and you can learn about cotton mills in their heyday in the Textile Gallery.

The Making of Manchester explores how the city developed from Roman times to the present and Underground Manchester, an exhibition about sanitation and sewerage, contains a reconstructed Victorian sewer - complete with sounds and smells!

In addition to exploring the past the museum also looks to the future. The Out of this World space gallery explores space - fact and fiction - and visitors can learn about science while having fun in Xperiment! the hands-on science centre. The museum is open from 10 to 5 every day of the year (except over Christmas).

Museum of Science and Industry 0161 832 1830.

Within easy walking distance of Castlefield is the **GRANADA STUDIOS TOUR**, the only attraction of its kind in Europe. Granada Television's headquarters are in Water Street, and the company had the brilliant idea of opening part of the studios to the public, so you can visit the set of Coronation Street, sit in a replica House of Commons bench, or discover what went on at 221B Baker Street, the residence of Mr Sherlock Holmes.

You can also experience 'out of this world' cinematic adventures with Motion Master, which takes you on an exciting journey into the 21st century. There's even a Sooty show for the younger visitors and opposite the entrance, across the car park, **CAPTAIN SALT** (yes, that's his real name) runs cruises up and down the Irwell.

Granada Studios Tour 0161 832 9090

However, Manchester City Centre is more than these things. You do not have to be in the city for very long, whether you arrive by train (the city lies in the centre of excellent network rail services, both Inter-City and suburban) or by car (there is an excellent system of well signed off-street parking) before you begin to appreciate that you really are in a great European city.

The introduction of Manchester's Metrolink, a new tram system which criss-crosses the city centre, adds to the increasingly cosmopolitan feel of the place. A superb heritage of late Victorian and early Edwardian warehouses and office blocks, some of them richly decorated and of monumental proportions, gives the streets of the city centre a sense of wealth and importance which later sky-scraper office blocks cannot match.

ALBERT SQUARE is an inevitable focal point. The city's magnificent Gothic **TOWN HALL**, designed by Alfred Waterhouse and built between 1871 - 1877 at a cost of £1 million, overlooks this now pedestrianised square named after Prince Albert, consort to Queen Victoria. Alfred Waterhouse also designed the Assize Courts, Strangeways Prison, Owen's College (now Manchester University) and the Refuge Assurance building on Oxford Road.

Sculptures in Manchester have been erected in the main to commemorate famous people linked with the history of the city. There are five in Albert Square. One, of Prime Minister Gladstone, depicts movement and has earned the title "The Dancing Prime Minister". The Town Hall's richly decorated interior includes wall paintings by the Pre-Raphaelite artist Ford Madox Brown, illustrating various aspects of the history of the city.

Tucked away on Mulberry Street, only a few yards from Albert Square, is the Roman Catholic **CHURCH OF ST. MARY**, known to many as the 'Hidden Gem'. The church dates back to 1794, the time of the French Revolution.

At first St. Mary's was in fields, surrounded by the shanty homes of the poor. As the town developed, the church became hidden by commercial buildings. Recent development however, has given the church a slightly more open aspect. The exterior is lovely, but the source of the name refers to its beautiful interior.

Close by is another architectural masterpiece, the **CENTRAL LIBRARY**, one of the largest Municipal libraries in Europe. This impressive circular building of white Portland stone, designed by the eminent architect Vincent Harris, was opened in 1934 by King George V. Visitors are recommended to take a few minutes to venture inside and admire the great hall. The circular dome is intricately decorated and gilded and the inscription, carved in gold letters, has inspired countless readers, students and visitors:

> *"Wisdom is the principal thing*
> *Therefore, get wisdom*
> *And with thy getting get understanding*
> *Exalt her and she shall promote thee*
> *She shall bring thee to honour when thou dost embrace her*
> *She shall give thy head an ornament of grace*
> *A crown of glory shall she deliver to thee."*

The basement of the library houses a small theatre, home to the

Barton Arcade, Manchester

LIBRARY THEATRE COMPANY. Throughout the year they produce an exciting programme of lunchtime shows, workshops, comedy, drama and world premieres.

Library Theatre Company Box Office 061 236 7110.

The **FREE TRADE HALL** in Peter Street is the City's main concert hall where Britain's oldest professional symphony orchestra, founded in 1857 by Sir Charles Hallé, performs.

The hall stands on a site which had a tragic association with the 1819 Peterloo massacre, where a crowd of 60,000, meeting to debate Reform in the House of Commons, were charged by local soldiers. The name commemorates Manchester's fight against the Corn Laws.

Just around the corner from here, on Windmill Street, is Manchester's **G-MEX CENTRE** - Greater Manchester Exhibition and Events Centre. The building was once Central Station, opened by the Midland Railway company in 1880 and was the last railway terminus to be built in the city. Coming right into the heart of the city, its construction swept away 225 houses, home to 1200 city dwellers. The 210 foot high iron and glass arch remains as impressive today as it was the day the first train arrived. Amazingly the whole station stands on massive columns and beneath it was the goods yard and a labyrinth of warehousing. The station saw its last train in 1968 and after years as a car park was finally redeveloped as a huge exhibition centre hosting shows, concerts and trade fairs nearly every day of the week.

Straight across the road from the station is the former **MIDLAND HOTEL**, now called the Holiday Inn Crowne Plaza Midland. This monument to excess rose between 1898 and 1903 and it boasted a Palm Court, Winter Gardens, its own Concert Hall and Theatre as well as 400 bedchambers. Outside, its walls are ornate opulence, featuring glazed brick, terracotta and polished granite, matched only by its lavish interior.

Close by, on Great Bridgewater Street is a unique, triangular pub, **PEVERIL OF THE PEAK.** The exterior is a joy to behold, a riot of colourful glazed tiling. The interior contains a magnificently restored stained glass and wooden canopy bar. Peveril of the Peak was built in 1830 and its first licensee was a former coach driver on the London run, who named the pub after his coach.

THE CROWN INN on Deansgate, the heart of Manchester's shopping district, is probably one of the oldest licensed premises in the city. However, it has not always stood in its present position. At the end of the last century, the original building was knocked down when Deansgate was widened and the present Inn built on the other side of the road. This grand Victorian red brick building, owned and personally run by Lindy and Paul Bradley, is full of character and style and you can be sure of a warm welcome. Open all day, everyday, the pub serves a range of excellent ales and beers including Samson, Vaux and a guest beer.

Lunch is available during the week and the menu includes hot pots and curries as well as tasty snacks. The Inn also has nine comfortable guest bedrooms, very reasonably priced, that make an excellent alternative to the large, chain hotels in the city. Evening meals are by arrangement. Whether you are in the city for business or pleasure this is an ideal place to stay.

The Crown Inn, 321 Deansgate, Manchester Tel: 0161 834 7301

For the finest Italian food and a sparkling continental style cafe bar you should visit the **RISTORANTE ISOLA BELLA** and **SAN GIORGIO CAFE BAR** in Crown Square, Manchester and the **PIZZERIA ITALIA** at 42 Deansgate. Evandro has been looking after diners in Manchester for twenty five years and the present businesses are truly family run. The premises for the Isola Bella and San Giorgio were completely refurbished prior to opening in 1987 and the interior has a wonderfully continental appearance. Although the restaurant can seat 100, bookings are preferred. Lighter meals can be enjoyed in the Cafe Bar. The Pizzeria Italia is open seven days a week (12.00 - 11.30) and boasts the best Pizza in Manchester. All the delicious, mouth-watering cakes and ice creams are home-made in Evandro's San Marco Pasticceria and are served in all the establishments. Top quality food, service and venues. Restaurant open lunchtime and evening , closed Sunday.

Isola Bella & San Giorgio, Dolefield, Crown Square, Manchester. Tel: 0161 8317099. Pizzeria Italia, 40/42 Deansgate, Manchester. Tel: 0161 8341541

Nearby is the **JOHN RYLANDS LIBRARY**, an imposing Victorian Gothic edifice in red sandstone, a cross between a college gatehouse and a cathedral. John Rylands was a cotton merchant who became Manchester's first millionaire. He was also a devout Congregationalist, and kept a small library of theological works at his home. After his death in 1888, his widow decided to create a much larger library in his memory. The Library was to be one of the first public buildings to be lit by electricity and even had a system for filtering the dirty Manchester air. Among the many fine collections of early printed books and magnificent oriental manuscripts one treasure is a fragment of the New Testament dating back to the second century, one of the earliest known pieces of New Testament writing in any language.

Also situated on Deansgate in the heart of Manchester City Centre is the **SAWYERS ARMS**, formerly the 'The Two Sawyers', which was one of the very first licensed premises in Manchester. The three storey building is much larger than is first apparent and both the external appearance and the interior have many attractive period features.

The Sawyers is a great meeting place where business people, visitors and locals can easily mix together and enjoy well kept ales and enjoy the good food. The decoration and furnishings have been upgraded and there is a nice welcoming atmosphere. Real ales include Theakstons, Websters and Theakstons XB. Open seven days a week - all day.

The Sawyers Arms, Deansgate, Manchester. Tel: 0161 823 2133

Links with old Manchester can be found in and around the city's 15th century **MANCHESTER CATHEDRAL** on Victoria Street not far from Victoria Station. Built in Perpendicular Gothic style and beautifully restored after 1940's war damage it has a wealth of delightful carvings and unusual 18th century wrought-iron rails. Located in the Cathedral is the Manchester Cathedral Brass Rubbing Centre. Visitors can choose from a vast selection of replicas of original brasses from English Churches.

Just across Fennel Street is the astonishing **CHETHAM HOSPITAL AND LIBRARY**, built on the site of a 14th century Manorial Hall, once home to the Lord of Manchester. The building contains one of England's oldest and most remarkable libraries, together with a 'bluecoat' school founded by Sir Humphrey Chetham, who left a bequest which was used in the 17th century to turn the manor house into a college for poor boys. Today Chetham's is a very well known school for gifted young musicians.

On Cheetham Hill Road, the other side of Victoria Station, is the **MANCHESTER JEWISH MUSEUM**. Manchester has had a Jewish community for over 200 years and the museum celebrates their contribution to the city. It is housed in the former Spanish and Portuguese Synagogue and as well as a permanent display of photographs, objects and recorded memories of Jewish life early this century, there are frequent temporary exhibitions. Visitors are also welcome in the synagogue itself, restored to its original splendour with Moorish decoration and fine stained glass windows.

The city has long been a centre of learning and scholarship. Among its great men are John Dalton, the founder of atomic theory, and the physicist James Prescott Joule. Their intellectual inheritance is reflected in the two great universities - Manchester University itself on Oxford Road, and the University of Manchester Institute of Science and Technology, which together with Salford University and two large polytechnics constitute one of the largest complexes of higher education in Western Europe.

Set back from Oxford Road, within its own pleasant gardens, is the imposing Victorian facade of **WHITWORTH ART GALLERY**. Inside, however, could not be more different, the interior is very much from the 1960s: spacious and airy. The galleries collection include contemporary art, drawings, prints, textiles and wallpapers and it is particularly renowned for its fine collection of British drawings which include works by Turner, Gainsborough and Constable.

The Gallery Bistro

Conveniently placed near the Gallery entrance is the **GALLERY BISTRO**. Owned and run by Rosemary Watts, this is a wonderful place to rest and refresh yourself whilst at the Gallery or just in the area. There is an excellent choice of regular, speciality or herb teas, coffees, juices and, more unusually, Elderflower Champagne. Daily, freshly prepared, home-made soup, based on seasonal produce, is offered along with a host of tasty, imaginative and freshly prepared dishes such as vegetable goulash, stuffed aubergines and succulent Sea Bass. Rosemary's unique Welsh Rarebit is high recommended. The memorable cakes are created by her son Richard and the selection, which may include candied lemon, carrot cake and sticky toffee pudding, varies daily depending on Richard's inspiration. Whether you are an art lover, a food lover or both, this is one stop you should not miss.

Gallery Bistro, Whitworth Art Gallery, Oxford Road, Manchester
Tel: 0161 273 1249

With such a large student population, it is not surprising that Manchester, Britain's City of Drama in 1994, is a major cultural centre, with two large Victorian theatres, **THE PALACE** and **THE OPERA HOUSE** which take opera, ballet and touring productions, as well as the **ROYAL EXCHANGE THEATRE** and the more experimental **GREEN ROOM** and **CONTACT THEATRES**.

The city also has a variety of jazz and folk clubs and a lively night life, and a truly cosmopolitan choice of restaurants.

Most great cities throughout the world have a **'CHINA TOWN'**, and Manchester is no exception. As one would expect, a thriving oriental pot pourri of restaurants, gift shops, warehouses and banks are to be found in this small area of Manchester. The Chinese influence on the area is signified by the enormous and beautiful pagoda style archway, which is the symbolic entrance to China Town. However, there are restaurants from all parts of the Orient to be found here, including Japan, Thailand, India, Hong Kong, and all places East!

Situated in Shambles Square, **SINCLAIRS** stands on the original site of The Punch House, which was started by John Shaw in 1738. However, records indicate that a building has stood on this site since the 14th century. The Punch House housed the first Gentleman's Club in Manchester, and was occupied by John Shaw until his death in 1796 at the age of 83 years. Around 1845, oysters were introduced to the premises, and alcoholic beverages some 20 years later. Fifteen square yards of the site of the old Punch house is now occupied by the north-west corner of Sinclairs.

Also in Shambles Square, **THE OLD WELLINGTON INN** is one of the places where the commerce that made Manchester great began. In it lived some of the men and women who founded the City's first bank and cotton industry, and built its first quay. Also born here was the inventor of Phonetic Shorthand, John Byrom. Other inhabitants helped to found at least one City church and a hospital. The exact date of the building is unknown. A spurious date of 1328 was once displayed at the Inn, but experts now put its construction date at around 1550. Literally, the greatest upheaval the building had ever seen took place in the summer of 1971, when it was 'lifted' four feet nine inches during the construction of the Shambles Square Market Place development.

Around Manchester

Manchester is not just a city centre, and it is surprisingly easy to escape into fine areas of countryside and small towns and villages, each with their own character and fine 'hidden places'.

DIDSBURY. The impressive **DIDSBURY WINE BAR** is situated in the heart of the village which is south of the city centre. This is a stylish and sophisticated establishment that is definitely one of the places to be seen. Open seven days a week from 11.30 am onwards the wine bar serves snacks and meals all day as well as offering an excellent selection of classic and new world wines, bottled beers, lager and draught beer.

Particularly busy at weekends, the atmosphere is lively though there is still room to hold an intimate dinner for two. The excellent food compliments the wine list and there is also an exciting and different Tapas menu as well as tasty dishes with flavours from around the world. A truly international bar, that you will be sure to enjoy.

Didsbury Wine Bar, 747 Wilmslow Road, Didsbury Tel: 0161 438 0064

Why not visit the **FLETCHER MOSS BOTANICAL GARDENS** also in Didsbury. The gardens and playing fields were officially given to the city early this century by the late Alderman Fletcher Moss. The location and southerly aspect of the rock gardens has made it possible to create a haven of botanical beauty. The garden contains many uncommon alpines, bulbs and shrubs as well a natural pond, orchid house and heather and wild gardens.

THE BARLEYCORN is an outstanding public house situated in West Didsbury, close to the end of the M56 motorway. Formerly a nightclub and a hotel, the Barleycorn was renamed in 1986 and it has been recently completely refurbished. Today, it is an establishment, full of

Hall i'th'Wood, Bolton

character and style, with a wood panelled drinking area, ceiling beams and lots of gleaming brass work. A friendly and popular meeting place, where you can enjoy a pint or two of well kept ale, with Tetley's and Burton's as permanent fixtures. Open all day, everyday, the Barleycorn also has a tasty and delicious lunchtime menu but do save some room for one of the mouth-watering puddings. A handy, well run pub to stop at for lunch or any other time of day.

The Barleycorn, 120/122 Barlow Moor Road, West Didsbury
Tel: 0161 445 3378

When Patrick Hannity first opened his restaurant **THE LIME TREE** nine years ago, it quickly became one of the premier restaurants in the area. Some years on, its fame has spread to a much wider audience and he now has additional restaurants in Rusholme and Chorlton.

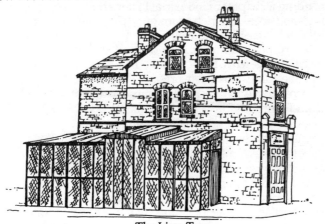

The Lime Tree

The Lime Tree demonstrates the ideal blend of imaginative dishes for the gourmet's palate at sensible prices. An inclusive menu is offered for lunch whilst a wider choice is available in the evening. The varied cuisine features dishes from all over the world. Sunday family lunch offers a treat of traditional English food; children are catered for at a very reasonable price. There is always a first class wine list with quality selections sold by the glass. Menus change frequently. Booking recommended.

The Lime tree, 8 Lapwing Lane, West Didsbury, Manchester M20. Tel: 0161 445 1217

HEATON PARK, can be reached either by road on the A576 (the link to the M62) or by the City's new high-speed Metrolink tram system to Bury. Acres of superb open countryside, a Regency house and formal gardens, boating lakes, a rare breeds centre and a restored old fashioned tramway system can all be found here.

Much beautiful countryside lies within the satellite Metropolitan Boroughs that form the county of Greater Manchester. Including the City of Manchester itself, there are no less than ten constituent boroughs around the central core, the others being Salford, Wigan, Bolton, Bury, Rochdale, Oldham, Tameside, Stockport and Trafford. All have their special qualities and areas of individual interest.

SALFORD is Manchester's twin across the River Irwell. Its art gallery in Peel Park in the Crescent by the River Irwell now contains **THE LOWRY CENTRE**, a tribute to L.S. Lowry, the great Lancashire artist who during the 1920s and 30s meticulously recorded a now vanished scene of industrial poverty and hardship. The old Salford of Harold Brighouse's 'Hobson's Choice' and Walter Greenwood's 'Love on the Dole' has echoes in Lowry's paintings.

AGECROFT, Greater Manchester's last coal mine closed a few years ago ending a chapter of industrial history that stretches back four generations and more. The rich seam of coal spread out from the city across southern Lancashire and well within living memory there were a dozen and more pits mining it. The story of the coal field is told at **SALFORD MINING MUSEUM** in Buile Hill Park off the A576.

One of the mines has been preserved - **ASTLEY GREEN COLLIERY** - just off the A580 East Lancashire road. It is looked after by volunteers and also provides a home for the **RED ROSE LIVE STEAM GROUP** who restore all kinds of steam engines.

The biggest change in Salford is the emergence of Salford Docks as a major tourist and residential centre. Renamed **SALFORD QUAYS**, the waterfronts now provide a backdrop to apartments, pubs and walkways, and are served by the Metrolink.

WORSLEY, at the other side of the city is home to a different kind of waterway heritage, the astonishing **BRIDGEWATER CANAL BASIN** (reached by bus or the A572 road from the City Centre). Here, in an area of lovely woodlands, you can see where the Duke of Bridgewater first opened his canal from his Worsley coal mines to carry coal to the centre of Manchester, in the 1760s. This new canal halved the price of coal and thus began the Industrial Revolution that helped to change the western world.

WORSLEY OLD HALL is the ancestral home of the Duke of Bridgewater. This splendid half-timbered 16th century manor house now provides the venue for conferences, wedding receptions and extravagant Jacobean banquets, where visitors can enjoy a candlelit evening of feasting and merriment in the company of knights and fine ladies. Situated in the vaulted cellars beneath the Old Hall is The Duke's Cellar Restaurant, which with its unique structure of arched alcoves provides the perfect setting for an intimate dinner.

The wonderful **RENDEZVOUS** licensed tea room and restaurant is a welcome addition to the picturesque village of Worsley. Standing opposite the Bridgewater Canal, Rendezvous, housed in a two hundred year old building, is owned and personally run by Janice and Graham Webb.

After completely refurbishing the building to create a cosy and intimate atmosphere with pleasant decorations, the tea room and restaurant opened in November 1995. In such a short time, Janice, Graham and their friendly, efficient staff have gained an enviable reputation as the place to meet in Worsley. Open between 10 am and 5 pm everyday except Mondays, the Rendezvous serves a wide variety of delicious meals and Daily Chef's Specials, all home-made including delicious desserts. From the Spring of 1996 they will also be opening in the evenings from Friday to Sunday and, already a popular tea room, we wish them every success with the restaurant.

Rendezvous, 17 Barton Road, Worsley Tel: 0161 793 1160

BOLTON, northwest of Manchester, is another mill town that defies expectations, its very fine Victorian town hall being the central point in a recently extensively refurbished pedestrianised shopping and leisure area with shopping malls, a restored market hall, a superb leisure centre including a swimming pool, the celebrated **OCTAGON THEATRE**, and an excellent local museum.

BOLTON FESTIVAL, at the end of August, is a very popular event. It runs for a whole week and there is a vast range of attractions, which include Morris Dancing and brass bands. The Victorian market is a favourite event, with everyone dressing up in full period costume.

LEIGH. **THE WATERSIDE INN** in the centre of Leigh is housed within a handsome 19th century corn mill and stands at the edge of the Leeds Liverpool Canal.

The Waterside Inn

The inn was completely refurbished by Watling Inns, the owners, two years ago, and great care has been taken to preserve all of its original features, including cast iron columns, exposed brickwork and timber beams. The interior of the inn is consequently very warm and inviting.

The inn is a free house, so a wide variety of real ales are always served. Food is also available at lunchtime, from 12.00am to 2.00pm and in the evenings from 5.30pm to 8.30pm, Monday to Saturday. A carvery is available all day on Sunday. The popularity that this inn enjoys is well deserved, for it is one of the best pubs in the area and should not be missed.

The Waterside Inn, Leigh. Tel: 01942 605005

THE RED BRICK INN, situated on Twist Lane in Leigh, is, without a doubt, one of the best inns in the area. Dating back to the early 19th century and formerly called The Oddfellows or 'Scotchies' to the locals, the inn changed its name in 1992 when it underwent a complete refurbishment. Graham and Joan Griffith, your hosts, came here three years ago with their family and, though this is their first venture in the licensing trade, they have made a roaring success of the Red Brick. This is a friendly, lively pub where, as a visitor, you will quickly become one of the family. Open everyday, all day, there is a good selection of real ales from the bar (the Red Brick is a member of CAMRA) and delicious food is served for residents. The letting rooms, of which there are eight, are available all year round and they vary in size to suit everyone's needs. There is something going on most evenings, darts, pool, quizzes and live entertainment, and you will certainly have a relaxing and pleasant time.

The Red Brick Inn, 94/96 Twist Lane, Leigh Tel: 01942 671698

WIGAN lies to the west and is the town that turned a music hall joke on its head. The old canal basin on the Leeds-Liverpool Canal had a coal wharf known as **WIGAN PIER**, jokingly referred to by George Formby, and by George Orwell in a documentary book about working-class life in the North in the 1930s, " The Road to Wigan Pier "

Wigan has used the complex of old warehouses and mills around the canal basin to create a new Wigan Pier, a major leisure attraction with its own Piermaster. There are canal boat rides, and remarkable exhibitions based on local social history of "The Way We Were", with costumed actors whose activities in the reconstructed schoolroom bring back vivid memories of childhood.

Wigan Pier

Within easy walking distance from the centre of Wigan, and close to the motorway network, lies the small and friendly **AALTON COURT HOTEL**. Owned and run by Malcolm and Susie Ellison, this bed and breakfast hotel, with fourteen bedrooms nine of which have en suite facilities, is situated in a quiet, tree lined street. Handy for Wigan Pier and the Heritage Centre and with several top class golf clubs nearby this is a lovely place to stop.

Aalton Court Hotel, 23 Upper Dicconson Street, Wigan Tel: 01942 322220

Wigan is not a town living in the past, but has a modern town centre, with fine countryside on its own doorstep such as the **DOUGLAS VALLEY TRAIL**. Even Wigan's coal mining past has interesting links with the natural world - **PENNINGTON FLASH**, a large lake caused by mining subsidence, is now a wildlife reserve and country park.

The Croal-Irwell Valley to the south of Bolton now forms part of one of the great countryside success stories of recent years. From **MOSES**

GATE COUNTRY PARK southwards, a former derelict industrial valley has now been turned into a beautiful green corridor of lakes, streams, woods and walkways, supported by a lively warden and recreation service.

To the north of Bolton lie magnificent moorlands, forming the southern edge of the West Pennine Moors, through which walking opportunities abound, varying from full moorland hikes to gentle strolls. For example, there are lakeside walks in **JUMBLES COUNTRY PARK** around Jumbles reservoir, the wide open moors around Winter Hill, and the lovely open parkland around Rivington and Anglezarke Reservoirs.

RAMSBOTTOM. In the Market Place of this traditional Lancashire village, opposite Grant Arms Hotel, is **RAMSBOTTOM VICTUALLERS AND THE VILLAGE RESTAURANT**. The building, dating from 1829, was originally workers' houses. Today, below street level, is a superb food and wine shop whilst the ground floor is an excellent and interesting restaurant. Both are owned and run by Ros Hunter and Chris Johnson who are real foodie fanatics. They are extremely knowledgeable and their passion is infectious.

Ramsbottom Victuallers and The Village Restaurant

The shop, recently enlarged, is packed full of unique tastes and fine ingredients from Britain and around the world including *Carluccio's* superb range of Italian specialities (Antonio Carluccio is the ebullient Italian chef who frequently appears on television. The fame of the shop has spread far and wide. This is no backwater but a hidden treasure trove which hosted an episode of Granada TV's 'Main Ingredient' programme. It has regularly featured in the national quality press and has been chosen as the 'Best Food Shop' in the whole of Britain by the BBC in their "Food Lover's Guide to Britain 1996/97". Occasional newsletters are enjoyable and informative, highlighting new lines as well as regular of food and wine tastings. All in all the shop succeeds in being much, much more than just another delicatessen and wine shop!

The restaurant, open for lunch and dinner from Wednesday to Saturday, and for lunch only on Sunday, compliments the shop beautifully. Ros Hunter, the chef of the partnership, produces imaginative, daily changing menus from fresh local ingredients in season. The Village Restaurant is a true gourmet experience, whether you have a light lunch or full blown dinner.....

Ramsbottom Victuallers and Village Restaurant, 18 Market Place, Ramsbottom Tel: 01706 825070

THE EASTERN EYE Indian restaurant, in the centre of Ramsbottom offers a wide range of Indian cuisine in pleasant, air conditioned surroundings. The menu, with helpful information for those unfamiliar with the dishes of the sub continent, ranges from the very hot Vindaloo curries to the mild and aromatic Kormas. A variety of side dishes, including many delicacies, are also available. Open seven days a week and with a special family banquet menu at Sunday lunchtime it is advisable to book as this is a very popular restaurant.

The Eastern Eye, 38 Bolton Street, Ramsbottom Tel: 01706 823268

The Millenium Clinic

Opposite the steam railway is the **MILLENIUM CLINIC**. Owned and run by Anne Earle, the Clinic is beautifully comfortable and tastefully decorated to ensure that all visitors gain as much benefit as possible from their treatments and time spent here. All the treatments use the latest technology and techniques and are performed by fully qualified practitioners. Available treatments include: homeopathy, hypnotherapy, psychotherapy, reflexology, aromatherapy, reflexology, aromatherapy, acupuncture, addition therapy and bereavement counselling.

Millenium Clinic, 9D Toll Bridge House, Bridge Street, Ramsbottom
Tel: 01706 827373

Also opposite the Railway Station in Ramsbottom is the delightful **RUMBLE TUMS TEA SHOP**. Owned and personally run by Mrs V McArthur this is a traditional cafe, open seven days a week, which offers a mouthwatering range of homemake cakes and delicacies. The building is itself has an interesting history and in its time has been a tailor's shop and a sorting office. This is an ideal place to relax and enjoy light refreshment in pleasant and relaxed surroundings.

Rumble Tums Tea Shop, 9E Bridge Street, Ramsbottom Tel: 01706 825232

The Andertons, Holcombe Village

HOLCOMBE VILLAGE is one of the oldest surviving communities around Ramsbottom itself, dating back to the 14th century. **THE ANDERTONS** restaurant follows a family tradition of eating houses in Ramsbottom going back some 50 years. The Andertons country restaurant is situated on the lower slopes of Holcombe Hill and was established by brother and sister Trevor and Julie Anderton in 1981.

The building which survived a Zeppelin bomb attack in 1916 has been converted from an old post office, which in turn was converted from three cottages. The tower on the hill behind the restaurant was erected in memory of Sir Robert Peel the founder of the modern police force. Trevor and Julie have preserved The charm and character of Holcombe Village in The Andertons' restaurant and also in their style of cooking - traditional English food at its best. Seasonal menus at modest prices. They also have an outside catering facility.

The Andertons, 18-22 Holcombe Village, Nr. Ramsbottom.
Tel: 01706 825702

RIVINGTON is entered across a long causeway that spans the huge two mile long reservoir, built in the 1850's to supply water to Liverpool. Half of the old village now lies beneath the water and of the remaining half only the stubby spire and weather-cock of the part-Elizabethan church are visible above the trees as you approach. Opposite the church is the village primary school, built in 1656 and just off the triangular village green is the handsome Georgian **FISHER HOUSE**, once home of John Fisher, who was vicar for half a century from 1763.

RIVINGTON HALL lies at the end of a long avenue of beech trees. There has been a hall on the site since Saxon times, the present house being built by Robert Andrews in 1780. In 1900 the house was sold to soap-magnate William Lever, later Lord Leverhulme, who restored the two vast Saxon tythe barns in the grounds. Both are of 'cruck' construction, with massive paired oaks supporting the roof and walls. They need to be big as they would have become a sort of 'Noah's Ark' during winter, sheltering the estates farm animals and all their fodder.

Lord Leverhulme had the grounds laid out as formal gardens with ponds, bridges, mock-temples, tower and hanging gardens, then threw them open to the public. He also had a replica of the long-vanished Liverpool Castle built overlooking the reservoir. The park is now gloriously overgrown and decaying, but holds a special attraction for being that.

Above the park is **RIVINGTON PIKE** with its 18th century lookout tower and towering over everything the television mast on Winter Hill, visable from most of the north-west on a clear day.

BURY shares this fine Pennine moorland backcloth and is a town famous for its black puddings. Like Bolton it enjoys an attractively refurbished town centre.

One fascinating development has been the reopening of the old railway line between Bury, Ramsbottom and Rawtenstall as the **EAST**

LANCASHIRE STEAM RAILWAY. The former Bolton Street Station is now a small museum, with regular steam services through the Upper Irwell valley at weekends and during holiday times.

East Lancashire Steam Railway

Travel along from HOLCOMBE village towards TOTTINGTON, Bury, and you'll find the village of GREENMOUNT. In an old cottage style shop dating back to 1870 (opposite the Bulls Head pub) is **COBWEBS,** an intriguing gift shop with speciality dolls for the collector, dressed in every type of costume and style each with an authenticity certificate. Collectors of the ever favourite Teddy Bears are not forgotten and many are found sitting about the shop awaiting their new owners. A selection of Lancashire pottery is on sale along with many items of table decoration.

Cobwebs also offer a picture framing service and stock a range of ready made miniature frames. A choice of quality gift cards and a variety of other attractive gift ideas makes this a worthwhile stopping point.

Cobwebs, 329 Holcombe Road, Greenmount, Bury, Lancashire.
Tel: 01204 885123

ROCHDALE has its origins in medieval times. It lies in a shallow valley formed by the little River Roch on the slopes of the Pennines, whose broad summits just above the outskirts of the town are often snow covered in winter. Another once prosperous cotton town, its handsome Town Hall rivals Manchester in style if not in size.

Rochdale, to the east of Greater Manchester, was the birthplace of both the 19th century political thinker, John Bright, and the celebrated entertainer Gracie Fields, but perhaps its chief claim to fame is with the birth of the Co-operative movement. In carefully restored Toad Lane to the north of the town centre, you'll find the world's first consumer Co-operative store, the Rochdale Pioneers. The Co-op movement now represents a staggering 700 million members in 90 countries, and the celebration of its 150th anniversary in 1994 focused worldwide attention on the original **CO-OPERATIVE STORE MUSEUM** on Toad Lane.

Between Rochdale and Littleborough lies Hollingworth Lake, originally built as a supply reservoir for the Rochdale Canal, but for many years a popular area for recreation known colloquially as "The Weavers' Seaport", for cotton workers unable to enjoy a trip to the seaside. It is now part of the **HOLLINGWORTH LAKE COUNTRY PARK** with a fine visitor centre, and you can still enjoy trips on the lake as well as walks around its shores.

It is well worth taking the A58 Halifax road from Littleborough to see the famous **BLACKSTONE EDGE ROMAN ROAD**, a stone causeway crossing this high Pennine pass. It is walkable from the roadside layby to the medieval cross, the Aigin Stone at its summit, a superb viewpoint over the entire Lancashire plain to the coast.

OLDHAM is still dominated by great square red mills, though many have now been put to new uses. The town, soon to be linked to central Manchester by the new Metrolink Supertram, is notable for its lively **COLISEUM THEATRE** and for its position close to superb scenery in the South Pennines and the Peak District, most notably the moorland villages of Delph, Denshaw, Dobcross and Uppermill.

UPPERMILL is the largest of these and lies in the upper reaches of the Tame Valley offering lovely walks along the Huddersfield Canal with boat trips in the summer. **BROWNHILL VISITOR CENTRE** situated just to the north of Uppermill, is an ideal starting point for a visit to Saddleworth and can provide a wide range of local information. Nearby Dovestone Reservoir, just in the Peak District National Park, is a popular sailing and birdwatching centre.

TAMESIDE was a name coined in 1974 to describe the district which includes the towns of Stalybridge, Ashton, Hyde and Denton, and other communities which fringe onto the Cheshire Pennine border. All have pleasant town centres with much of interest.

ASHTON is notable for a remarkable example of medieval stained glass at The Church of St. Michael and All Angels.

Situated in the town centre, in the Victorian Town Hall, is the **MUSEUM OF THE MANCHESTERS**. Opened by the Queen mother in 1987 it tells the story of the Manchester Regiment in the context of the local community that its soldiers came from. You can discover what life was like for troops and civilians during the time of the Peterloo massacre, in the trenches of the First World War and during the Blitz. The Town Hall stands on the Market Place and the museum is open Monday to Saturday 10am to 4pm.

DENTON is noteworthy for **ST LAWRENCE'S CHURCH**, which has the nickname 'Th'owd peg' because reputedly neither nails nor metal were used in its construction, only wooden pegs.

The Tame and Etherow Valleys, both higher tributary valleys of the River Mersey, have been kept as attractive linear green spaces and walkways through otherwise busy urban districts, and contain some lovely areas of unspoiled countryside on the edge of both the Peak District and the South Pennines.

Country lovers will discover a beautiful oasis at **ETHEROW COUNTRY PARK**, which is situated at Compstall on the B6104 between Romiley and Marple Bridge. Once part of the estate belonging to George Andrew who built Compstall Mill in the 1820s, the park covers an area of 240 acres. A haven for ramblers and birdwatchers, the park lies at the halfway point of the Etherow-Goyt Valley Way Footpath. The Goyt Way, a ten mile trail to Whaley Bridge, also starts here. The park provides an ideal habitat for a rich variety of bird and wildlife as well as many different plant species. The nature reserve here, which is managed by Cheshire Conservation Trust, has been designated a Site of Special Scientific Interest.

Etherow Country Park, Compstall, Stockport Tel: 0161 427 6937

The Duke of Yory, Romiley

ROMILEY. The outstanding **DUKE OF YORK** lies on the main Bredbury to Marple Bridge road in the village of Romiley. Once a recognised coaching inn, you can still see the archway through which horses and coaches passed to the stables behind, the pub has been serving the weary traveller since 1786. Painted in the traditional black and white, the Duke of York retains much of the character and charm of those bygone days.

Today, the pub is run by Jenny and Jim Grindrod and, though this is their first venture in the trade, they have certainly started well. Open all day, everyday, excellent well kept ales including Directors, John Smiths, Websters Green Label and Ruddles County will help to quench your thirst. At lunchtime and in the evening, except Sundays, there is an delicious menu of mouth-watering hot and cold snacks and meals supplemented by a specials board. For those that like to test their general knowledge, Monday night is quiz night and all are welcome.

The Duke of York, Stockport Road, Romiley, Stockport Tel: 0161 430 2806

THE BRIDGE CAFE is situated adjacent to a bridge crossing the Peak Forest Canal. This charming and friendly establishment was refurbished by the owners Penny and Warwick when they took possession of it ten years ago, and since then its popularity and reputation have gone from strength to strength, due in no small part to the excellent standard of the dishes which are served.

The cafe is open from 9.00am to 3.00pm from Monday to Friday and its menu caters for all tastes and appetites, from freshly made sandwiches to delicious lunchtime specials. In addition Penny will specially arrange a 'gourmet evening' for parties of twelve or more booking in advance.

To the rear of the premises is a lovely garden where, on warm days, meals can be enjoyed in in a peaceful and tranquil atmosphere.

The Bridge Cafe, 164 Stockport Road, Romiley, Cheshire. Tel: 0161 430 5937

MARPLE. **THE CROWN** overlooks the village green at Hawk Green on the outskirts of Marple. Featured in many good food guides, the pub has been personally run for the past 12 years by Beryl Lane and has plenty to offer both visitors and locals alike.

Dating back to the mid 19th century, The Crown has been a house, inn and a smithy in its time. In fact, it was only in 1984 that the derelict barn where the smithy once stood was converted and added to the inn. Viewed from outside, The Crown is as pretty as a picture with hanging baskets and window boxes adding great splashes of colour in the summer. The interior is equally impressive, beautifully decorated and furnished throughout with many picture windows and a wooden dance floor whose wood came from the old Co-op shop in Stoke-on-Trent.

Renowned for its excellent and delicious food, the menu is supplemented by a daily list of mouth-watering specials. Everything is home-cooked and do make room for one of the naughty puddings. Open all day, everyday with food available at lunchtimes and from 6.30pm. evenings and all day Sunday this is a super place to come to eat and drink.

The Crown, 1 Hawk Green Road, Hawk Green, Marple Tel: 0161 427 2678

MARPLE BRIDGE lies just north of Marple and here on Town Street you will find **GRAYS CAFE BAR**, the perfect place to call in for a refreshing cup of tea or a tasty meal.

Grays Cafe Bar

Karen Thorpe is the friendly hostess who specialises in good home baking and delicious cream teas, using only the finest fresh produce. Attractive surroundings and a warm, friendly atmosphere create the perfect environment in which to savour your chosen dish from an extensive and reasonably priced menu. From the range of all day breakfasts, soups, sandwiches, salads, hot potatoes and filled baguettes, the speciality teas and aromatic coffees and the traditional afternoon teas, there is something mouth-watering to tempt everyone. The Café, recently extended to accommodate about 50 people, is closed on Mondays though open throughout the winter for Sunday lunches. The delicatessen, next door to the Café, supplies a wonderful range of foods as well as a takeaway menu service.

Grays Café Bar, 22 Town Street, Marple Bridge Tel 0161 449 0132

DISLEY. **THE DANDY COCK** public house is situated in the centre of Disley and is just a few minutes drive from the wonderful countryside of Derbyshire and the Peak District National Park.

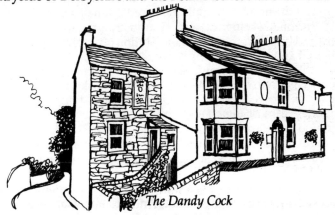

The Dandy Cock

Dating back to the early 19th century, the inn was named after the old fashioned sport of cock fighting which was prevalent in the area. Jon Greenwood and Gill Cope , your hosts, took over the tenancy here at the beginning of the year though Jon, a local lad, has worked at the pub for some time. Open all day, everyday, there is a wonderful range of real ales including Robinson's Best, Old Stockport Bitter and Hatter's Mild that will quench your thirst. However, if you are feeling hungry, the Dandy Cock serves delicious, home-cooked lunches and dinners everyday except Sunday and Monday evenings in a cosy and intimate restaurant. Conveniently situated only 2 minutes from the railway station and 30 minutes from Manchester town centre, this is a popular pub with locals and visitors to the area and a great place to stop after exploring the local countryside.

The Dandy Cock, 15 Market Street, Disley Tel: 01663 763712

STOCKPORT, a town famed for its 700 year old market, part of which is held in a handsome Victorian market hall, is dominated by the 27 arch railway viaduct built by the Manchester & Birmingham Railway and opened in 1841. Its two tracks soon became congested and a second almost identical viaduct was built next to it in 1898, the two are so close in fact that it's hard to tell they're separate. The two structures contain 22 million bricks hold the record for being the biggest brick built structure in Europe.

Stockport's potential was first recognised by the Romans, but it wasn't until the arrival of the Saxons that the town gained its name. However, there is no mention of it in the Domesday Book, the reason for this being unclear. Stockport, however, rose again, still under the leadership of the Normans, to claim a place in many chapters of British history.

Up to the beginning of the 18th century it continued to be an attractive and prosperous market town, but all this changed with the start of the Industrial Revolution. By 1760 there were seven silk mills in the town, and the number of mills increased dramatically following the arrival of cotton spinning. Like most industrial towns of that period, Stockport had its problems, with the evolution of organisations pressing for industrial and social reform.

In 1938, prior to the outbreak of World War II, a labyrinth of passages was cut into the soft, red sandstone of Stockport town centre to provide an extensive system of underground air raid shelters. They survive today, almost intact, and you can visit them on a fascinating underground tour. You are provided with a helmet and lamp, and an expert guide will point out and explain the many interesting features: the wardens' area, toilet and washing facilities, first aid area and original bunk-beds! Tours are on the first Sunday of every month in the afternoons. For details ring *0161 474 4460*.

Stockport was once a great hat town, with many factories sending everything from bowlers to pith helmets all over the Empire. One of the biggest and most famous, **CHRISTIES**, survives to this day and is the last hatters in Britain still making traditional bowlers. Incidently the phrase 'mad as a hatter' comes from the industry's use of highly poisonous mercury for treating the felt used in the hats.

People all over the country stand on another Stockport product. Before its closure Needhams Foundry produced hundreds of thousands of cast iron man-hole covers, grids and the like, which have found their way all over the country.

Just as Rolls-Royce had humble beginnings in Manchester, Jaguar cars can be said to have begun in the Stockport suburb of Woodsmoor. William Walmsley began building motorcycle sidecars there before moving to Blackpool in the 1920's. In the seaside resort he met William Lyons, began full-time manufacture, expanded into building car bodies and finally complete cars; moving to Browns Lane in Coventry in 1928. The rest is, as they say, history.

One of Stockport's more unusual hidden places is strictly for gentlemen only. **THE QUEENS HEAD** pub, on Great Underbank, not only has a very ornate bar and very civilised reading room, with an impressive glass skylight but also boasts having the smallest gents urinal. With standing room for one, and a pretty small one at that, it's certainly a fascinating curiosity in a very pleasant pub.

HEATON CHAPEL. **THE HIND'S HEAD** in Heaton Chapel is,

without a doubt, one of best pubs in the area. Looking at the building you could be forgiven for thinking that it had been here for years but, in fact, the building is relatively new and it used to be the Poco a Poco nightspot. Personally run by June and Alan Preston, the Hinds Head is a picture to look at, both inside and out, with plenty of tables and chairs outside for pleasant al fresco drinking in the summer.

The Hinds Head

The Hinds Head also has its fair share of awards which include the Civic Society Award for the best enhanced building in Stockport and Pub of the Month from CAMRA. With these commendations you can be assured of an excellent pint of real ale and there of plenty to choose from with Higson's, Marston's Pedigree, Castle Eden, and a regular guest beer on tap. Renowned for its beers, the Hinds Head also has an enviable reputation for serving delicious meals. The dishes are all individually prepared and, along with a children's menu and ever-changing specials board, there is plenty to tempt you. This really is a smashing pub that is well worth visiting.

The Hinds Head, Manchester Road, Heaton Chapel Tel: 0161 431 9301

HAZEL GROVE. **THE WOODMAN** stands on the main A6 road in Hazel Grove, just two miles off the M6 and close to Stockport.

The Woodman, Hazel Grove

Formerly part of a row of cottages that dated back to the mid 19th century, it became a licensed premises at the turn of the century. Today's landlady, Lorraine Birtwistle, came here in 1985 and she runs a wonderful, friendly establishment. Open all day, everyday, the Woodman offers the very best in beers, including Robinson's Best and Three Shires Mild. Food is also available all day and, if she has the ingredients, Lorraine is happy to cook whatever you fancy. Finally, to complete this perfect picture, Lorraine also has four letting rooms, one of which is en-suite, where children are welcome and dogs by arrangement. A smashing pub, where you will soon feel at home.

The Woodman, 60 London Road, Hazel Grove, Stockport Tel: 0161 483 7186

BRAMHALL. Tucked away in the heart of Bramhall is **LITTLE RED RIDING HOOD**, a clothes shop with a difference.

Little Red Riding Hood

Owned and run by Sandra McRoberts, Little Red Riding Hood is a busy and bustling boutique for fashion conscious children, and their parents. Stocked to the brim with day and night wear for babies and children to the age of ten, the shop supplies such labels as Sarah Louise and Petit Boy.

Christening outfits are also a speciality and the range extends from the traditional gown to more up-to-date styles. Mothers-to-be are not forgotten and Little Red Riding Hood stocks a range of high fashion and designer maternity clothes and lingerie that are flattering as well as comfortable and practical. With children's shoes, babies booties and soft toy characters like Jeremy Fisher, Paddington Bear and Peter Rabbit, this is the ideal shop for children, mothers-to-be and anyone looking to buy baby a present.

Little Red Riding Hood, 10 Bramhall Village Centre, Bramhall, Stockport Tel: 0161 439 7777

Close to Bramhall you will find a very special place which should feature high on your list of essential places to visit. Probably one of the finest and most attractive properties in Cheshire, **BRAMHALL HALL** is a splendid black and white timbered manor house dating back to the 14th century. Many changes and alterations over the past 500 years mean that visitors today can admire the varying architecture, design and decoration of five centuries. Oak furniture and ornate, wood-panelled walls abound, each of the rooms having its own distinctive style and appeal, especially the Victorian Kitchens. The Great Hall with its enormous fireplace and flagstoned floor, reveals its medieval origins, although later alterations have added Tudor influences. Outside, the 70 acres of parkland provide a peaceful oasis in which to walk and watch the leisurely activities of waterfowl on the lakes and for younger members of the family, there is an enclosed play area to enjoy. The 'in-house' Gift Shop is a browser's haven, full of tempting mementos. At The Stables Café you can sample mouthwatering homemade cakes, snacks and light meals to appeal to every taste.

Bramhall Hall, Bramhall Park, Bramhall, Stockport. 0161 485 3708

HIGH TOWN. **THE HORSESHOE INN** is situated on the A6 at High Town, just five miles from Stockport and close to the Peak District National Park. Dating back in parts to the late 18th century, the inn was formerly called The Blacksmith's Arms when it also had accommodation and stabling. Today, the inn is personally run by Rose and Alan Green who came here in 1995. They have, in their short tenancy, created an inn with a warm and friendly atmosphere where the locals welcome visitors warmly. A Robinson's house, The Horseshoe has several real ales on tap, including regular guest beers, all of which are kept in tip top condition. Meals are available every lunchtime and on Thursday, Friday and Saturday nights. The delicious set menu is supplemented by an ever-changing specials board. This is a wonderful pub and we wish Rose and Alan every success.

The Horseshoe Inn, 1 Buxton Road, High Town Tel: 01663 766747

TRAFFORD is a borough which encompasses everything from Victorian terraces to green belt farmland, all within a few miles of the city centre. Driving down the M56 from Stockport to Chester you will pass the turn off for **MANCHESTER INTERNATIONAL AIRPORT**. A huge

Bramhall Hall

Dunham Massey Hall

expanse of buildings and a recently opened second terminal give the area an unrivalled communications network.

SALE. If you are of the widely held opinion that craftsmanship is dead and that new buildings cannot match the style or quality of their Victorian counterparts then you would be well advised to visit **THE KING'S RANSOM** in the centre of Sale. This pub has only just been constructed, but it is already apparent that this is one of the most stylish pubs in the area. You could be forgiven for thinking that it is as old as the adjacent Bridgewater Canal or the railway arch that it is partly built into.

The King's Ransom

The interior is a real 'eye-opener', with lots of reclaimed timber and open fires to enhance its warm and inviting atmosphere. The King's Ransom is owned by Watling Inns (also owners of The Waterside Inn in Leigh) so you can be assured that this fine pub serving real ales and good food is certainly worth a visit.

The King's Ransom, Britannia Road, Sale.
Tel: 0161 969 6006 Fax: 0161 969 6776

HALE and HALE BARNS house a wealth of excellent restaurants and some good hotels convenient for the airport.

SAN ROCCO, a genuine Italian restaurant, lies just a few yards of Ashley Road, in Crown Passages, the heart of Hale Village. Purpose built in 1992 San Rocco is one of the five restaurants that Sergio Stefanuto owns and runs in the region. This popular eating place has an extravagant and unusual interior decor that adjusts well from lunchtime eating to evening dining.

Whether you are here for a party or an intimate dinner for two the atmosphere will just right. It is advisable to book at the weekends not to avoid disappointment and when you taste the food you will see why it is so popular. The menu, a delicious list of mouth-watering dishes changes regularly and contains many familiar favourites as well as house specialities. As with all Italian cooking, fresh produce plays an important part and the daily specials reflect the seasons as well as the best in Italian cuisine.

San Rocco, Crown Passages, off Ashley Road, Hale Tel: 0161 929 8024

Further up the main street, Ashley Road, the recently refurbished **EVERGREEN** is an elegant Chinese eatery (telephone 0161 928 1222)

HALE WINE BAR, on the main road through the village and almost opposite the Victorian station, is well known in the area for its fine selection of classic and new world wines as well as for its appetising, menu.

Owned and run for the past 12 years by John Buckley, ably assisted by his son Jean-Christophe, its well earned reputation makes it one of the places to be seen in the area. The low key, symmetrical frontage hides the interesting and atmospheric interior, where, on two floors, there are plenty of tables and chairs on which to sit. Open for lunch and again in the evening, it is an ideal place to come to when taking a break from the office or to enjoy a pleasant and relaxing glass of wine and meal in the evening.

Hale Wine Bar, 108 Ashley Road, Hale Tel: 0161 928 2343

In the heart of Hale is **MULBERRY AND ZWECH,** a wonderful delicatessen and café with a true continental feel. Enter the shop and you could be anywhere in Europe; Paris, Rome, Athens or Berlin. All the bread and pastries are baked at the back of the shop and include traditional Italian ciabatta, croissants and patisserie. The delicatessen counter is stocked full of cheese, with creamy French brie, tangy goat's cheese, Gruyere and feta, cooked meats, with wonderfully luscious smoked hams, juicy salamis and bacons, and a whole range of other foods from around the world..

Mulberry And Zwech

The relaxed and informal café, open like the delicatessen, all day everyday and for much of Sunday, serves a mouthwatering selection of filled ciabatta and baguettes, with imaginative fillings such as feta and roasted vegetables, ham and Gruyere with Dijon mustard, and hummous, olives and charred peppers. With a healthy range of fresh salads and hot filled croissants and ciabatta this is an ideal place for a tasty lunch break. For those with a sweet tooth the creme patisserie tarts and other French pastries are too tempting. Finally, the aroma of coffee is hard to resist whether you prefer cappuccino or expresso, Mulberry and Zwech also serves a range of regular and herbal teas. With a lunchtime ordering service this is an ideal place to stop and sample the delights of the Continent.

Mulberry and Zwech, 24 Victoria Road, Hale Tel: 0161 929 7661

In the heart of the village of Hale Barns you will find **THE BULL'S HEAD,** which offers the very best in cuisine, ale and comfort. Over the last three years the Bull's Head has been completely refurbished, this work has been sensitively executed and great care has been taken to ensure that all of its original features are retained. The pub has a traditional stone floor and a series of colour themed rooms, each with its own antique marble cast iron or carved wooden fireplace and log fire. Excellent food is served and a wide selection of well kept ales is always available. Live entertainment is provided every Wednesday night.

By the end of 1996 a building project to add 21 en-suite letting rooms will be complete, and, if they are up to the same high standard as the rest of the pub, will be well worth investigating. All in all this is a super pub which you would be well advised to visit.

The Bull's Head, Wicker Lane, Hale Barns, Cheshire. Tel: 0161 980 3050

ALTRINCHAM is a busy town and whilst only a few minutes from Manchester and a mere 20 minutes on the new Metrolink tram system it has retained a market town feel to it. All the major high street names are here, but there are still a good number of individually run enterprises which saves you from having that "haven't we been here before" feeling, so common now as many town and city centres have nothing but chain stores to offer the shopper. Altrincham has a busy market and some good places to eat.

Cadoro, Altrincham

One of the most original and interesting shops in Altrincham's fine shopping centre is **CADORO**. Situated on Oxford Road, Cadoro, which means 'House of Gold' in Italian, aims to make art works more accessible to the general public. Original, high quality works of art from all over the world, including glassware, paintings, etchings, studio ceramics, sculptures and individually designed pieces of jewellery are for sale at prices which are affordable. Specially commissioned one-off pieces by local artists hang from the wall alongside work by well renowned overseas designers and painters.

If you are considering changing the look of your home you would be well advised to employ a skilled Interior Designer. A number of top hotels around the country use Cadoro's expert soft furnishing and design service for this very reason. From curtains and couches, to bedrooms and bathrooms, Cadoro's experienced and talented designers can transform your house into the home that you have always wanted.

Cadoro Gallery and Interiors, 31 Oxford Road, Altrincham.
Tel: 0161 929 8120

Just off the main shopping street in Altrincham, in the small but vibrant Kings Court, is **GALLIPOLI TURKISH RESTAURANT**. As Manchester's first ever regional Turkish restaurant owner, Unal Capli takes great pleasure in introducing the unique taste of Turkish food to new and valued customers.

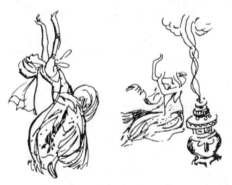

Gallipoli Turkish Restaurant

Dining here is very much an experience. Fortunately, the menu provides English translations to the wealth of dishes which are all prepared in an authentic manner from fresh produce. The comprehensive wine list includes labels from France and Italy as well as Turkey and the Turkish beer is a house speciality. Open for lunches and dinners, party bookings are welcome and, to add further to the already exciting atmosphere, a belly dancer can be arranged. After your Dolmalar (meat stuffed vegetables), Kebab which ever one of the mouth-watering dishes you finally decide upon, why not end your meal with an authentic Turkish coffee?

Gallipoli Turkish Restaurant, 4 Kings Court, Altrincham Tel: 0161 928 6983

The outstanding **JASPERS WINE BAR** lies hidden away in the

Kings Court development in Altrincham. Standing on the site of an old corn mill, the wine bar features an internal exposed brick wall that was the old exterior wall of the mill.

Owned and personally run by Ruth Fletcher and Arturo Biviano, over the past four years they have turned Jaspers into the place to eat, drink and be seen in the town. Outside, there is a lovely terrace, floodlit in the evenings. Inside you will find stone tiled floors, open fireplaces and an interesting display of prints. As well as having a wonderful atmosphere, Jaspers is renowned for its exciting and delicious cuisine, complemented by superb wines. Open throughout the day, this is an ideal place to come for a cup of coffee, a light lunch or an intimate dinner.

Jaspers Wine Bar, Kings Court, Altrincham Tel: 0161 941 6241

The outstanding **BRICKLAYERS ARMS** lies in George Street, the main pedestrian walkway through the centre of Altrincham. With an eye-catching exterior this is just the place to quench the thirst and fill that hungry gap. Inside the pub is a picture, with wooden floors and lots of memorabilia hanging from the ceilings and displayed on the walls. Very popular both for the food and for the excellent selection of beers and ales it has a warm and friendly atmosphere. The menu contains many favourites and ranges from snacks to full meals but its is the daily specials board that makes the Bricklayers so popular with its diners.

Bricklayers Arms, George Street, Altrincham Tel: 0161 928 1567

Tucked away in Goose Green Courtyard, just off the busy main shopping street in Altrincham, lies **SNOCKERS ON THE GREEN**. This unusually named restaurant is owned and run with enthusiasm and style by Chris Hyde and Jon Scoltock. Dating back to the 19th century, the building was once railwaymen's cottages and the name Goose Green comes from a time when geese were let loose here. This is a peaceful, tranquil spot, full of character, and, when the weather is fine, diners can enjoy the pleasure of eating outside.

Snockers on the Green

The interior of the restaurant has been extensively refurbished to create an intimate atmosphere which complements the imaginative menu. Open every day except Monday evenings and Sundays, Snockers on the Green specialises in high quality English cuisine.

There is a light lunch menu, a full a la carte evening menu and a daily specials board. With dishes such as Bury Black Pudding and Golden Delicious Apples encased in puff pastry with Green Peppercorn and Calvados Sauce and Tiger Prawns with toasted Coconut on Sweet Honey and Ginger Syrup this really is a dining experience not to be missed. The wine list, featuring a fine selection of European and new World wines of quality and value, complements the menu beautifully.

Snockers on the Green, 9 Goose Green, Altrincham Tel: 0161 929 8929

OLD MILL HOTEL is an outstanding Victorian property which overlooks Altrincham railway station and is just a few minutes walk from the town centre. As the name suggests, the hotel was originally a mill, but for many years was known as The Barrington.

Recently, the Old Mill has been thoroughly renovated and refurbished and now looks a picture, inside and out. Though a peculiar wedge shape, the hotel offers the very best in comfort for all its guests. The fourteen en-suite bedrooms are top quality and the hotel is open seven days a week to non residents who can enjoy, along with guests, excellent food and warm and friendly hospitality.

Old Mill Hotel, 2 Barrington Road, Altrincham Tel: 0161 928 2960

On The Downs, a road running from Altrincham to Bowden, is the popular **"THE FRENCH"** and opposite its sister restaurant **"THE BRASSERIE"**. Both offer classic french cuisine with The French being a more formal restaurant, while the Brasserie caters for more informal dining

The French & The Brasserie 0161 928 0808

Up the road in Bowden is a good family eating place called **DECKERS**. It has a wide choice and very generous portions, all reasonably priced.

Deckers 0161 941 5253.

BROADHEATH, **THE OLD PACKET HOUSE**, at Broadheath near Altrincham, is a delightful olde worlde inn dating back to the late 1700s.

The Old Packet House

Recently renovated, none of the inns striking original features have been lost and the original open fires, dark panelling, tiled floors and exposed brickwork create a homely atmosphere. Once a staging post along the famous Bridgewater Canal, the same warm and friendly welcome is extended to all guests ensures that they return again and again. There are four en-suite bedroom providing the ultimate in comfort and relaxed living and the food and ales here are of excellent quality and value.

The Old Packet House, Navigation Road, Broadheath, Altrincham
Tel: 0161 929 1331

GATLEY. THE RED LION, situated in the heart of the village of Gatley, is a Whitbread Managed House. It is full of character and charm and, although it has been refurbished, if you took out all the modern fittings with would look just as it did 200 years ago. There are a mixture of flagstone and wooden floors and plenty of old oak beams. This is very much the village local but the warm welcome is whole heartedly extended to visitors. Food is available at lunchtime and evenings, except Sunday evening, from a mouth-watering menu and there is no need to book. With a specials board and children's menu there is something for everyone. The Red Lion also keeps a good variety of beers and ales to quench that thirst. As well as good food and drink there is always something going on, Wednesday night is Quiz night and there is are darts, crib and football teams.

The Red Lion, 63 Church Road, Gatley Tel: 0161 428 4344

DUNHAM MASSEY. Tucked away in a corner, bounded by the M56 and M6 motorways is Dunham Massey which is home to **DUNHAM MASSEY HALL** and Park. Excellent walks can be had here and there are often craft fairs held in the hall and grounds.

CHEADLE. THE ASHLEA stands on the main road into Cheadle and opposite the now redundant Cheadle Railway Station. The pub started life many years ago as estate worker's cottages to nearby Abney Hall and until November 1990 it was known as The Railway, for obvious reasons! One of Henry's Table chain of pub restaurants owned by Boddington Brewery, you know you can be sure of excellent food and beer. The interior of the Ashlea has been beautifully decorated and furnished: there is plenty of wood with half-panelled walls, comfortable tables and chairs, feature fireplaces and an octagonal conservatory. Whilst soaking up the atmosphere, there is an extensive menu of delicious and mouth-watering dishes to choose from as well as the daily specials board. A popular place for all the family it is always a good idea to book a table for Saturday evening and Sunday lunchtime.

The Ashlea, 14 Manchester Road, Cheadle Tel: 0161 428 0413

Of course these are only some of the many attractions within the Greater Manchester region and it is worth exploring further before making your way across the border into East Lancashire which is where the next chapter begins.

CHAPTER TWO

East Lancashire

Haworth Gallery, Accrington

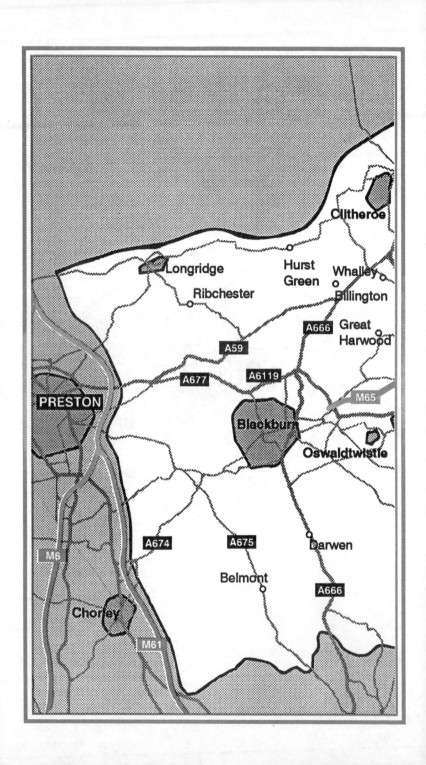

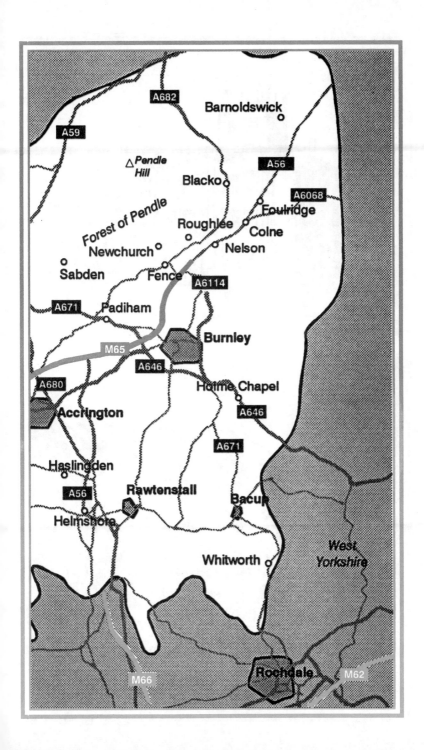

Gawthorpe Hall, nr Burnley

Townley Hall Art Gallery and Museum, Burnley

CHAPTER TWO

East Lancashire

If Manchester is Cottonopolis, East Lancashire is the Cotton Capital's hinterland, a series of densely populated towns crowding into the Pennine valleys, each with its own special character and close to open moorland landscape of desolate grandeur.

PENDLE HILL, that great whaleback of a mountain, dominates the northern part of this region. It is a constant feature on the skyline, giving its name to the District which includes the towns and villages on its eastern flank.

This is an area rich in legend and history - none more evocative than the tragic story of the Pendle Witches. The infamous witches were mainly old women who dabbled with plants and herbs and knew those plants that could heal and those which spelt certain death when taken.

Early in the year of 1612 several people were imprisoned at Lancaster Castle. At the trial, chilling accounts of evildoings were brought to light as families and villagers accused each other. On August 20th ten women and one of their sons were found guilty and were hanged in front of huge crowds. Years later, in 1633, there were more trials. Several died in prison and four others were taken to London to be put on show.

Something of that old, dark tragedy still broods around Pendle and many memories and places which hark back to that time still remain. Find out more by visiting **WITCHES GALORE** at NEWCHURCH and see if you can find the grave of Alice Nutter who was hanged on that fateful day in 1612 in St. Mary's churchyard.

Look up at the mysterious Eye of God carved on the tower to protect parishoners from the evil they feared lurked in the shadow of Pendle Hill.

There are many books inspired by the Witches of Pendle, you will find a good selection at Nelson Tourist Information Centre. A full list of Tourist Information Centres in the region is at the back of the book.

For all of its mysterious history, this is countryside of intimate beauty. You can take a choice of routes north of Burnley or Nelson into BARROWFORD and on to BARLEY where there is a car park and a small Visitor's Centre and from where there is a popular, well marked path to the summit of Pendle Hill.

The steep climb affords a magnificent viewpoint across to the coast and on clear days, Yorkshire's Three Peaks and the Lakeland mountains beyond. There are delightful walks along the little valley formed by Pendle Water, perhaps to **WHITE HOUGH** and Mistress Nutter's home - now a farmhouse - in Roughlee, or around the nearby reservoirs of Lower and Upper Black Moss, the brooding outline of Pendle Hill always a presence.

ROUGHLEE. In the centre of the picturesque village of Roughlee is the eye-catching **BAY HORSE INN**. The oldest part of the building dates back to the 17th century though it was a farmhouse prior to becoming a public house in the late 18th century. This free house, owned and run by Val Graham, is beautifully decorated and furnished throughout and includes exposed brick walls and a feature stone fireplace that all conjure up images from the past. As well as serving a selection of well kept ales the restaurant offers a range of tasty and imaginative dishes that have made the Bay Horse famous in the surrounding area. Children are very well catered for and there is an excellent purpose-built adventure playground at the rear of the pub. This is a real family inn.

The Bay Horse, Blacko Bar Road, Roughlee, Nelson Tel: 01282 613683

BLACKO. Situated up on a hill overlooking the village of Blacko is **BLACKO LAITHE FARM** guest house. Set in 48 acres of farmland in the heart of Pendle Witch country, there are unrivalled views in all directions which include the legendary Pendle Hill. In the late 1980s, your hosts Ernest and Sandra Greenwood, opened the guest house, with the help of John Lee MP the then Minister of Tourism, which had been converted from a 300 year old barn.

Blacko Laithe Farm

The guest house has seven double bedrooms including three with en suite facilities and there are also family rooms if required. The attractive gardens and trees create an atmosphere of peace and tranquillity though the Farm is not far from the M65 and close to many places of historical interest.

Blacko Laithe Farm Guest House, Blacko Bar Road, Blacko, Nelson
Tel: 01282 694642

COLNE is one of East Lancashire's mill and market towns, with lines of sloping grey roofs stretching along a gentle hillside above the valley formed by Colne Water. Here you'll find a monument on the main road near the War Memorial to one Wallace Hartley, who had the misfortune to be bandmaster on the Titanic in 1912. He heroically stayed at his post, conducting the band in 'Nearer my God to Thee' as the doomed liner was sinking beneath the icy Atlantic.

Whilst in Colne be sure to visit **THE BRITISH IN INDIA MUSEUM**, situated on Newtown Street. The exhibits cover many aspects of the British rule of India from the 17th century to the granting of idependence in 1947. *Tel: 01282 870215*

FOULRIDGE It's only a short way from Barrowford along the Leeds-Liverpool canal to Foulridge, near Colne. A stroll or boat trip along the canal almost inevitably includes dropping in to the **HOLE IN THE WALL INN** for a refreshing pint of real ale and a sustaining bar snack.

The Hole in the Wall Inn

Locally known as The Gap, the inn was rebuilt in the late 18th century following a fire which destroyed most of the original building. Peter and Jean, your hosts, came here in the summer of 1995 and bring with them many years experience in the trade. Jean is the cook and the menu, simple and all home-made, is just the thing when out and about exploring the local area.

The darts board and pool room are among the inn's other attractions, and musical guests are encouraged to share their talent on a rather fine organ. Pictures adorning the walls include one of a local by-gone celebrity - 'Buttercup' the cow. The story goes that when this hapless animal fell into the canal, she was to swim a mile before finally being rescued near the inn and successfully revived with a tot of whiskey! Anglers will be pleased to known that there is also the opportunity to catch fish!

The Hole in the Wall, 1 Towngate, Foulridge, Near Colne Tel: 01282 863568

WYCOLLER, reached either from the main A6068 Keighley road at Laneshaw Bridge, or via the mill village of Trawden is an almost deserted Pennine village which was once a thriving handbook weaver's settlement that lost most of its inhabitants when new factories took trade away.

WYCOLLER HALL, now a ruin, was the inspiration for the setting of Ferndean Manor in Charlotte Bronte's 'Jane Eyre'. The Brontes, keen walkers, would often have walked over here from Haworth. Much remains of interest in the village - a lovely old hump-backed packhorse bridge crossing Colne Water, and above the village, a single slab gritstone bridge, Clam Bridge, thought to be Iron Age in origin.

The settlement now forms part of WYCOLLER COUNTRY PARK, and you must leave a car in the car park to walk a few hundred yards down the hill into the village. At Hall Barn Information Centre there are displays about village and local natural history, and a choice of easy walking trails in and around the Country Park is available.

BURNLEY, to the south, is a cotton town, rich in history and the largest town in East Lancashire. Incorporating an area of some 50 square miles, visitors will be amazed by Burnley's wealth of contrasts, from some of the best preserved industrial landscapes in Britain, to magnificent countryside with rugged moorlands and deep gorges.

The town was first established around 800AD and nestles in a basin between the River Calder and the River Brun from which it gets its name.

With the Industrial Revolution and the building of the Leeds and Liverpool Canal, Burnley grew in stature and by the end of the 19th century was the world's leading producer of cotton cloth. Take a walk along the canal towpath through the area known as the Weaver's Triangle and you step back into the 19th century. Here are to be found former spinning mills and weaving sheds; foundries where steam engines and looms were made; canal-side warehouses; domestic buildings, including a unique row of worker's houses; and a Victorian school.

The WEAVERS TRIANGLE VISITOR CENTRE on Manchester Road is housed in the former wharfmaster's house and canal toll office. The centre is open to the public, free of charge, on several afternoons each week during the summer months and on most bank holidays.

Weavers Triangle Visitors Centre. Tel: 01282 30055

You can take a step back in time and explore history by boat as you travel along the **LEEDS-LIVERPOOL CANAL.** This famous waterway cuts dramatically through Lancashire's Hill Country, from the lush farmland south of Blackburn to the fine summit stretch in Pendle before it strides into the Pennines.

From the Weaver's Triangle the huge Burnley embankment carries the canal across the town. Known as the "straight mile", it is in fact only three quarters of a mile long, but no less exciting for that, and at sixty feet high is one of the most impressive features of the canal system. On a misty day you almost feel as if you are floating above the clouds.

Situated on the Todmorden Road on the outskirts of Burnley, **TOWNELEY HALL ART GALLERY AND MUSEUM** provides a fascinating and enjoyable day out for the whole family.

The Hall was the home of the Towneley family from the 14th century to 1902 and parts of the present building date back to the 15th century, the oldest being the lower part of the south-east wing containing two stone spiral staircases and a Gothic window. Visitors to the Hall can explore the kitchen with its open fires on which many a banquet was cooked and then passed through to the Servants' Hall before discovering the fascinating family history in various other rooms. Towneley Park which surrounds the Hall extends to some 284 acres with facilities for golf, pitch and putt, tennis, bowls and other outdoor sports. The art collections, the Whalley Abbey Vestments and the museum of local crafts and industries, which is housed in the former brew-house and laundry, are all worth visiting while you are here.

Towneley Hall Art Gallery and Museums, Todmorden Road, Burnley
Tel: 01282 424213

Over the centuries people have turned to nature to cure their niggling aches and pains and provide relief from the symptoms of any number of complaints and illnesses. In fact, homeopathy and other alternative medicines are not really an invention of the late 20th century but rather a recognition of much older treatments used by our forebearers. Here in the heart of Burnley, **BARLOW'S HERBALISTS**, have been offering old fashioned remedy's for over 100 years. Established in 1882, the shop was originally owned by the Barlow family. Today, with a renewed interest in the remedy's of previous generations the shop is in a renaissance period. The shelves are stocked with vitamins and minerals supplements and healing herbs in ointment, tablet, dry and liquid form to help promote a healthy body and mind. The staff, all extremely knowledgeable, are a mind of information and very willing to offer advise and help. The shop also offers a mail order service for which a catalogue is available and is happy to agree bulk prices. This really is an interesting and very informative place, with a wonderful mixture of aromas, and a visit could just be the pick-me-up you need!

Barlow's Herbalists, 27 Standish Street, Burnley Tel: 01282 423374

Just outside the centre of Burnley, on the A682, lies the elegant, stone mansion **ROSEHILL HOUSE HOTEL**. Standing in its own grounds in a quiet residential area, the house was built in 1856 by the prominent local businessman, Adam Dugdale. He brought in Italian craftsmen to build the solid marble fireplaces and the extremely ornate moulded ceilings, all of which remain as lasting features in the hotel.

Rosehill House Hotel

Owned and run by Jacquie and John Doherty, the accommodation is suitable for both business and pleasure. All the 20 bedrooms are en suite and fully central heated with other modern comforts you expect from a top class hotel. On the ground floor are two comfortable lounges and a large cocktail bar, together with two tastefully decorated dining rooms for non-resident's use. The restaurant is renowned in the area for its fine cuisine and offers an excellent choice of English and international dishes. A charming establishment that comes highly recommended.

Rosehill House Hotel, Rosehill Avenue, off Manchester Road, Burnley
Tel: 01282 453931

Around Burnley

There are many charming villages around Burnley, each with their own particular points of interest and it is worth spending some time branching out from here along the winding country lanes and exploring some of them.

HOLME CHAPEL is an unspoilt village situated in the beautiful **CLIVIGER GORGE** three miles south east of Burnley on the A646. The church is of particular interest and is the burial place of General Scarlett who led the charge of the Heavy Brigade at Balaclava.

CLIVIGER has a few old legends connected with it . The Towneley boggart of 'Boggart Bridge' was attributed to the restless, remorseful spirit of Sir John Towneley who enclosed 194 acres of land illegally, and forcibly ejected local tenants. The Holme too is said to be haunted.

REEDLEY HALLOWS is set between Burnley and Brierfield. It is a place with historic connections. Old Chattox, one of the Lancashire witches, had associations with Greenhead Farm, and Laund House was the home of John and Robert Nutter, Catholic priests who were persecuted in the 16th century.

PADIHAM, to the west of Burnley, with its narrow winding lanes and cobbled alleyways, still retains characteristics of the early Industrial Revolution. It existed well before the Norman Conquest and was a market town where produce from Pendleside was bought and

The Hare and Hounds Inn

Standing 100 yards back from, what used to be, the main street in Padiham is the **HARE AND HOUNDS INN**. Known locally as the

'Coachy', this former coaching inn is run by the charming Sandie Crosbie. Inside the inn is full of character and divided into three intimate and cosy rooms which help to create a wonderfully warm and friendly atmosphere. As well as serving a fine selection of ales and beers, there is an extensive menu of bar snacks with special menus for children and vegetarians. Bed and breakfast accommodation is also on offer in four tastefully decorated and well furnished, comfortable, en-suite rooms.

Hare and Hounds, 58 West Street, Padiham Tel: 01282 774749

For lovers of historic houses, one place well worth visiting while you are in the area is **GAWTHORPE HALL**. Situated on the eastern outskirts of Padiham on the edge of the Pennines, this splendid 17th century house was restored to Victorian elegance by Sir Charles Barry during the 1850s.

The present house was started in 1600, but Gawthorpe had been the home of the Shuttleworth family for 200 years prior to this. Beautiful period furnishings are enhanced by ornately decorated ceilings and original wood panelled walls, providing the perfect setting for the nationally important Kay-Shuttleworth collections of needlework and lace.

The Hall also houses a major collection of 17th century portraits on loan from the National Portrait Gallery. The lovely gardens surrounding the Hall are open all year round and in the shop you will find a range of quality goods providing you with the ideal memento of your visit.

Gawthorpe Hall, Padiham, Near Burnley Tel: 01282 778511

HUNCOAT is one of only a few local places listed in the Domesday Book and in 1986 celebrated its 900th year. The nucleus of the old village can be seen at Town Gate, together with the village stocks which have existed since 1722. It was in this same year that local man John Hacking invented the cotton carding engine.

Of further historic interest, situated off Burnley Road, **HUNCOAT HALL** is of medieval origin, and the King's Highway is the ancient road to Manchester used by John Wesley.

FENCE, the unusually named village of is not far away to the north-east of Padiham. The name of this small settlement strung out along the fields of Pendleside recalls the enclosure in which stags were kept when hunting was abandoned in Pendle Forest.

Just a couple of hundred yards off the main A6068, in the village of Fence, is the **FENCE GATE INN** and Banqueting Centre. This is the premier place of its type in the area and Kevin Berkins, the owner, has put in a lot of hard work to establish this reputation. Over the years he has extensively refurbished and extended these historic premises. As well as the inn and brasserie, there are two outstanding banqueting rooms. The Fence Gate is stylish and full of character and, whether you are here just for a drink or to attend an elaborate function the food, drink and service is second to none.

Fence Gate Inn, Wheatley Lane Road, Fence, Near Burnley
Tel: 01282 618101

At Fence Gate, there is a **SLATE AGE CRAFT CENTRE**, situated in a converted farm building now used for the manufacture of slate giftware. There has been a slate craft centre here for 22 years.

This small family run company manufactures high quality slate giftware which is exported all over the world. The slate can be seen in its 'raw' state and then through the various machine and hand processes until the finished product is achieved.

Marble and granite are also on show in the form of hearths, fireplaces, kitchen worktops, vanity units etc. which are all produced to customers own requirements.

Visitors can look around the workshops and visit the craft shop where there is a wide choice of unusual gifts. Admission is free.

Slate Age, Fence Gate, Fence, Nr Burnley.
Tel; 01282 616952
Fax: 01282 619058

The brothers, Jonathan and Clive Seedall, took over **THE FOREST INN** at the beginning of 1993 and have turned it into the impressive establishment it is today. This former farmhouse did not become a pub until the late 19th century but the buildings date back a lot further. During the 1950s this was the place to come as it had the first TV in the area and visitors came from far and wide to watch a programme.

Now fully refurbished and with a charming conservatory, the Forest Inn is once again popular. This time people come here for the excellent food, good ale and pleasant and charming atmosphere. It is always a good idea to book a table to avoid disappointment and besides the set menu there are numerous blackboards with tempting and mouth-watering dishes. Open all day, everyday this is a place full of character, style and class.

The Forest Inn, Cuckstool Lane, Fence, Burnley Tel: 01282 613641

HIGHAM, another delightful Pendle village, is nearby . Higham has been associated with Jonal Moore of White Lea, mathematician Surveyor-General of Ordnance and co-founder of the Greenwich Observatory.

Keep an eye out for the Four Alls Inn. The sign outside bears four pictures and the legends: "I govern all" next to the king, "I pray for all" next to the clergyman, "I fight for all" next to the soldier, and finishes with a rather rueful looking worker and the words: "I pay far all".

SABDEN is set beneath the impressive Pendle Hill, only a mile or so from Higham. Here George Fox, founder of the Quakers, had a vision which led to the foundation of that movement.

The local handloom weavers of old were said to weave parkin using oatmeal as the warp and treacle as the weft! Now it is possible to visit the **SABDEN TREACLE MINES** to meet the small furry treacle miners, immortalised in a children's television series.

The interestingly named **CHICKEN PIRI PIRI**, situated in Sabden, is housed in what was once a pair of 18th century cottages. This fine restaurant specialises in Portuguese food and is owned and run by the Fortuna family.

Eduardo, his wife Gillian and their sons John and Cristian established the restaurant in 1994 and have completely refurbished it taking care to enhance its existing features such as exposed stone walls and ceiling beams. The result is warm, inviting and full of character, surroundings that certainly will enhance your enjoyment of the delicious food.

The menu includes such exquisite dishes as Bitoque Com Ovo A Cavalo (Portuguese Fried Steak with Egg), Frango de Piri Piri (Chicken marinated in a traditional hot Portuguese sauce) and Bifes de Espadarte Grehados (Charcoal Grilled Swordfish Steaks). If you have never savoured the delights of Portuguese food then be sure to pay this excellent restaurant a visit.

The restaurant has a good reputation and often gets busy, so be sure to book in advance.

Chicken Piri Piri, 6 Whalley Road, Sabden, nr Clitheroe. Tel: 01282 777547

Situated in the centre of this scenic village, **BEECH COTTAGE** provides comfortable, stylish B & B accommodation suitable as a base for your exploration of this area. Helen, the hostess prides herself on the warm, friendly atmosphere which the establishment possesses. The food is of the best quality, evening meals are available on request.

Beech Cottage B & B, 12 Wesley Street, Sabden, near Clitheroe. Tel: 01282 772348

PENDLE ANTIQUES CENTRE is another popular attraction, housed in an old mill. The centre has a constantly changing stock of antique furniture and bric-a-brac from British and European sources, most of which are refurbished on the premises.

Standing high up at Sabden, on the Clitheroe Road, and with the most outstanding views is **WELLSPRINGS INN**. From this former farmhouse can be seen, to the rear, the Forest of Bowland and, to the front, the Forest of Pendle with its famous history. The farmhouse became an inn in the 19th century when it was famous for brewing its own nettle beer. Today Paul and Elaine Brown still keep the character and atmosphere as it should be but modernisation has brought the facilities up to date. The restaurant seats up to 100 comfortably and its delicious food is a favourite with everyone.

Also owned by Paul and Elaine is **FRYERS**, a hot food take away in the heart of Clitheroe. Open each evening from Tuesdays to Saturdays.

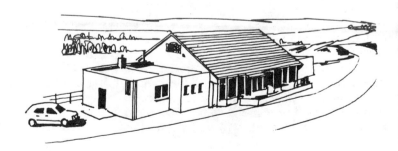

Wellsprings Inn, Clitheroe Road, Sabden Tel: 01200 23870

ROSSENDALE is one the most picturesque, varied and interesting areas of Lancashire's Hill Country. Nestling in the unspoilt beauty of the Irwell Valley, the market towns of Rawtenstall, Haslingden and Bacup are time capsules from Britain's industrial past.

RAWTENSTALL is where visitors can discover the **WEAVER'S COTTAGE**. The building was purpose built for hand loom weaving in 1780 and is one of the last remaining buildings of its kind. It is open to the public every Saturday and Sunday, between 2 and 5, April to September.

Look out for the **NEWCHURCH TUNNELS** - an impressive symbol of the determination of Victorian railway companies and their engineers to overcome obstacles in the pursuit of business and profit.

These tunnels were built in 1857 to take the line from Rawtenstall to Bacup through the narrowest part of the Irwell Gorge.

Not far outside Rawtenstall is **SKI ROSSENDALE**, the North West's premier ski centre, open all year round - whatever the weather! The centre is ideal for beginners and experts alike, and tuition is available. Adjacent to Ski Rossendale is Whitaker Park and the Rossendale Museum.

ROSSENDALE MUSEUM is housed in a Victorian mill owners' mansion formerly known as Oakhill. There are impressive collections of natural history, fine art and furniture, ceramics and local industrial and domestic bygones.

The extensive grounds of Whitaker Park contain something for everyone, including a bowling green, tennis courts, playground area, aviary and domestic animal enclosure. You could also enjoy a stroll amid the pleasant and well kept gardens.

At one end of the town, you will find a new railway station marking the end of a very old railway - the **EAST LANCASHIRE RAILWAY**. The original line opened in 1846 and ran until 1980 when the last coal train went to Rawtenstall. Seven years later, and with plenty of hard work and dedication from the East Lancashire Railway Preservation Society, the railway began to carry passengers again.

The East Lancashire Railway

The steam trains offer an enthralling 17 mile round trip along the River Irwell, between Rawtenstall and Bury via the picturesque market town of Ramsbottom. Trains run every weekend, with additional services in the summer. Ask at Tourist information Centres for more details.

HASLINGDEN With such interest in antiques and curios these days, a stop at **SOMETHING OLD - SOMETHING NEW** in Haslingden could provide the answer for that special gift or addition to your home. The shop and mill has a an extensive array of period furniture, antiques, period dolls and attractive pottery, pictures and curios. Gift opportunities are everywhere and browsers will enjoy the challenge of that special find. coincidentally, the business is close to the Pennine Walks and for motorists the M65 gives easy access to the town. Open six days a week - closed Wednesdays.

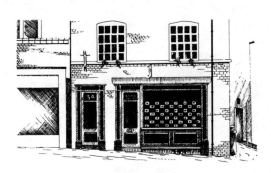

Something Old - Something New, 30 Blackburn Road, Haslingden, Lancs.
Tel: 01706 221976

HELMSHORE. Situated on Holcombe Road, the fascinating **HELMSHORE TEXTILE MUSEUMS** offer the opportunity to discover Lancashire's Textile Heritage.

Re-live the nostalgia and visit the historical working museum with demonstrations of machinery, a magnificent water wheel and Hargreaves' Spinning Jenny. There is a wonderful museum shop where you can but a momento of your visit.

BACUP. To the East is the town of Bacup. Built in the 19th century for the single minded purpose of cotton manufacture, Bacup is perhaps the best remaining example of a 19th century cotton town in England.

Strolling through the town centre you will discover beautifully restored homes and shops, the grander homes of mill owners and elegant commercial and municipal buildings hint at Bacup's proud and productive past.

WHALLEY. Back towards Pendle Hill, and a town that few visitors wish to miss is Whalley, with its grey ruined **CISTERCIAN ABBEY**, founded in 1296 and rich in historic and architectural interest.

The grounds are open to the public. The town of Whalley itself has great character and charm, and lanes link it to the village of Sabden, from where a steep and scenic pass crosses Nick o' Pendle, a notable viewpoint and hair-raising descent towards Pendleton, Clitheroe and the Ribble

Valley.

Arriving in the historic village of Whalley is always a delight since it seems so little changed from its early days. Although somewhat dominated by the railway viaduct with its 49 arches, the village has a much older history with its ruined Cistercian Abbey founded by the monks in the 13th century.

With many places of interest to visit around Whalley what better place to aim for refreshments than **THE TOBY JUG TEA SHOP** on King Street. This is a quaint Grade 11 listed building with oak beams and panelling from the abbey which authenticates its age and adds a special touch to the homely atmosphere of the tea shop. Opened some ten years ago, the business soon developed and the earned a good reputation for its home made fruit pies, cakes and traditional afternoon teas. Although the selection changes regularly, the walnut cake, lemon gateaux and fresh cream cakes remain firm favourites. Wholemeal sandwiches of home-cooked chicken and ham with salad are freshly made to order and the extensive menu offers further selections of home-made soups and speciality lunches. Although the owners will be delighted to see you at any time, the weekdays offer a more relaxed pace. Good wheelchair access. No smoking please. Closed Mondays and Tuesdays.

The Toby Jug Tea Shop, 20 King Street, Whalley, Lancashire.
Tel: 01254 823298

Look out for **WHALLEY VIADUCT**, a major landscape feature more than 600 metres long and up to 21 metres high.

There are 48 arches in total, and the viaduct is built of 7 million bricks, all made locally. It was built to carry the Blackburn-Clitheroe railway line across the Calder Valley in 1850.

Where it crosses the lane to Whalley Abbey, three of the arches have been given Gothic details to harmonise with the nearby 14th century gatehouse.

Ideally situated for touring the surrounding Lancashire country-side, **THE SWAN HOTEL** at Whalley, features in many good guide books. Steeped in history there has been a drinking establishment here since the times when nearby Whalley Abbey was a place of pilgrimage. Rebuilt in its present form between 1800 and 1810, The Swan Hotel has, over the years, been known as The Swan Inn, The White Swan and Posting House, The White Swan, The Swan and Commercial Hotel before taking its present name. Captain Harry Barlow and his lovely wife Carol came here four years ago and have created a wonderful, friendly establishment. Open all day there is an extensive range of homestyle country food available along with well kept beers and ales. The couple also offer en-suite bed and breakfast accommodation.

The Swan Hotel, 62 King Street, Whalley Tel: 01254 822195

THE DOG INN on the main street in Whalley dates back, in parts, to the 17th century but there first appeared a licensed premises of that name on the Town Census in 1830. A former farmhouse, the Dog Inn sits right in the heart of historic Whalley.

The Dog Inn

Personally run for the past three years or more by Norman and Christine Atty, it is a real picture with an olde worlde appearance and bygone memorabilia decorating the walls. At lunchtime food is available with the menu displayed on three blackboards. Cooked to order and absolutely delicious your meal can be enjoyed whilst listening to the

Packhorse Bridge, Hurst Green

Haworth Gallery, Accrington

classical music playing in the background.

In the evenings things change a little: there is no food, just a selection of excellent well kept ales, lagers and wines to enjoy.

The Dog Inn, King Street, Whalley Tel: 01254 823009

RIBCHESTER, a litte further to the west is an ancient riverside village, built on the site of the Roman station of Bremetennacum.

Estimated to have covered six acres of ground, a large portion of the remains lie under the old church and churchyard. **THE ROMAN MUSEUM** has recently been extended and provides interesting displays about Roman life in the area.

THE WHITE BULL can be found in Ribchester near to the Roman Bath House and Roman Museum. originally built and used as the local courthouse, the exact date of the building is not known although the 1707 datestone was placed after an early rebuilding. The pub has an imposing porch supported by Roman pillars that were salvaged from the River Ribble. the cosy, but open interior has a lounge bar with the local's snug off to one side and the dining room to the other.

The varied menu is available in the bar and dining areas and The White Bull is famous for its casseroles, stews and fish dishes. There is a selection of unique and exciting specials which are changed regularly and there is always a guest cask ale. There are open fires throughout and a fox going through the wall complements the unusual, but traditional decor. There is a beer garden to the rear. Families are most welcome and the pub offers a separate menu for children.

The White Bull, Church Street, Ribchester. Tel: 01254 878303

The **MUSEUM OF CHILDHOOD** contains a wonderful collection of toys, models, dolls, doll's houses, miniatures and curios including a 20 piece working model fairground. The museum has twice been voted best small attraction in the North West.

Also in this historic village, alongside the River Ribble, **STONEBRIDGE BISTRO** has a really picturesque situation. Formerly four farm workers cottages, the bistro is owned and run by Maria and

Stephen Joyson and their family. The couple both have plenty of experience in the business and Maria's father opened the first Greek restaurant in Lancashire. Beautifully decorated throughout, furnished to a high standard and seating 60 comfortably it is necessary to book you table at the weekend to avoid disappointment.

The menu is varied and extensive and is supplemented by a special's board that changes with the seasons. Home-cooking is the priority here and you can be sure of a very memorable meal in a pleasant and friendly atmosphere.

Stonebridge Bistro, 19 Blackburn Road, Ribchester Tel: 01254 878664

Hidden in Stonygate Lane, situated just off the main road at Ribchester, is the internationally renowned **STYDD NURSERY**, specialists in old-fashioned rose varieties. The staff are knowledgeable and will help you to select the best plants for your garden. Even if you have little interest in gardening, a visit to this pleasant nursery is certain to be rewarding.

Stydd Nursery, Stonygate Lane, Ribchester. 01254 878797

HURST GREEN. This picturesque village lies to the west of Whalley on the main B6243 and is celebrated for its **PACKHORSE BRIDGE** and **STONYHURST**, its famous Roman Catholic public school.

The magnificent buildings are set in extensive parkland with two huge ponds which were excavated in 1696. Cromwell stayed here in 1648 and in 1811 the building became the first public building to be lit by gas.

Sir Arthur Conan Doyle is among the famous ex-scholars of the college. Stoneyhurst is open to the public on certain days of the year and tours of the building can be arranged.

BLACKBURN, lying further south, is the largest town in East Lancashire, notable for its modern shopping malls, its Market Hall, its celebrated three day market, its modern cathedral incorporating the nave of the 1826 building, and Thwaites Brewery, one of the largest independent brewers of real ale in the North.

Other points of interest in this busy market town are **THE LEWIS**

TEXTILE MUSEUM which is dedicated to the cotton industry and **THE MUSEUM AND ART GALLERY,** appropriately situated in Museum Street, which has among its many treasures eight paintings by Turner, the Hart collection of medieval manuscripts, an outstanding collection of Japanese prints and antiques, and the finest collection of Eastern European Icons in Britain.

BILLINGTON. Situated a mile off the A59 on the edge of the village of Billington is the luxurious **FOXFIELDS COUNTRY HOTEL.** Its location puts within easy reach, travel to the Lake district, Yorkshire Dales and the Fylde Coast. The Motorway is a short drive away as are the historic towns of Whalley and Clitheroe. This delightful country hotel has long enjoyed an enviable reputation as a superb restaurant of the highest quality and holds the coveted A A Rosette for excellence. Recently extended and elegantly appointed it boasts the first all-suite accommodation outside London, these provide a large comfortable bedroom, separate sitting room and luxuriously appointed bathroom. Each suite is fully equipped with all the comforts you would expect. Final touches are being applied to the new leisure facilities which include a swimming pool, sauna/steam room and exercise equipment. AA - 4 Crown.

The Foxfield Country Hotel and Restaurant, Whalley Road, Billington, Blackburn, Lancashire. Tel: 01254 822556 Fax: 01254 824613

HOGHTON. A little to the west, about half way between Blackburn and Preston is this charming and much acclaimed parish.

Undoubtedly one of the most celebrated buildings in English History is the stately home of **HOGHTON TOWER** where, legend has it, King James I made his celebrated knighting of a particularly delicious joint of beef, with the eternal phrase 'I dub thee Sir Loin'! An Inn within the parish was promptly named after the event and still stands today.

ACCRINGTON. Before leaving this south-eastern corner of Lancashire, it is worth also visiting this town.

It has an outstanding Victorian town centre and is now a conservation area based on a splendid market hall and traditional shops.

There is also a popular policy of free parking for all and the new road network has made it easily accessible by car.

Accrington is home to one of the most attractive art galleries in the North of England. **HAWORTH ART GALLERY** is set in beautiful parkland and houses the largest collection - 130 pieces - of Tiffany Glass in Europe.

The collection was presented to the town by Joseph Briggs, an Accrington man, who went to New York to work with Louis Tiffany for almost forty years. Having joined the Tiffany studios in 1890, his rise through the company ranks was swift and he soon became a foreman and then manager of the Mosaic Department.

Later he held the prestigious post of Art Director and Personal Assistant to Louis Tiffany himself.

As the fashion for Tiffany Glass waned after the First World War, Louis Tiffany became despondent and concentrated his efforts on the development of an art school at Laurelton Hall, where students could learn about his personal concept of beauty. In 1924 Tiffany handed over the studios to his two managers, Douglas Nash and Joseph Briggs.

The stranglehold of the economic depression in the 1920s and changing tastes and fashions eventually forced the closure of Tiffany Glass. Douglas Nash bought the Corona Glass Works and continued trading under his own name, so Joseph Briggs was left with the sad task of trying to sell off the remainder of Tiffany stock.

He returned to his native Accrington in 1933, bringing his collection of Tiffany Glass with him, half of which he gave to the town, whilst the rest he distributed amongst his family.

Today, visitors to the Haworth Art Gallery can view this stunning collection and learn the fascinating history behind it.

Having explored some of the fascinating towns and villages of East Lancashire, we now make our way into the next chapter by travelling north to the beautiful area of the Forest of Bowland, and the Ribble Valley.

CHAPTER THREE

The Ribble Valley

Slaidburn Bridge

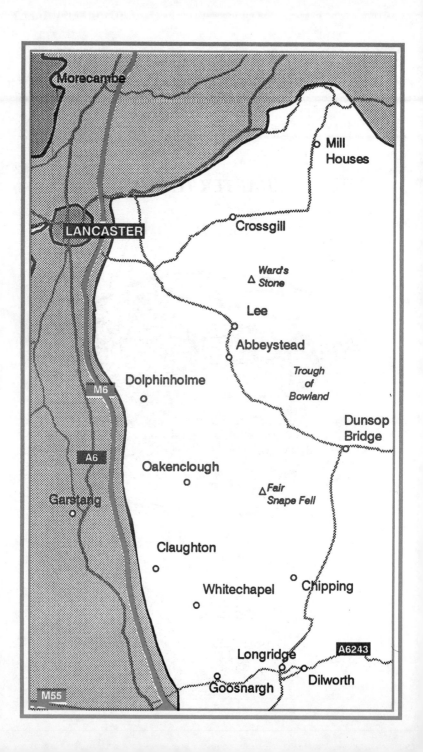

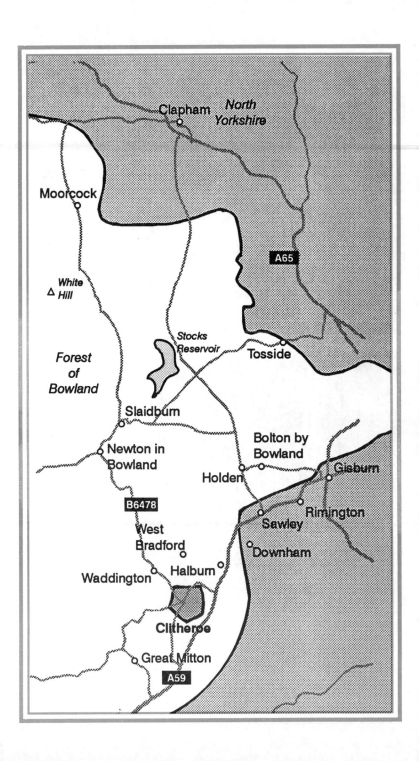

The Forest of Bowland

CHAPTER THREE

The Ribble Valley

Extending across the northern half of Lancashire, the FOREST OF BOWLAND is a region of scenic splendour. Designated an Area of Outstanding Natural Beauty in February 1964, this is a veritable paradise for walkers and country lovers, dotted with picturesque villages.

The eleventh largest of such designated areas, The Forest of Bowland is situated mainly in the county of Lancashire, although part of the area does extend into North Yorkshire.

Somewhat a misnomer, the term "forest" derives from the latin "foris" which was formerly used to denote a royal hunting ground, an unenclosed tract of land, rather than a distinct wooded area.

Its present landscape provides numerous clues to its past history. The remains of a Roman road can be clearly seen from the viewpoint at Jeffrey Hill on Longridge Fell and further clues are provided in the village names. Names such as Grindleton, Waddington, Caton and West Bradford date back to the Saxon period and Norse names are also common, such as "beck" (meaning stream) or "laithe" (meaning barn).

SAWLEY. During the 13th century Cistercian Monks travelled from Fountains Abbey in Yorkshire and settled here, just to the north of Clitheroe.

They toiled for years building the abbey, clearing trees and cultivating the land to grow crops. Ridge and furrow cultivation patterns can still be seen today.

The influence of the Monks reached across the whole landscape of Bowland through their clearance of land for farming sheep.

The 18th and 19th centuries saw the enclosure of land by drystone walls and hedgerows. Industrial activities also influenced the landscape with stone quarries, lead, and silver mines being developed. Lime was produced locally, burnt in kilns and after crushing, spread on the farmland to improve soil fertility.

The protected status of the area means it is a real haven for a wide diversity of animal, bird and plant life. Controlled burning maintains a healthy heather moor and a good grouse population.

This plays a particularly important role in the preservation of the threatened Hen Harrier, a rare bird of prey which requires substantial tracts of undisturbed heather moorland and feeds partly on grouse, of which there is a plentiful supply. Traditional field borders such as hawthorn, blackthorn, crab apple, holly and other shrubs, rising up to the levels of traditional drystone walls on the higher fells, help to maintain this natural, unspoilt picture. If you want a taste of nature at her finest, this really is the place to come.

The Forest of Bowland was chosen as one of the first places in the country to develop a chain of camping and bunkhouse barns, and there are now five Youth Hostel Association camping barns available in the Forest of Bowland. Bookings should be made in advance. Ring the Bowland Barns Reservation Office on *01200 28366*.

CLITHEROE. The old stone town of Clitheroe is the capital of the Forest of Bowland. Like Lancaster, it too is dominated by an 800-year-old castle on the hill, set on a limestone crag high above the little town. Little more than a ruin in a small park, when you stand inside the keep, hidden voices relate aspects of the castle's history with suitable sound effects. The **CASTLE MUSEUM** has collections of local geology and history, including a clogger's workshop, a printer's shop and a lead mine.

The **PLATFORM GALLERY**, opened in May 1994, is housed in a newly refurbished railway station building which was originally completed in 1870. As well as offering a regular changing programme of exhibitions the gallery aims to encourage greater appreciation of contemporary craft and to promote new works.

The Platform Gallery

The town's narrow, winding streets are full of character. You'll find old pubs and award winning shops, many of which have been owned and run for generations by the same families. You will also find narrow alleyways and steps and an excellent **TOURIST INFORMATION CENTRE**. Car parking in the town is free.

An unusual feature is the **CIVIC HALL CINEMA**, an unspoiled 1920s cinema lined in plush velvet. It is still in use as the town cinema.

Tourist Information Centre, 12-14 Market Place, Clitheroe Tel: 01200 25566

Clitheroe Castle

Clitheroe

Only yards from Clitheroe Castle, and housed within a simple Victorian building is **CAPRICE TEA SHOP**. This fine tea shop is owned and run by Peter and Joyce Jenkinson, who are justly proud of its elegant and refined interior, reminiscent of a bygone age, and the warm and friendly atmosphere which is immediately noticeable.

All of the dishes and specialities on the menu are prepared on the premises from the freshest ingredients, locally produced wherever possible. Caprice is open from 9.30am to 4.30pm with daily special lunches available from 11.30am to 2.00pm. Closed Wednesday and Sunday.

Caprice, 6-8 Moor Lane, Clitheroe. Tel: 01200 22034

Opposite the Castle Walls, in Parson Lane, is the impressive **NEW INN**. Its name is a little deceptive as the building, in parts, has been here for 250 years. Formerly a coaching inn, called the Market Hotel, the building is now listed. Alan Lees, your host, ensures that all visitors receive the same warm and friendly welcome that is a trademark of this establishment.

The New Inn, Clitheroe

The feature fireplaces and interesting prints of bygone Clitheroe make for an intimate and nostalgic atmosphere in which to enjoy one, or two, glasses of one of four real ales kept here in superb condition. From early 1996 food will be available and this will no doubt be yet another bonus to an already excellent pub.

New Inn, Parson Lane, Clitheroe Tel: 01200 23312

Situated on the main street through Clitheroe is the **ETHOS GALLERY**. This place really is something special and is much more to offer than most galleries. Owned and run by Frank and Pat Barnes, through an lot of hard work, have managed to built up a splendid reputation which, once you visit, you will see is richly deserved. The knowledgeable and friendly staff are on hand to guide you through the rooms. Downstairs there is a magnificent display of porcelain, pottery and crystal: Royal Doulton, Royal Crown Derby, Royal Worcester, Spode, Wedgewood, Caithness, Royal Brierley Crystal and Moorcroft Pottery to name a few. The two upstairs floors also show many original paintings by artists from all over the world. This is a real treasure trove and is certainly not to be missed.

Ethos Gallery, York Street, Clitheroe Tel: 01200 427878

Clitheroe is full of interesting small shops, one of the very best (not only because it stocks *The Hidden Places Series*!) is **KAYDEE BOOK-SHOP**, now part of Bookland Ltd. For the past fifty years this shop has sold a remarkably diverse range of books, indeed the shop boasts that any book currently in print can be ordered for you if it is not in stock. Fancy goods, stationery, artist's materials, greetings cards, toys and games are also stocked.

Kaydee Bookshop, 26-30 Moor Lane, Clitheroe. Tel: 01200 22698

Another of Clitheroe's top class shops is **STANSFIELD DELI**, owned and run since 1994 by Melanie Atkinson. The shop has an enviable reputation and specializes in fine foods including cooked meats and home-made pies. Particularly tasty are the special muffins which are filled with a cooked meat and topped with a delicious salad.

Stansfield Deli, 36 Castle Street, Clitheroe. Tel: 01200 23227

After ten years working as an operations manager with Tetley's Brewery, Harry Landless took on the historic **SWAN AND ROYAL HOTEL** on Castle Street. In the two years since then, Harry has not looked back and the success he has created is plain to see. As well as serving a good range of ales, bar snacks are available at lunchtimes and the hot sandwiches are a house speciality. The Swan and Royal building dates back to the 1830s when it replaced a much older inn from the 15th or 16th century. A recently found solid oak door leading to the cellar was found in such a good condition that it is now displayed in the town's Castle Museum. Harry has a new cellar door. The inn's original stables and associated buildings were converted into an attractive shopping arcade in 1970.

Swan and Royal Hotel, Castle Street, Clitheroe Tel: 01200 23130

On King Street in Clitheroe is **HARRISON & KERR** a specialist, family run butcher's shop.

Harrison and Kerr

Stuart Kerr came here as a 15 year old and now, some 36 years later, he and his wife Marilyn own and run the shop ably assisted by their family and Brian Hodges, another long serving member of the team. Traditionally run, Harrison and Kerr offer the best in fresh produce and also a personal service that is hard to find these days. As well as the more usual cuts of meat, Stuart ensures that there is a wide range of game and seasonal meats available. The cooked meats, all prepared on the premises, make a mouth-watering display. The traditional Lancashire black puddings are made in the old fashioned way, the bacons and hams are cured here and the quiches and pies all home-made. Whatever your meat requirements, Stuart and his knowledgeable staff are keen to help and advise you.

Harrison and Kerr, 11-13 King Street, Clitheroe Tel: 01200 23253

In the heart of the Clitheroe, on King Street, lies **THE APRICOT MERINGUE**, a charming tea shop that has a small Victorian frontage hiding a spacious interior. With three separate dining areas, one in a lovely conservatory at the rear of the property, intimacy is maintained whilst satisfying the many customers. For the past six years partners, Terry Wild and Christopher Sharp, have been catering to the needs of shoppers and visitors to the town with a mouth-watering array of home-made, freshly cooked dishes.

Along with the more traditional hot and cold sandwiches, the menu also has a selection of delicious bistro-style dishes that cater for every taste and in particular to the hungrier client. The warm and friendly atmosphere makes this a superb and stylish place to stop.

The Apricot Meringue, 15 King Street, Clitheroe Tel: 01200 26933

Further along King Street is the outstanding **D.BYRNE & CO.**, recently voted the best independent wine merchant of the year by *Which? Wine Guide*. This family run shop has been in existence for over 105 years and is now run by the fourth generation of the Byrne family who demonstrate a wealth of expertise in the goods which are stocked. The style of the shop has altered little over this time, it still has all of the atmosphere that you would associate with Victorian times and a standard of service which elsewhere has vanished.

The interior of the shop has a wonderful aroma of fresh coffee beans and tea, twenty varieties of each are stocked. Down in the cellars, over 1500 different wines and from all over the world are expertly stored and displayed, paradise for connoisseurs of fine wine and whisky.

A wide variety of home mixed tobaccos are also available. Be sure to visit this charming shop whilst you are in Clitheroe

D.Byrne & Co., 12 King Street, Clitheroe. Tel 01200 23152

BARKERS PRIMROSE NURSERIES AND GARDEN CENTRE, on the edge of the town centre, has extensive and ever changing displays of plants, herbs, shrubs and gardening related items. The staff are keen gardeners themselves, so are only too pleased to help you select the right plants for your garden. This is a wonderful place to spend some time. Open every day 9am to 5.30pm. situated on Whalley Road leading out of Clitheroe.

Barkers Primrose Nurseries and Garden Centre, Whalley Road, Clitheroe.Tel: 01200 23521 Fax: 01200 28160

Around Clitheroe

THE EDISFORD PICNIC AREA can be found just outside of Clitheroe. Once a battle ground between the Scots and the Normans, this is now a pleasant family area on the banks of the river, with a miniature railway, children's play area, cafeteria and pitch and putt course.

SHIREBURNE PARK, situated in the Forest of Bowland within walking distance of Clitheroe and overlooking the River Ribble is ideally located as a base for a family holiday spent exploring the area. This picturesque woodland park offers an extensive range of new and used holiday homes for purchase, each with its individual plot.

Touring caravans are welcome with both seasonal and overnight stays accepted. Luxury caravans are available for hire. The park has excellent facilities, these include a licensed clubhouse, with family room, shop and launderette. Golf and fishing are available close by.

Shireburn Park, Waddington Road, Edisford Bridge, Clitheroe. Tel: 0200 23422 or 25323

GREAT MITTON. South of Clitheroe on the B6246, is a particularly attractive village. Until 1974 Great Mitton, with its church, was in Yorkshire, but the other part of the village, Little Mitton, divided by the River Ribble, lay in Lancashire.

The tiny hamlet of Mitton is situated on a limestone rise above the River Ribble near to its junction with the Hodder. The 13th century **CHURCH OF ALL HALLOWS** has the Shireburn Chapel with effigies of members of that family, sculpted by William Stanton, one of the foremost sculptors of his period. The Chancel Screen that came from Sawley Abbey is also an interesting feature.

Mitton Hall

A sweeping drive leads to **MITTON HALL**, which is a stone's throw from the medieval church at Mitton. This imposing Manor House, with stately mullioned windows, was built for a cousin of Henry VII in about 1514. It stands in woodland surroundings, extending to nearly 18 acres in all, with the River Ribble flowing by. Today Mitton Hall offers accommodation in the Mitton Hall Lodgings as well as a restaurant and an inn.

THE OLD STONE HOUSE RESTAURANT, open every evening and all day at the weekend, serves a wide range of dishes, many with an Italian flavour, in the magnificent surroundings of a Great Hall. **OWD NED'S TAVERN**, with its stone flagged floor and dark oak beams, open from 6.30 am, serves breakfasts and also carries at least seven real ales.

Mitton Hall, Mitton, Whalley Tel: 01254 826544

BASHALL EAVES, the quaintly named village on Clitheroe road, has a super place to call in, or indeed stay at, if you are in the area. The village, is still in fact owned by the Lord (or in this case Lady) of the Manor, and it is here that you will find a true hidden gem in the form of **THE RED PUMP INN AND RESTAURANT** run by Alison and John Fisher.

The Inn has a lot to commend it as there is an excellent restaurant and comfortable accommodation in a marvellous 18th century setting .

Alison and John have won many awards for their cooking and this is reflected in the quality of the food on offer. Places this tucked away have to be good in order to attract custom and this is well worth the detour.

The Red Pump Inn & Restaurant Clitheroe Rd. Tel: 01254 826227

GRINDLETON. Situated in the village of Grindleton is the magnificent **BUCK INN**. Dating back to the 18th century it was formerly a house and farm buildings for a head groomsman to the local lord of the manor. Licensed during the 1870s it retains all its character, style and atmosphere and is full of bygone memorabilia of the village.

Run by Margaret Evans and Joyce West, the inn is renowned for its excellent and different menu. Who could resist Boozy Bread and Butter Pudding or indeed Normandy Pancake. So popular has the Buck Inn become under the leadership of these two lovely lady hosts that it is imperative to book in the evenings.

The Buck Inn, Grindleton, Near Clitheroe Tel: 01200 441248

GISBURN. **THE STIRK HOUSE HOTEL** at Gisburn was originally a 16th century manor house. It is now a superb, lavishly equipped, privately owned hotel, '. The elegant split level dining room is widely known for its intimate ambience and fine cuisine. This is a great place for a romantic, candle-lit meal accompanied by soothing piano music played live.

The rooms are very well equipped with colour TV (including satellite channels), radio, direct-dial telephone and tea/coffee making facilities. They all have private bathroom facilities. Additionally the hotel boasts a sports complex which includes a heated indoor swimming pool, squash courts, sauna, solarium and exercise room.

Stirk House Hotel, Gisburn, near Clitheroe. 01200 445581

If you go eastwards from Clitheroe, you will reach **PENDLE HILL** and the villages in and around its western slopes, including Downham, one of the most attractive villages of all in a region of exceptionally fine villages.

DOWNHAM. If you visit Downham village, near Clitheroe, for the first time do not worry if you feel a touch of déjà vu. It is quite likely that you have seen the village before for this was the location used in the famous film 'Whistle Down The Wind' and little has changed since the young Hayley Miles walked its streets. More recently BBC Television's 'The Likely Lad' was filmed here. The unspoilt nature of Downham is due, in no small part, to Lord Clitheroe who still resides at Downham Hall which the Assheton family bought, along with the Lordship of the Manor, in 1558.

DOWNHAM POST OFFICE CAFE, owned and run by Dianne and Stephen Smith, is still the village Post Office; Dianne is the Post Mistress. But here along with stamps you can also buy provisions, hand-made crafts, books and gifts from the shop as well as sample some of Dianne's delicious home-made cakes, scones and tarts in the café. Tasty light meals and snacks are also available.

If you would like to stay a little longer, Dianne and Stephen can also offer you either bed and breakfast accommodation in the Post Office or self-catering in the **STABLE LODGE HOLIDAY COTTAGE**. Originally a stable, the cottage has been converted to retain all its character, having open beams throughout and it provides a cosy atmosphere as well as panoramic views across Pendle Hill from the first floor lounge.

Downham Post Office Café, Downham, Clitheroe Tel: 01200 441242

Purchased by the Assheton family in 1558, along with Whalley Abbey, Downham is without doubt one of the loveliest villages in Lancashire. It has been maintained in virtually its original condition by the Assheton family.

The present squire, Lord Clitheroe of Downham, still refuses to permit the skyline to be spoilt by TV aerials, satellite dishes or even dormer windows, which are all strictly prohibited. The church tower is a splendid example of 15th century architecture.

Situated off the A59 in the middle of Downham village, opposite the church, is **THE ASSHETON ARMS**. There are records of licensed premises on this site going back as far as 1765. Look out for the initials carved over the stone fireplace, they are believed to be those of the original builder.

The pub has a very olde-worlde feel to it, with low ceilings, exposed beams and open fires. The Assheton Arms has an excellent reputation for food, the menu is extensive and impressive and usually includes a surprising variety of fresh seafood specialities. The ales are traditional and all hand-pulled. If you happen to notice the wooden busts of guardsmen wearing 'busby' hats, they are in fact newel posts from the Busby family's department store, which later became Debenhams in Bradford.

The Assheton Arms, Downham, near Clitheroe. 01200 441227

CHATBURN. Situated in Chatburn, in a beautiful old stone toll house is **HUDSONS HOME MADE ICES.** Ice cream has been made here since 1947; Irene and Maurice Smithson took over 8 years ago and have continued to make the real thing, with no preservatives and additives so the true flavour is brought out. Made in various varieties up to 12 in the summer - take your pick from gooseberry, toffee, melon and ginger, mandarin sorbet and traditional vanilla. As well as selling their ice cream, the shop also offers a wide selection of high class provisions including home cooked meats. Open seven days a week.

Hudsons Home Made Ices

Three years ago the couple opened Hudsons Ice Cream Parlour in the nearby village of Gisburn. Run by their daughter Aimée, this delightful tea room offers light meals and home made cakes as well as the delicious ice cream, sundaes, pancakes and waffles.

Hudsons Home Made Ices, Chatburn, Clitheroe Tel: 01200 441305

RIMMINGTON.   Carrying on to the East you will reach Rimmington. Delightful countryside is to be found here and at the adjoining hamlets of Stopper Lane, Martin Top, Newby, Middop and Howgill.

This area was the home for many years of Francis Duckworth, the famous composer of hymn tunes, including one called 'Rimmington"

BOLTON-BY-BOWLAND.   Just the other side of the River Ribble is a tranquil village with a village green, stone cross and old stocks.

The church has many ornamental carvings and a tomb dating from 1500 which has the arms of Pudsey, Percy Tempest, Hammerton and other families. The famous Pudsey tomb has an engraved figure of Sir Ralph Pudsey in full armour with the figures of his three wives and 25 children.

In this pretty Lancashire village is the charming old corner shop, **FARMHOUSE ANTIQUES**. This Aladdin's Cave, owned and run by Marian Howard, has two claims to fame: it is believed to be Britain's smallest antiques shop and also, it contains the largest selection of antique textiles in Lancashire. People travel from far and wide to see and buy her specialist lines which include glass beadwork, quilts, lace trimmed table and bed linen, cushions, samplers and christening gowns. Unlike many other antiquities, needlework items deteriorate over the years and Marian is always seeking items with which to replenish her stock. A farmer's daughter, and for many years a farmer's wife, Marian also has a particular affection for farmhouse antiques and there are also fine examples of brass ware, Staffordshire figures and old porcelain. A visit here will delight everyone.

Farmhouse Antiques, Corner Shop, 23 Main Street, Bolton-by-Bowland,
Clitheroe Tel: 01200 441457

HOLDEN. Not easy to find but well worth the effort, **BAYGATE FARM** lies just a mile out of Bolton-by-Bowland in the hamlet of Holden. This charming farmhouse bed and breakfast establishment is run by Ethel Townson who ensures that all visitors receive a warm welcome.

Set high up in the hills in the ancient Forest of Bowland there are breathtaking views from all the windows. Baygate Farm is a working sheep and beef farm of some 130 acres that also offers peace and quiet in splendid surroundings. The bedrooms are spacious and warm, with good facilities, and there is a magnificent English cooked breakfast in the morning. Though evening meals are not available there are some excellent pubs and restaurants nearby.

Baygate Farm, Holden, Bolton-by-Bowland Tel: 01200 447643

WEST BRADFORD, a little to the east, is a village with a long history of rugged independence. A stream runs deep alongside the road through the bottom half of the village and access to the houses bordering the beck is by means of quaint stone bridges.

In West Bradford you will find the traditional 400-year old English Village pub, **THE THREE MILLSTONES.**

The Three Millstones

Complete with low beamed ceilings, open fires and a wealth of antique furniture and brasses, this former coaching inn is a must for visitors to the area. There is even a resident ghost - a former highwayman known as Kirkam Jack. The restaurant seats 32 and has an interesting and varied menu featuring smoked oysters, fresh fish and the famous sticky toffee pudding.

Michael is your host and chef; food is available every night from 6.00p.m. There are also two bedrooms available for bed and breakfast and golfing and pony trekking breaks can be arranged.

The Three Millstones, West Bradford, Clitheroe, Lancashire.
Tel: 01200 23340

THREE RIVERS PARK, in the village of West Bradford just off the A59 near Clitheroe, makes an ideal base for a visit to this interesting area. Set in 45 acres of peaceful and tranquil woodland the park offers luxurious, well equipped holiday homes for hire. Additionally there is ample space for touring caravans and tents and these are provided with electric hook-up facilities, toilet block, shop and launderette.

Three Rivers Park, Eaves Hall Lane, West Bradford, Clitheroe. 01200 23523

WADDINGTON. The next village is, one of the Ribble Valley's best known villages, and the attractive Coronation Gardens have appeared on many a postcard and even on biscuit tins.

King Henry VI (Henry the Good) lived for a year, in secret, at **WADDINGTON HALL** before being betrayed to the Yorkists. He allegedly escaped via a secret panel and staircase from the dining room, only to be captured at **BRUNGERLY BRIDGE**, down river near Clitheroe.

In the lovely village square you will find **HIGHER BUCK INN**, a characterful, cosy and welcoming establishment, full of style. Bernadette and Steve have only recently taken over the running of the pub, but already they have enhanced its reputation. The inn stocks good, traditional Thwaites Ales and also serves delicious home cooked 'pub grub', reasonably priced and prepared from fresh locally produced ingredients. Food is available during lunchtimes and Friday, Saturday and Sunday evenings.

As an added bonus, the inn also boasts two delightful letting rooms, one family size, the other a twin room. Where better to take a break at any time of the year than here in the heart of the Ribble Valley

Higher Buck Inn, The Square, Waddington, Nr Clitheroe. Tel: 01200 23226

LONGRIDGE. **THE ALSTON ARMS** in Longridge, when visited in the summer, is as pretty as a picture. In fact, it is a three times winner of the Longridge Chamber of Trade Hanging Basket Competition. This former farmhouse was licensed during the late 19th century and is now run by Dave and Elaine Wright, who extend a warm welcome to all visitors.

As well as serving well kept Theakston and Matthew Brown ale, delicious home-cooked food is available with special dishes for children. In fact, children are particularly well catered for. At the rear of the building is 'Bertie' a double decker play bus, an adventure playground and a pet's corner with a donkey, goats and fowl. A delightful place for all the family.

Alston Arms, Inglewhite Road, Longridge, Preston Tel: 01772 783331

Situated on the edge of the Ribble Valley, near Longridge, is the magnificent **SPOUT FARM NURSERY** and the **WOODCUTTERS**

RESTAURANT. When Denis and Mavis Lambert came here in the early 1980s the 7 acre site was derelict but, with plenty of vision and a lot of hard work they have turned the establishment into a delightful place to visit, with something for everyone.

The well stocked nursery changes with the seasons growing flowers, shrubs and trees. The couple have refurbished a magnificent old barn which houses the garden shop. Everything for the gardener and knowledgeable staff are on hand to help the beginner.

Upstairs is the wonderful **WOODCUTTERS RESTAURANT** Open throughout the day this is stylish place to enjoy a light snack or a three course dinner. Fresh food is prepared daily with the emphasis on traditional English fayre, and may be chosen from the special's board or the à la carte menu. Booking is recommended.

Spout Farm Nursery and Woodcutters Restaurant, Preston Road, Longridge
Tel: 01772 784010

DILWORTH. Where the B6243 meets the B6245 in the tiny hamlet of Dilworth, near Longridge, is **THE CORPORATION ARMS** which has be run by the same family since 1951.

The Corporation Arms

Currently, Anthony and Stephanie are the owners in charge of this inn of sheer quality and character. The stone built property originates from the 17th century having formerly been a farm and subsequently the Black Bull until 1865. The restaurant was created from the old outbuildings and its large feature window was the entrance for the carriage or cart.

The food is highly recommended in the local area and the well prepared menu offers a really first class selection. The inn is currently extending its facilities to include accommodation which will provide a superb location to stay in this lovely area.

The Corporation Arms, Lower Road, Dilworth, Longridge, Preston, Lancashire. Tel: 01772 782644'

GOOSNARGH. Situated in the village of Goosnargh is **SOLO**, a fine restaurant with a friendly, welcoming atmosphere. Vincent and Susan, their daughter Adriana and her husband Stefano are the owners. Together they have built up an enviable reputation for the high standard of service and exceptional quality of the food. This popular restaurant serves a wide variety of delicious dishes including; Lune Smoked Salmon, Lamb Osso Bucco and Roasted Gressingham Duckling to name but a few. The dishes are prepared using only the very best ingredients, and you can be sure of a memorable meal whatever you decide to select from the menu.

A good selection of wines are available to accompany your meal. It is advisable to book in advance since the restaurant can get quite busy. Ample parking is available. No smoking is permitted in the dining room.

Solo, Goosnargh Lane, Goosnargh, Preston. Tel/fax: 01772 865206

YE HORNS INN is a premier country inn and restaurant in the lovely Ribble Valley at Goosnargh. Established in 1782, this inn has character, style, class, and a wonderful feeling of friendship. The resident owners are Mark and Denise Woods whose family have owned the inn for the last forty years. Ye Horns Inn is dived into many rooms, all are cosy and very intimate. The inn can seat about 100 people in its restaurant and dining room and provides a good Table d'hôte and a'la carte menu at a very reasonable price. Six well furnished double bedrooms are available with en-suite facilities and all modern comforts. Full English /Continental breakfast, lunches and dinners are served daily. Three Crown - ETB.

Ye Horns Inn, Goosnargh, Nr. Preston, Lancashire. Tel: 01772 865230

Close by is **CHINGLE HALL**, a small moated manor house, built in 1260. This was the birthplace of Saint John Wall 1620. It has been described as one of the most haunted houses in Britain as has featured on countless TV and radio programmes. It has a fine rose garden and is well worth a visit.

CHIPPING. A picturesque village on the slopes above the River Loud to the north of the town of Longridge.

In Medieval days no less than five watermills were sited along Chipping beck. Several attractive inns are to found in the centre one of which is the **SUN INN**, to which there is a legend. Lizzy Dean was a serving wench at the Sun Inn, engaged to be married to a local man.

On the morning of her wedding, on hearing the church bells, she looked out of the window of her room in the Sun Inn and saw her bridegroom leaving the church with another bride on his arm. She hanged herself in the attic of the pub.

Her last request was that her grave be dug in the path of the church so that her ex-boyfriend had to walk over it every Sunday. She died in 1835 aged 20 and is said to still haunt the Sun Inn.

In the centre of Chipping, in the heart of the Forest of Bowland, and on the west side of the Hodder Valley, you will find a former coaching inn, **THE TALBOT HOTEL.** The Talbot's claim to fame is that they have a resident ghost here. It isn't actually seen, but there is a distinct smell of lavender whenever it is around! The pub has recently been refurbished with quality furnishings and decor though the original beams have been retained throughout.

There is a separate restaurant area although the same menu is available in the bar area as well. The Talbot's food is varied and reasonably priced. Additionally daily blackboard specials are offered together with a 'children's choice' menu. There is a garden to the rear which is very peaceful and has a pretty stream running through it.

The Talbot Hotel, Talbot Street, Chipping, Lancashire.
Tel: 01995 61260 & 61083

Situated on the edge of this picturesque village in the heart of the Ribble valley is the magnificent **DOG AND PARTRIDGE INN.** Dating back at its oldest part to the very early 16th century, it has been during its lifetime; a farmhouse, courthouse and a coaching inn and has had a variety of names including 'The Clividger' and 'The Green Man'. This inn has a wonderfully friendly atmosphere and a warm welcoming interior which features a magnificent original stone fire-place. Peter and his sister Lisa, the owners, can rightly boast of the good food and superb traditional ales which are served. The meals are delicious and very reasonably priced, so unsurprisingly the restaurant is apt to get busy. It is a good idea to book in advance.

Children are welcomed and there are good facilities for disabled persons. No smoking is permitted in the dining areas.

Dog and Partridge, Hesketh Lane, Chipping, Preston. Tel: 01995 61201

Slaidburn Bridge

The **GIBBON BRIDGE HOTEL** , near Chipping in the Forest of Bowland, is probably the finest in the area.This warm, charming and luxurious country hotel offers top class accommodation, the very best of local food and international cuisine and a level of professionalism beyond compare.

The individually designed bedrooms, with their open fires and oak beams have an authentic olde worlde character, are superbly appointed and include four pos ter, half tester and gothic brass beds and Jacuzzi baths, together with the most astounding panoramic views of the surrounding countryside.

The unsurpassable restaurant has a beautiful conservatory and a wonderful ambience, your enjoyment of a delicious meal will be enhanced by freshly baked bread and the melodious sound of a grand piano. The hotel also boasts its own unique garden bandstand where special musical events and civil wedding ceremonies take place. Additional facilities include a beauty salon, fitness room, tennis court and helicopter landing pad. From Chipping, turn right at T-junction for Clitheroe, the hotel is three-quarters of a mile down this road.

The Gibbon Bridge Hotel, Nr Chipping, Forest of Bowland, Lancs.
Tel: 01995 61456 Fax: 01995 61277

THE HODDER VALLEY. In the southern corner of Bowland is certainly somewhere to linger - it has an intimate beauty that contrasts with the wild moorland of the hilltops. You'll find here a series of lovely villages.

Whitewell is known locally as 'Little Switzerland' because of its location in a deep, wooded valley. A church, an Inn and a few cottages grace this very attractive spot.

DUNSOP BRIDGE. A little further along the valley has been officially declared by Ordnance Survey to be the nearest village to the exact centre of the British Isles and its associated islands.

NEWTON - IN - BOWLAND. The best way to approach this next village is said to be from the south over Waddington Fell.

The views are breathtaking. John Bright the Quaker spent two years of his early life here.

Enjoying a pleasant location with wonderful views, on the hill just below Newton Village, **THE PARKERS ARMS** with its impressive black and white frontage is a charming and traditional country pub.

Originally the stables for Newton Hall, it is full of character, with open fires, oak beams and stuffed birds all enhancing a cosy, country atmosphere. In the warm, welcoming ambience of the bar you can choose from a selection of hand-pulled real ales and in the comfortable beamed restaurant, which seats up to 55, an imaginative and varied menu tempts the most discerning palate. You can also choose from the delicious daily specials on the blackboard. We recommend that you book a table in advance for Saturday evenings or Sunday lunchtimes.

For guests seeking a bed for the night, there are also three attractively furnished guest rooms, each equipped with a hairdryer and hot drinks facilities.

The Parkers Arms, Newton-in-Bowland, near Clitheroe. Tel: 01200 446236

SLAIDBURN. Just a few miles from Newton this compact village with a fine 15th century church, notable for its great three-decker pulpit and unusual Jacobean chancel screen.

The village has rows of cottages that indicate its links with weaving, and a famous pub, the **HARK TO BOUNTY**. This splendid inn dates back to the 13th century and until 1895 was known as The Dog. Apparently the squire of the village, who was also the parson, had a pack of hounds: one day while out hunting, he and his party called at the inn for refreshments. Their drinking was disturbed by loud and prolonged baying from the pack outside and high above the noise could be heard the squire's favourite hound, which prompted him to call out "Hark to Bounty".

The inn also housed the ancient Moot Courtroom of the Forest of Bowland which was still in use as recently as 1937. Being the only courtroom between York and Lancaster, it was used by visiting Justices from the 14th century onwards and is said to have been used by Oliver Cromwell when he was in the area. The records still remain in the archives at Clitheroe Castle as well as the county archives at Preston.

On the edge of the village of Slaidburn, amidst beautiful country-side and panoramic views, stands **PAGES FARM**, a wonderful small-holding that was formerly a working farm. In a homely and peaceful atmosphere, Mary and Peter Cowking offer award winning, traditional, farmhouse bed and breakfast accommodation that is hard to match anywhere.

Pages Farm, Woodhouse Lane, Slaidburn Tel: 01200 446205

Slaidburn is a good centre for country walks. A network of beautiful, little visited lanes, hardly wide enough for a small car, radiate westwards into the high fell country, or eastwards into the main Ribble Valley to the charming village of Bolton-by-Bowland.

TOSSIDE. If you venture along the B6478 you will soon reach Tosside, a small hamlet on the edge of the Forest of Bowland, half in Lancashire and half in Yorkshire. Just over into Yorkshire is the delight-fully named village of Wigglesworth.

CLAPHAM. Carrying straight along the B6478 will bring you to the A65 road to Kendal. Turning north it will bring you here. It is worthwhile pausing your journey in Clapham village where there is a car park and National Park Information Centre enabling you to leave your car and follow the Nature Trail walk which leads to Clapham's **INGLEBOROUGH CAVE**, the outlet cave of the famous Gaping Gill system. It contains some impressive cave formations, underground streams and naturally formed passages, with magnificent displays of cave coral and illuminated pools, all providing a unique underground experience.

HIGH & LOW BENTHAM. Travelling west from Clapham along the B6480, you will pass through these two small villages. Evidence of the antiquity of these quaint villages abounds.

Near West End Farm in Low Bentham you can see remains of a Roman road which ran from Ribchester to Burrow and Castleton.

In the Parish Church of St. John the Baptist there is a fragment of a crucifix, apparently of Saxon origin, thus at least a thousand years old, and the church itself receives mention in the Domesday Book, although nothing of the original building remains, it having been destroyed in the 14th century by the marauding Scots. A "Plague Stone" between High and Low Bentham is a grim reminder of the pestilence of 1597 and 1598 which played havoc with the district. A short distance away is HIGHER TATHAM. Continuing southwards following the beautiful Lune Valley you can trace a picturesque route along quiet roads via WRAY and CLAUGHTON, perhaps taking in CATON, which has the remains of an ancient cross, and its twin village Brookhouse.

From here we travel to the northern end of the Lune Valley and the town of Kirkby Lonsdale, which is where we begin the next chapter.

CHAPTER FOUR

North Lancashire
and Lancaster

Hornby Castle

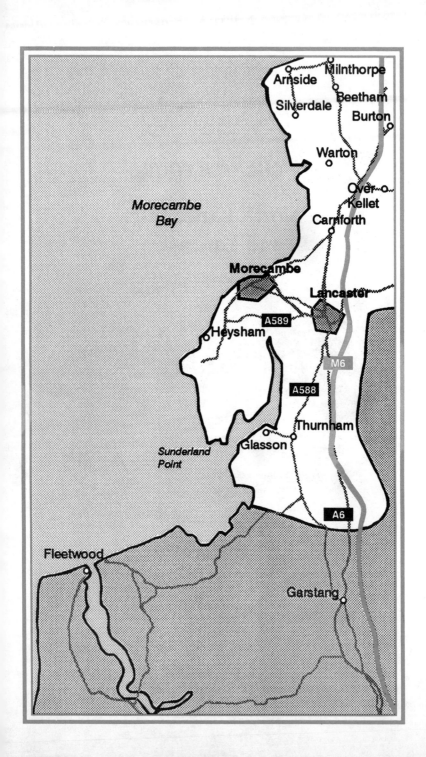

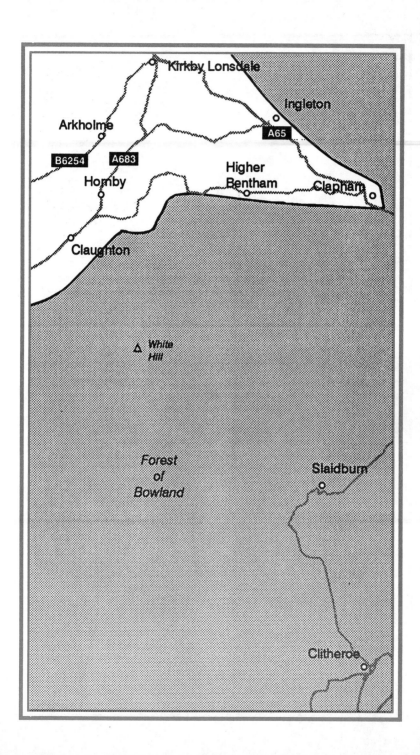

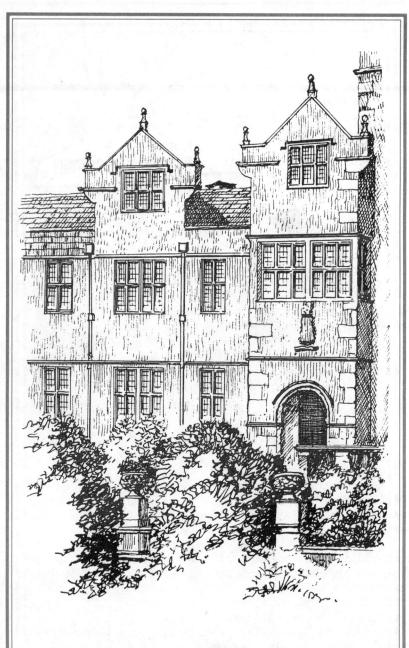

Borwick Hall

CHAPTER FOUR

North Lancashire and Lancaster

The northern edge of Lancashire sweeps from Morecambe Bay up along the valley of the River Lune to the edge of the Yorkshire Dales.

Indeed, high up on Leck Fell east of Kirkby Lonsdale, you are in true Dales country, with a typical craggy limestone gorge along the little valley of Leck Beck, as well as one of the most extensive cave systems in the British Isles for the experienced potholer to explore.

INGLETON is, in fact, over the county border, in North Yorkshire. Well worth a visit and we make no apology for mentioning it in two books in the series for it is here you will discover **INGLETON WA-TERFALLS**, one of the noted natural Beauty Spots of the North.

The Falls Walk is a spectacular four mile stretch leading up the glen, over the hills and returning down the other glen to Ingleton. The First Pecca Falls and Pecca Twin Falls are a delight to behold, as is Hollybush Spout. Thornton Force, the Triple Spout of Beezley and the Rival Falls are equally impressive, with individual splendour and beauty, and from here the rushing waters plunge and roar through Baxenghyll Gorge and over Snow Falls before returning to the village.

KIRKBY LONSDALE. Again situated just over the Lancashire border in the county of Cumbria, but it serves as a focal point for the whole of this part of the dale.

Architecturally, this little town is a jewel, with a considerable number of fine Georgian, Regency and early Victorian houses and shops.

As you approach the town along the main A65 from the east, your first sight of the town is across **DEVIL'S BRIDGE**, a slender, triple-arched bridge across a wooded gorge of the River Lune.

Records show this bridge being in existence as far back as 1365 when a grant of pontage - the ability to collect a toll from travellers crossing the bridge - was granted to the vicar, who in return had to maintain it.

The bridge apparently takes its name from a legend about the Devil and an old lady who wanted to get her cattle to the other side of the river. The Devil promised her a bridge provided he could have the soul of the first creature to cross it. Next morning, the Devil lay in waiting for his victim, but was thwarted by the ingenuity of the old lady, who before crossing herself, threw a bun across the bridge.

Her little dog chased it across and the Devil had to be content with the animal's soul instead.

Kirkby Lonsdale is a delightful little market town growing up on an old packhorse route, and during the 18th century an annual hiring fair was held there. It has a fine Market Square (market day is Thursday) with a tall Market Cross, and the attractive narrow streets radiating from the

Square are lined with shops, cafés and public houses.

Take some time to admire the views - the town is wonderfully situated on a high bank overlooking the River Lune. The glorious views from the Churchyard and Ruskin's View up the valley to the Howgills and Casterton Fells have drawn many artists, including JMW Turner, and were described as "one of the loveliest scenes in England" by John Ruskin.

A natural route from Kirkby Lonsdale to the county town of Lancaster is marked by the River Lune. For those who enjoy walking, the best way to enjoy this area of Lancashire is to follow the Lune Valley Ramble. The booklet that accompanys the walk (available from Kirkby Lonsdale Tourist Information Centre) provides detailed maps and plenty of information on the places which you pass. The Lune Valley Ramble allows you to explore the valley's intimate pastoral setting, with walking through woodland, meadows and along the riverside itself. You can also enjoy picturesque villages, castles and ancient churches along the way. The booklet is designed to be followed from Lancaster to Kirkby Lonsdale, however the maps are detailed enough for the route to be followed easily in either direction.

There is a lovely network of quiet lanes and roads leading out of this green and sheltered valley to delightful villages such as WHITTINGTON WENNINGTON, MELLING, TUNSTALL, WRAY, and GRESSINGHAM, all of which repay exploration handsomely.

HORNBY. On the other side of the Lune Valley, south of Kirkby Lonsdale on A683, Hornby has many historic connections. Its position by a bluff overlooking the valley commands a fine panoramic view of the Lune Valley and this strategic position has been utilised over the centuries for defence purposes. Just to the north of Hornby is the attractive stone built **LOYN BRIDGE** The bridge takes the road over the Lune to Gressingham and was built in 1684 replacing a ford. Situated beside the bridge is the **CASTLE STEDE** which presents the best example of a Norman motte and bailey castle in Lancashire, built at a point which clearly controls the crossing of the Lune.

The romantically situated **HORNBY CASTLE**, which can be viewed from the village, was immortalised in a painting by Turner, although it was only built last century, incorporating the ruins of an older castle, and transformed into a grand and picturesque country house

CLAUGHTON. Continuing south on the A683, shortly before entering the village (pronounced Clafton) look out for the **OLD TOLL HOUSE GARAGE** where early this century the garage owner painted the first white lines on the road at the nearby corner because of the many accidents there. After much debate their value was recognised by King George V and from then the use of white lines became accepted, eventually spreading worldwide.

Continuing on this road just before you reach the M6 take the road to the right signed to Halton, which soon crosses the lovely stone Crook

O'Line bridge. A little way over the bridge on the right there is a car park where you can leave the car and take a short stroll along the Caton footpath, created from the old Lancaster-Wennington rail line.

From the old rail bridges magnificent views of the Lune and wooded banks can be enjoyed on this part of the river known as the Crook O'Lune. Gray and Turner have both acknowledged the delight of the scene.

LANCASTER, on the River Lune is the capital of this beautiful county. It proudly boasts of its 'Legacy', which extends back many centuries. Unlike York, which has long been internationally known as a tourist attraction, its Red Rose cousin has taken longer to be discovered.

In fact, Lancaster has an equally important place in English history and there is much for the serious visitor to explore. It's also a surprisingly compact city, easily reached by either road, just off the M6, or by rail from a centrally positioned station where most Intercity trains call.

Within yards of the railway station you'll find **LANCASTER CASTLE**, a great medieval fortress, founded by Normans to keep out Scottish invaders, and strengthened by John of Gaunt, Duke of Lancaster, in the 15th century.

Standing proudly atop a hill, this great medieval castle has an imposing presence and dominates the skyline above Lancaster. Its huge square keep dates back to 1200 and was raised in height and impregnability at the time of The Armada.

Astonishingly perhaps, most of the building still functions as a prison, but certain sections are open to the public, including the 18th century **SHIRE HALL**, the cells, where the witches of Pendle were imprisoned, the Crown Court, Hadrian's Tower and, a touch of the macabre, the Drop Room where prisoners were prepared for the gallows.

Close by, sharing the hill with the Castle, is a building with less grim associations - the lovely **PRIORY CHURCH OF SAINT MARY**, which once served a Benedictine Priory established here in 1094. Most of the present church dates from the 14th and 15th centuries, and particularly interesting things to see are fragments of Anglo-Saxon crosses, magnificent medieval choir stalls, and some very fine needlework. Nearby is a link with Roman Lancaster - the remains of a bath house which also served soldiers as an inn.

A short walk from the Castle leads into the largely pedestrianised city centre, for shops, the market and much besides. **THE CITY MUSEUM** in the Market Place occupies the Old Town Hall, built between 1781-3 by Major Jarrett and Thomas Harrison.

As well as the city's art collection and an area of changing exhibitions, you'll find displays and collections of material illustrating aspects of the city's industrial and social history. Also here is the **MUSEUM OF THE KING'S OWN ROYAL**, a regiment which was based in Lancaster from 1880 onwards.

In Church Street is the **JUDGES LODGING**, a beautifully proportioned building dating from the 1620s when it was built as a private house for Thomas Covell, but later used for judges during the Lancaster Assizes. It now houses two separate museums; the **MUSEUM OF CHILDHOOD** containing the Barry Elder doll collection, and a **FURNITURE MUSEUM** containing many examples of the workmanship of Gillows, the famous Lancaster cabinet makers. In fact it was Richard Gillow who designed the Maritime Museum.

The Judges Lodging, Lancaster

Around the corner in Sun Street is the **MUSIC ROOM**, an exquisite early Georgian building originally designed as a pavilion in the long vanished garden of Oliver Marton. It is notable for some superb decorative plasterwork.

The Blue Anchor

The **BLUE ANCHOR**, situated in the pedestrianised centre of this historic town, is regarded by many as being one of the best pubs in Lancaster. The pub, as its name implies, has a nautical theme throughout and if you look carefully many interesting relics can be seen; the three cast dolphins legs that support the bar, came from the compass of the first steamship to navigate the River Lune, and the actual binnacle is on display under the restaurant stairs. The bar area is shaped like a boat hull and everywhere you get the feeling that you could actually be on board a ship, so convincing is the use of nautical memorabilia. In addition to the bar area, the Blue Anchor also has a fine restaurant which is situated upstairs and resembles a captain's cabin. The food and the ales which are served are of the very highest quality and you can be sure that you will enjoy your visit. This 'hidden place' should not be missed.

The Blue Anchor, Anchor Lane, Lancaster. Tel: 01524 66898

As you walk into **J.ATKINSON & Co**. on China Street, you can be forgiven for feeling you have slipped into a timewarp, for this delightful tea and coffee merchant's is exactly as it has been for generations, with assistants in brown overalls, old machinery and even the original tins on the shelves bearing the Lancaster City coat of arms, all adding an air of bygone days. Established in 1837, the year that Queen Victoria came to the throne, this wonderful shop specialises in coffee which they roast on the premises daily and a glorious aroma hits you the minute you walk in. Among the many people they supply is the Sunbury Coffee House.

J. Atkinson & Co., China Street, Lancaster Tel: 01524 65470

Tucked away close by in Music Room Square, is a little gem called **SUNBURY COFFEE HOUSE**, owned by Gill and John Constable.

Sunbry Coffee House

The Georgian theme extends from the attractive stone facade to the elegant interior with its marble table tops and this provides the perfect setting in which to enjoy the finest selection of tea and coffee accompanied by delicious freshly prepared snacks. A diverse range of coffees are always available including Colombian, Kenya Blue Mountain, Costa Rica, New Guinea and Decaffinated. The food is excellent and ranges from jacket potatoes with a choice of fillings to open sandwiches and savoury filled croissants, not to mention a mouthwatering display of homemade cakes and pastries, Sunbury Coffee House is a very tempting stopping-off point as you explore the wonders of this historic city.

Sunbury Coffee House, Music Room Square, 28 Sun Street, Lancaster
Tel: 01524 843312

Lancaster has grown up by the River Lune, navigable as far as Skerton Bridge, so there has always been a strong association between the town and its watery highway. It was in the late 17th and 18th centuries that Lancaster's character as a port fully emerged.

The splendid buildings of the 18th century 'Golden Age' were born out of the port wealth, and the layout and appearance of the town was much altered by this building bonanza. Lancaster as a port gradually declined throughout the 19th century so that many buildings put up for specific maritime purposes were taken over for other uses. Naturally the city has been affected by the arrival of the canal, the railways and 19th century industry; yet the hallmark of Lancaster, its Georgian centre, remains as the product of this maritime prosperity.

Lancaster's rich maritime history is celebrated at St. George's Quay, which with its great stone warehouses and superb Custom House, is now an award-winning **MARITIME MUSEUM**. In Georgian times this was a thriving port with the warehouses receiving shiploads of mahogany, tobacco, rum and sugar from the West Indies.

Visitors today are given a vivid insight into the life of the mariners and quayside workers, with opportunities for Knot tying and other maritime skills. Every year, over the four days of Easter weekend, St. George's Quay is the site home to the Lancaster Maritime Festival with Smugglers, Sea Songs and Shanties. If you're in the area, or even if you're not, it's well worth a visit.

On the banks of the river near the Maritime Museum, in the heart of the old port area of Lancaster, is **PIERRE VICTOIRE** Part of a national franchise, the first Pierre Victoire restaurant was opened in Edinburgh and the outlets have established a good reputation for high quality, imaginative French food with a matching informal, continental atmosphere at a price that is just right.

The restaurant is staffed by a team of young and enthusiastic people which adds to the bustling, yet relaxed, air of the establishment. The rustic style furnishings and continental pictures and decorations could easily belong in any number of cafés and restaurants the length and breadth of France. The food is excellent, all cooked to order, and there are special three course, set lunches at £4.90 and an à la carte menu for the evening. The menu changes daily. As you might imagine, wine is taken seriously but the emphasis is on enjoyment and the list is well worth reading. Naturally, this is a real find, but its success is no secret so booking is necessary at the popular times.

Pierre Victoire, 27A St George's Quay, Lancaster Tel: 01524 843199

Built between 1797 and 1819, the **LANCASTER CANAL** stretches 57 miles from Preston through the centre of Lancaster to Kendal.

Today it is navigable between Preston and Tewitfield, north of Lancaster, the longest lock-free stretch of canal in the country. The canal offers a diversity of scenery and wildlife with opportunities for long distance trips and short circular walks with fine views through peaceful countryside.

With 41 lock-free miles it offers relaxed boating with canalside pubs, restaurants and boat-hire facilities. It provides a good touring route for canoeists and is excellent for coarse fishing.

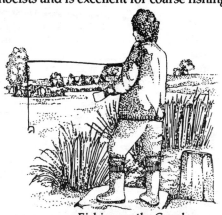

Fishing on the Canal

Another place the whole family can enjoy is **LANCASTER LEISURE PARK** on Wyresdale Road. Set in 42 acres of landscaped parkland, the site includes a mini-marina, a Wild West adventure playground, miniature railway, rare breeds unit, children's farmyard, pony rides, gift shop, tea garden and pottery shop.

While exploring the city it is worth travelling via East Road and Wyresdale Road on the eastern edge, to Williamson Park. Here you can see the impressive **ASHTON MEMORIAL** - a great green copper-domed building, a kind of miniature St. Paul's - standing on a hilltop in the centre of a wonderful Edwardian park.

It forms a landmark seen for miles around and gives a magnificent viewpoint across Morecambe Bay, the Lakeland Hills and the Forest of Bowland. It now houses exhibitions and multi-screen presentations about the Life and Times of Lancaster's Lord Ashton and The Edwardians. There is also a delightful Tropical Butterfly House in the former conservatory.

MORECAMBE. Featuring prominently on the Lancashire coastline, Morecambe has long been one of the most successful and popular seaside resorts in the North, and it can truly be said to enjoy one of the finest views from its promenade of any resort in England - a magnificent sweep of coastline and bay, looking across to the Lakeland mountains.

Like other resorts, Morecambe has changed with the times, and major new attractions include the multi-million pound **BUBBLES LEISURE PARK** and **SUPERDOME**, as well as a **WILD WEST THEME PARK**.

WOMAD, Morecambe's annual world music festival, attracts visitors from across the globe. There are also popular seafront Illuminations in late summer, together with all the usual lively shops and variety of entertainment associated with a busy seaside resort.

Arnside Tower, near Morecambe

Chapel of Saint Patrick

Church of Saint Peter

It's worth strolling along the promenade as far as Heysham Morecambe's twin, with its quaint old main street which winds down to the shore.

It is also a town with considerable historic associations, because it was here in the 8th century that Christian missionaries arrived from Ireland to convert the heathen Viking settlers in the north of England. They built the **CHAPEL OF SAINT PATRICK** on a rock on the sea edge. Its ruins, with coffin-shaped rocks - one of the most curious graveyards in England - can still be seen.

The little **CHURCH OF SAINT PETER** on the headland is equally interesting. It dates back to Saxon and Norman times, with an Anglo-Saxon cross on which the Madonna and other figures have been crudely carved by 9th century masons, and there is a rare Viking hog-back gravestone.

Alongside these antiquities is the modern port of Heysham, with regular car-ferry sailings to the Isle of Man and to Northern Ireland.

SUNDERLAND POINT. For anyone with a sense of the past, it is worth making your way further down the peninsula formed by Heysham and the River Lune, via Middleton and Overton, from where you can either walk or drive (though be careful - the road is closed at high tide, and parking is extremely limited in the village) to Sunderland Point. This is, unbelievably, an old port and seaside resort, which flourished until larger berthed ships, silting channels and the growth last century of rail-served Morecambe caused it to decline.

A little wharf, quiet cottages, some with faded and evocative elegance, a sandy shore where sea thrift flourishes among the pebbles, are all that remains. The estuary is now a Site of Special Scientific Interest because of its wildlife value.

You are likely to see such birds as redshank feeding on the rich food supplies of worms, shellfish and shrimps on the saltmarshes, while a variety of wildfowl such as shelduck, wigeon and mallard, are to be seen in autumn.

A particularly sad story is associated at Sunderland with **SAMBO'S GRAVE**, Sambo was a sea captain's servant at the time of the Slave Trade into Lancaster, who probably died of a fever in 1736 after a long and difficult voyage from the West Indies. Because he was not a baptised Christian, he was not allowed to be buried in consecrated ground. In later years, his death and grave became a potent local symbol of the anti-slavery cause.

His grave can be still seen, in a field at the west side of the point. It is reached by walking along The Lane from the village foreshore, past Upsteps Cottage where Sambo died, and turning left at the shore then over a stile on the left which gives access to the simple gravestone. Fresh flowers are usually to be seen here, mysteriously placed on the grave.

On the opposite side of the Lune estuary from Sunderland Point (and only reached by a long road journey through Lancaster) is **GLASSON DOCK.** The silting of the Lune that ended Lancaster's importance as a port was the reason for the building of Glasson Dock in 1787 to hold 25 seagoing ships. In 1825, the Lancaster Canal was built to provide a better link between the city and the docks, and this was, in turn, supplemented by a railway line in 1883. This railway is now the footpath and cycle way to Lancaster's St. George's Quay.

However, the village of Glasson is now a sailing centre, with the old canal basin a popular marina, and the old wharves and warehouses transformed into an attractive leisure area, with pubs and shops serving a different kind of sea-going clientele.

You can walk, cycle or drive from Glasson past **PLOVER SCAR** where a lighthouse guards the estuary, and where you'll find, near the point where the little River Cocker flows into the Lune, the ruins of **COCKERSAND ABBEY**. The Abbey was founded in 1190 by the Premonstratensian Order on the site of a hospital.

This had been the abode of a hermit, Hugh Garth, before becoming a colony for lepers and the infirm. The Chapter House of the Abbey remains, and was a burial chapel for the Daltons of Thurnham, descendants of Sir Thomas More.

THURNHAM. A little way from here, just off the A588, lies the village of Thurnham.

The local Hall at Thurnham is worth a look and dates from the 13th century, although the main part of the building is 16th century and later.

If you are looking for somewhere a little different as a holiday base, or just seeking good food in pleasant surroundings, then at **THURNHAM MILL HOTEL** you won't be disappointed.

Thurnham Mill Hotel

This Four Crown Commended establishment enjoys a lovely canalside location close to Lancaster Golf Club.

Originally a 19th century corn mill, sympathetic conversion in 1991 has preserved the building's unique character whilst providing every modern amenity. Huge beams and original flagstone floors together with traditional furnishings enhance the olde worlde ambience which extends into the eighteen en-suite guest rooms.

You can relax with a drink on the canalside terrace and the restaurant which is open to non-residents offers a superb menu combined with friendly efficient service. All these factors make Thurnham Mill a popular venue with locals and tourists alike.

Thurnham Mill Hotel, Conder Green, Nr Thurnham.
Tel: 01524 752852.

HEST BANK. Venturing north from Morecambe you will come to the quiet village of Hest Bank where, tucked away up Hatlex Lane between the village and the A6 road to Carnforth, you will discover **WHITEWALLS RESTAURANT**- another 'hidden' gem well worth seeking out.

With ready access for disabled visitors, this superb restaurant is set within a listed building once the home of local character William Stout, a Lancashire shopkeeper.

The surroundings are sumptuous without being impersonal, with many extra little touches which ensure that it provides the perfect setting in which to savour an extensive and imaginative à la carte menu plus a range of daily specials which incorporate the finest English and Continental cuisine.

It comes as no surprise therefore to learn that Whitewalls has won the Best Kept Restaurant award several times, a factor which makes eating here such a joy.

Whitewalls Restaurant, Hatlex Lane, Hest Bank, Lancaster
Tel: 01524 822768

CARNFORTH. To the north of Lancaster, the town of Carnforth lies around what used to be a busy crossroads on the A6. It has a choice of inns and shops, including one of the largest bookshops (new and secondhand) in Lancashire.

Carnforth was once a busy railway junction town whose station has a claim to fame as the setting for the 1940s film classic 'Brief Encounter'.

Though the station has declined in importance, being an unstaffed halt, the old engine sheds and sidings are now occupied by **STEAMTOWN** one of the largest steam railway centres in the north of England. You are

Carnforth Steam Railway

likely to see such giants of the Age of Steam as the Flying Scotsman or an A4 Pacific being stabled here, together with a permanent collection of over 30 British and Continental steam locomotives. There are steam rides in the summer months on both standard gauge and miniature lines.

Just a mile from Carnforth, on a quiet holiday home park at Netherbeck, you will find a lovely place to stay at **THE LODGE**, a distinctly upmarket pine-built lodge which carries a Four Keys Highly Commended rating. Furnished and equipped to a very high standard, the Lodge has all you need to ensure a totally relaxing holiday and enjoys a peaceful location with views across open farmland towards Warton Crag. Lying at the gateway to the Lake District, it makes an ideal touring base from which to explore the surrounding countryside. Managed by Red Rose Cottages - telephone 01200 27310 for a brochure.

The Lodge, Netherbeck, Carnforth Tel: 01200 27310

In the most northern part of Lancashire is Morecambe Bay and the Kent estuary. The villages of SILVERDALE and ARNSIDE (actually in Cumbria) are small and mainly residential, but are worth visiting for the network of footpaths crossing the escarpments whose limestone woodlands are a joy for the botanist, being rich in wild flowers in spring - primroses, violets, orchids, bird's eye primroses, rockroses and eglantines abound.

You can take a choice of footpaths from Arnside village to the summit of the lovely little limestone hill called Arnside Knott, to enjoy breathtaking views of the Kent Estuary, and across Morecambe Bay.

Another footpath follows the shoreline around the little peninsula, following a miniature cliff above the muddy estuary which is particularly rich in birdlife - both seabirds and a variety of waders. If you continue inland by quiet lanes or footpaths you will soon reach **ARNSIDE TOWER**, a 14th century pele tower, built during the reign of Edward II.

BEETHAM. On the A6 further inland, has an unusual 19th century Post Office with a distinctive black-and-white studded door. Within earshot of a waterfall is the **CHURCH OF ST MICHAEL AND ALL ANGELS**, approached through a pergola of rambling roses.

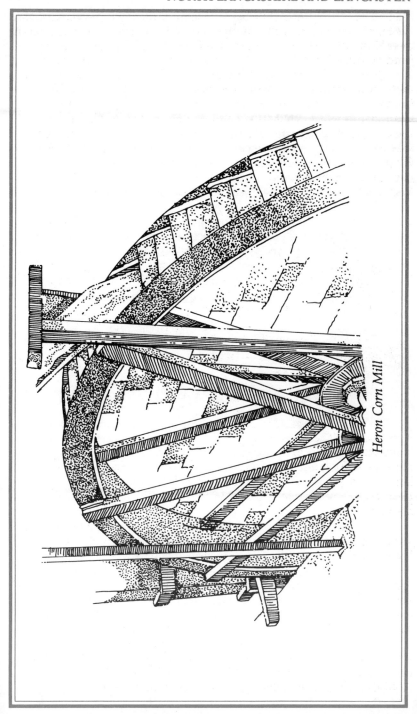

Heron Corn Mill

The church dates from Saxon times and during restoration work in 1834, a hoard of about one hundred old coins was discovered. The coins were from the reigns of Edward the Confessor, William the Conqueror and William Rufus.

In the Civil War the church was badly damaged, its windows smashed and effigies broken. However, a glass fragment of Henry IV in an ermine robe has survived.

HERON CORN MILL, nearby, is a restored and working watermill, with fully operational grinding machinery. There is an exhibition about its history and the processes of milling. Just outside the village, on the Arnside road, a sign points the way to Fairy Steps, a curious rock formation in the woods.

LEIGHTON MOSS. Near Silverdale is a nationally known RSPB Bird Sanctuary, while bird lovers will also enjoy a visit to nearby **LEIGHTON HALL.** As well as being a handsome neo-Gothic building with exceptional collections of Lancaster-made Gillow furniture, the Hall has extensive grounds which are used for displays of falconry in the summer months.

From here we turn southwards and make our way to the lovely districts of Fylde and Wyre and thus into the next chapter.

CHAPTER FIVE

The Fylde and Wyre

Greenhalgh Castle, Garstang

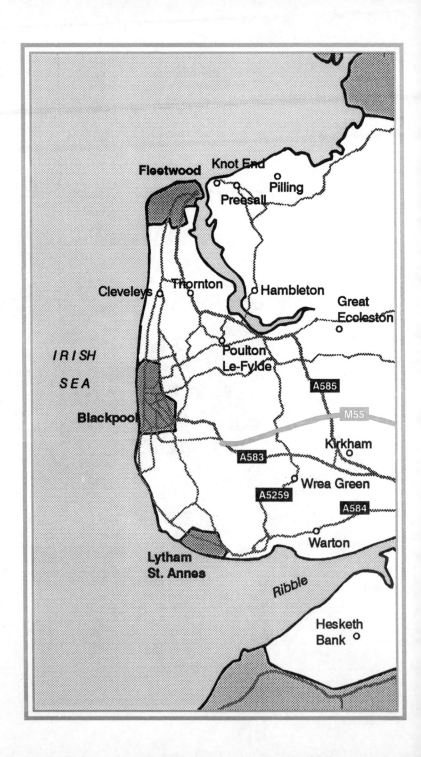

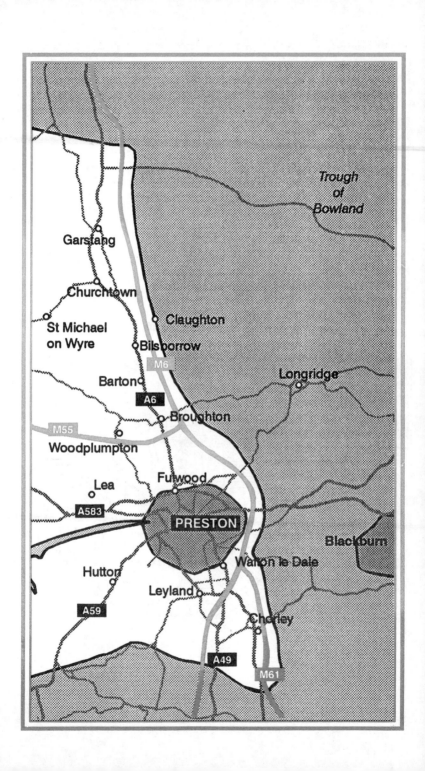

Windmill at Thornton Cleveleys

CHAPTER FIVE

The Fylde and Wyre

GARSTANG, south of Lancaster, just off the A6, is an ancient, picturesque town whose market dates back to the time of King Edward II, who gave monks the right to hold a market here. It was also important as a stage coaching town on the great high road to Scotland, and Bonnie Prince Charlie is reputed to have stayed in the town in 1715.

The main road, later the A6, now by-passes the town, as does the M6. Garstang also had a period of glory as an inland port on the Lancaster Canal and there are a number of fine canalside features, and trip boats operate on the canal during the summer time.

On Thursdays, the weekly market takes over the town, and the High Street and Market Hall become a hive of activity.

A visit to the centre of Garstang will bring you to **TH'OWD TITHEBARN RESTAURANT AND AGRICULTURAL MUSEUM,** a renowned restaurant and place of interest throughout Lancashire and beyond. A Tithebarn has stood on this site since the year 1110, the present one having been built in 1710. The location is alongside the Lancashire canal, and entering through the large wooden doors you are immediately aware of the great character of this building and its extensive exhibition of bygone agricultural memorabilia.

The central feature of the restaurant is the long table with pew style seating where delicious wholesome food is served by happy and smiling staff. Eunice and Kerry have been the managers here for eleven years and will ensure your visit is a memorable one.

Th'owd Tithebarn, The Wharf, Church Street, Garstang, Lancashire.
Tel: 01995 604486

Garstang has an excellent **DISCOVERY CENTRE** in the High Street, which deals with a variety of aspects of the region, including the canal and countryside history, both in Over Wyre and the nearby Forest of Bowland.

Next to the parish church of St Helen in the centre of the village stands the award-winning **PUNCHBOWL INN AND RESTAURANT**. This really is a first class hostelry, from its attractive black and white exterior which entices you inside, to the lovely character of the bar, with its exposed oak beams and open log fires enhancing the warm, friendly atmosphere.

A former 16th century coaching inn, The Punchbowl is renowned for its excellent food, and welcoming hosts David and Pat Singleton have won the Huntsman Awards prestigious title 'Licensee of the Year'. In the cosy surroundings of the three bars you can enjoy a pint of fine hand-pulled ale and to the rear of the pub, the lovely restaurant provides a relaxed setting for an excellent home cooked meal. Families are most welcome and smaller portions are available for children and those with smaller appetites.

The Punchbowl Inn, Church Street, Churchtown, Garstang.
Tel: 01995 603360

Alongside the River Wyre, in Garstang, is the cosy and intimate **WYRESIDE** licensed restaurant. Valerie, the chef, and Clarence Blagden have had Wyreside for some sixteen years and have built up an enviable reputation for excellent and imaginative food served with flair at a very reasonable price.

The Wyreside, Bridge Street, Garstang Tel: 01995 605914

About half a mile east of the town on a grassy knoll are the ruins of **GREENHALGH CASTLE**, built in 1490 by Thomas Stanley, the first Earl of Derby. The castle was severely damaged in a siege against Cromwell in 1645-46, reputedly one of the last strongholds in Lancashire to hold out against him.

A little to the north on the A6 look out for the remains of a stone built

TOLL HOUSE, probably dating from the 1820's when parts of the turnpike from Garstang to Lancaster and beyond were re-aligned - the old road snakes from side to side of the present A6. More than usually interesting because the posts for the toll gate still exist on either side of the road.

On the edge of Garstang, not far from the main A6 route, is the eye-catching **CHURCH INN**. Originally called the Rose and Crown, the inn changed it name when the nearby church was built in around 1753. Judith and Roger Gerrard came here a couple of years ago though they have plenty of experience in the trade. This pub is full of character; the exposed oak beams add to the atmosphere, there are some wonderful prints and other memorabilia dotted around the walls and a smashing feature fireplace.

Judith is the cook and the Church Inn is renowned for its excellent home cooked dishes. Meals are served every lunchtime and evening and can be washed down with a superb choice of well kept cask conditioned ales.

Church Inn, 33 Bonds Lane, Garstang Tel: 01995 602387

When driving through the area try and keep an eye out for the **GARSTANG MILESTONES**. They are to be seen to the North and South of Garstang on the A6, and are the finest turnpike milestones in the County. To the south, they are round-faced stones with cursive lettering dating from the 1750's. To the north the stones are triangular, with Roman lettering associated with the realignments of the 1820's.

BILSBORROW. In Bilsborrow, on the main A6, there is a picturesque stopping-place for bed and breakfast called **OLDE DUNCOMBE HOUSE**. With white walls, contrasting black sills and hanging baskets, it lies within well-kept gardens spreading alongside the Lancaster Canal. Cruising boats and walkers can now enjoy the tranquillity of this stretch of water, which was constructed last century for transporting coal and stone.

Jayne and Alec Bolton came here twelve years ago, and soon found that their house had an interesting history. Its name refers back to the time when Bilsborrow was actually the village of Duncombe. The house was originally three cottages and a barn, and probably dates back to the 1500s.

Long ago, the barn sheltered some of Bonnie Prince Charlie's men overnight, but in modern times, it forms the lounge and bedrooms of the main building.

Beautifully furnished, the cottage style emphasises the character of the house, with spacious bedrooms that are most attractive and extremely well equipped. Pine furniture features throughout, and each room is quite individual. Exposed beams and pictures on the walls enhance a warm and peaceful atmosphere. Jayne and Alec give extraordinarily good value for money.

The beams in the dining room are old ship's timbers and the traditional English breakfasts served here are substantial! Although Jayne and Alec can provide evening meals, this service is rarely needed - four neighbouring restaurants and inns cater for most tastes. For the more independently minded, there is a Certified Caravan Park for five vans, all with electric hook-ups and water, open all year round, adjacent to the house.

Finally, Jayne and Alec also offer a wide range of trips and cruises along the canal on 'The Bilsborrow Lady'. The craft was designed specially for smaller parties, to a maximum of twelve, who wish to travel in style and comfort.

Olde Duncombe House, Garstang Road, Bilsborrow Tel: 01995 640336

As many will know, who have driven along the route between Preston and Lancaster to the 'Lakes', **THE ROEBUCK HOTEL** on the A6 at Bilsborrow is an old established inn and restaurant of many years standing. In the 18th century it was frequented by Engine Drivers and Firemen who would slip down for a 'toothful' while awaiting a train from another direction on the single line track.

Nowadays the Roebuck provides excellent food and drink seven days a week, it's open all day and welcomes children. As with all Pennine Inns, the Roebuck has quality decor and provides a friendly atmosphere

Greenhalgh Castle

for all the family. Food is varied with lots of tasty dishes and additional daily selections on the chalkboard. The challenging 32oz. Rump Steak is the speciality of the house. Full compliment of fine wines and ales. Turn off the M6 for this route and enjoy the difference.

The Roebuck Hotel, Garstang Road, Bilsborrow, Nr. Garstang, Lancashire.
Tel: 01995 640234

In an idyllic setting adjacent to the Lancaster Canal, **GUY'S THATCHED HAMLET** is an establishment with plenty of character and charm. Owned and run by Roy Wilkinson and his two sons Sean and Kirk there is plenty here for everyone. Guy's Eating Establishment, a restaurant where the emphasis is on informality, offers a range of tasty dishes from Scotland, Italy and beyond. The flagged floored, thatched, country style tavern, Owd Nell's, is renowned for its wholesome meals, fine cask kept ales, and wines and lagers from around the world.

Guy's Thatched Hamlet

In the olde worlde atmosphere of Guy's Lodgings you will be sure of a peaceful and relaxing night's sleep. All the rooms are delightfully decorated and with en suite bathrooms and all the other facilities of the hi-tec 1990s. Finally, take a stroll through the Thatched elegance of Spout Lane and School House Square and visit the many craft shops before stopping for a well earned ice-cream at Owd Nell's Ice Cream Parlour.

Guy's Thatched Hamlet, St Michael's Road, Bilsborrow, Preston Tel: 01995 640010 Fax: 01995 640141

CHURCHTOWN, south of Garstang, is a delightful village with many buildings of architectural and historical interest. The **CHURCH OF ST HELENS** dates back to the Norman Conquest and includes architecture from almost every period since then. There is a museum of dolls and toys from the last 100 years at the local school. Find out much more about Churchtown - pick up a village trail leaflet from the church.

Crossing to the other side of the M6 you will find yourself on the edge of the FOREST OF BOWLAND, area of natural beauty. This western area of Bowland lies within a network of quiet lanes, with hidden villages such as Claughton, Calder Vale and Oakenclough. From the higher lanes along the moorland edges, you get sudden, unexpected views of the Fylde Coast, and often magnificent sunsets looking across the Irish Sea. Best of all, this is an area to explore on foot. Leaving the car and the tarmac roads, you can take a choice of footpaths, for example, winding along the little River Brock, or onto the higher fell country around Bleasdale.

CLAUGHTON. In the village of Claughton, lovers of fine clothes will discover a real haven at **COUNTRY VOGUE**. Lizzie and Trevor, the shop owners, have spent a great deal of effort in restoring what were almost derelict stables when they bought the property. In their heyday they were the home of prizewinning Shire horses.

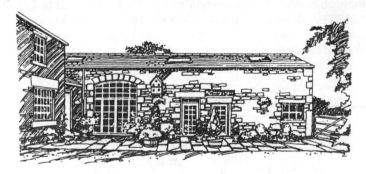

Country Vogue

The finished result is a great success and now houses a vast collection of quality country clothing, sold direct from the manufacturers at discounted prices. The shop stocks range from designer labels to wax jackets and include handbags and accessories. You can choose from a selection of classic pure wool knitwear, all cotton shirts, handcrafted leather shoes and other beautiful items made from the finest yarn and cloth, be it alpaca, silk or cashmere; all of which look quite at home in rooms where flagstoned floors and beamed ceilings retain the original character of these old buildings.

Country Vogue, Garstang Road, Claughton-on-Brock, Garstang. Tel: 01995 640622 Fax: 01995 640288

Just a little to the east is **BEACON FELL COUNTRY PARK**, one of the most popular countryside destinations in this part of Lancashire. This is a beautiful wooded hill top, commanding magnificent views of the Bowland Fells. There are well-signed car parks, picnic places and a choice of well-marked walks across the summit and through the woodlands, and the area is rich in wildlife interest.

ST MICHAEL'S-ON-WYRE, a few miles beyond Churchtown on the A586 has a superb church, mainly 15th century, but with Jacobean pews and some unusual stained glass.

GREAT ECCLESTON which lies in the centre of the Fylde plain, is 10 miles from Blackpool and 12 miles from Preston. Every Wednesday the busy **OPEN AIR MARKET** held in the picturesque Village Square attracts local villagers, residents from neighbouring villages and even coach parties from outside the rural area. The parish council began negotiations to have a market in 1971, and by 1974 they were successful. Some 20 - 30 stalls sell a variety of goods and are open for business from 10am to 4pm.

The village of Great Eccleston has, in more recent years, become a great attraction for visitors, being conveniently situated between the Trough of Bowland and the coast. Refreshments and gift shops are usually high on the visitors agenda and both can be found in **CHARLOTTE'S TEA ROOM AND GIFT SHOP** in the Square. Housed in the attractively converted outbuildings of an old Public House, it has been completely refurbished in traditional style. Here you can take morning coffee, light lunches or afternoon teas.

Charlotte's Tea Room and Gift Shop

Charlotte's also has a tempting selection of quality country crafts and gifts attractively displayed on old dressers and tables.

Across the road is **M.M.J's** offering a further selection with clothes of distinction; everything for the lady, including separates, dresses and evening wear, by top designers. Open Tuesday to Saturday 10.00am to 5.00pm. Credit cards accepted.

Charlotte's Tea Room & Gift Shop, The Square, Great Eccleston, Preston, Lancashire. Tel: 01995 671108

POULTON-LE-FYLDE is a kaleidoscope of colour and old world charm. This ancient market town with its cobbled streets, market place complete with medieval stocks, and historic church makes the perfect setting for the superb floral decorations that adorn the town each year. Small wonder that Poulton has twice won the prestigious Britain in Bloom, small town category.

Poulton-le-Fylde is mentioned in the Domesday Book and once famous for its market, the town grew around the Parish Church of **ST CHAD'S** which is surrounded by several old pubs - no doubt a legacy to the days when hostelries had to cater for the thirsts of visiting farmers and market traders! Poulton's fascinating history can be traced on one of the regular Town Trails organised by the local Historical Society, details of which are available from Tourist Information Centres.

In contrast to its ancient centre, Poulton has superb 20th century style shopping arcades, a modern swimming centre, and with ample free parking in the heart of the town, all amenities are easily accessible for visitors. For the more active, Poulton has one of the Wyre's superb golf courses - a testing 9 hole course surrounded by farm and fields.

It's hard to imagine the town of Poulton as a seaport today, after all, it is miles from the sea. But in bygone times, ships sailed up the Wyre to **SKIPPOOL CREEK**, Poulton - and to **WARDLEY'S CREEK** across the river at Hambleton. Now Skippool is home to the Blackpool and Fleetwood Yacht Club and you can stroll by the river and see the ocean-going yachts that compete in major races around Britain.

THORNTON CLEVELEYS. Thornton was listed in the Domesday Book, but neighbouring Cleveleys is a child of the 20th century.

Thornton, on the banks of the Wyre, was a farming area and in 1794 **MARSH MILL** was built to grind corn. Now, the magnificent mill with its machinery restored and new sails fitted, is the centrepiece for a new development with the creation of attractive leisure facilities on land beside the mill.

A visit to the speciality shops in the complex is a must. Look out for the fascinating **NORTHERN CLOG MUSEUM.**

The **BLACKPOOL FLEETWOOD TRAMWAY** link is unique, and it runs right through the middle of Cleveleys. Hop off at Victoria Square and you're in the heart of one of the busiest shopping areas in the Borough of Wyre, with a range of goodies on offer all along Victoria Road West.

Cleveleys seafront has long been a holiday haven with plenty of sand and lots to do. There's history here too. Cleveleys began to grow after an architectural competition was organised in 1906 and prizes were given for the best designs. Among those involved was the future Sir Edwin Lutyens, designer of modern Whitehall.

FLEETWOOD, a typical Victorian resort, has endured the transformation from wild sandhills into a busy seaport in just 160 years and now stands on the threshold of a new century with plans to further develop the new marina complex into a spectacular harbour village.

Over a century and a half ago, local Squire, Sir Peter Hesketh Fleetwood hired Decimus Burton, a leading architect of the day, to draw up a grand design for the town. Plans included **QUEENS TERRACE**, the spectacular **NORTH EUSTON HOTEL** - still as elegant today - a railway station to bring visitors from Northern Industrial towns, and a splendid port that was set to rival Liverpool.

Here, "where the river winds down to the sea", is a town that owes much of its prosperity to the sea. In the early days mighty ships brought in cargoes of cotton and grain from America. Gradually a new cargo took over as sailors turned their skills fishing and Fleetwood developed into the country's third largest fishing port.

Watersports are becoming increasingly popular and the town is now a major centre for the sport of sailboarding. Alternatively, you could board the popular "Steam Packet Boat" to the Isle of Man.

Look out for some of the town's more unusual features, such as the **PHAROS LIGHTHOUSE** in the middle of the street and the unique public tramway system that runs through the heart of the town.

For something completely different walk across the road to the **MOUNT SEASIDE PARK** and stand inside the huge clock while the wheels whizz around and bells chime! This unusual building houses the Fleetwood Civic Society display and a craft centre where you can by a wide range of quality goods. The tower affords splendid views of the town and a panorama across Morecambe Bay to the Lakeland Hills.

While in the area, you will find an enjoyable trip is to take the passenger ferry across the Wyre estuary to **KNOTT END**. Although Knott End is little more than a hamlet, the estuary itself and the coastline are particularly interesting, with areas of mud flat, salt marsh and dunes, all rich in birdlife. Much of the area has been declared a Site of Special Scientific Interest for its unique environmental quality, and you can follow the public right of way along the coastline almost as far as Pilling, overlooking **PRESSALL SANDS**.

Knott End also marks one end of **THE WYRE WAY**, Fleetwood being the other. The Wyre Way is a 16 mile walk that explores the history and wildlife of the estuary and surrounding countryside, from the estuary mouth inland as far as the Shard Bridge.

The route is easy to follow with clear markers - watch out for very high tides which may effect parts of the walk. For more details contact the nearest Tourist Information Centre.

PILLING, a little further along the coast, is a quiet scattered village on the edge of richly fertile marshland. For many years, the village was linked to its market town of Garstang by a little winding single-track railway, known affectionately to locals as the 'Pilling Pig'.

Pilling is said to be the second largest village in Britain and is steeped in history. **THE OLDE SHIP INN**, for example, which can be found in the centre of the village, was built in 1782 by Geirge Dickson, a slave trader. Originally an inn, this listed building is reputed to be haunted by a lady dressed in Georgian attire, wandering around with a pale and worried look on her face!

PREESALL is an ancient settlement built on a hill and one of the larger villages of Over Wyre. The name of Preesall comes from the Celtic for 'hill with brushwood growing on it'.

Rather than taking a ferry across from Fleetwood, an alternative way of crossing the Wyre is to take the A588 at Shard Bridge.

The 325 yards long **SHARD BRIDGE** built in 1864 is on the original site of a ford across the narrow part of the River Wyre. Finds at the site certainly date it back to Roman times, and it is possible that the ford goes back even further to the Iron Age, around 500 BC.

The Victorian bridge still operates a toll charge which has been paid over the decades by local residents who otherwise had to rely on the ferries or take their chances of being swept away, 'wagons and all', even at low tide!

HAMBLETON. The road shortly brings you to Hambleton, from where a network of quiet and sometimes extremely narrow lanes wind through a countryside of great charm. In Medieval times Hambleton was a centre for shipbuilding.

STALMINE VILLAGE, on the A588, between Hambleton and Preesall, is where can take tea in **THE OLD TROUGH** organic tearooms situated in a traditional farmyard dominated by a superb example of a Tudor Barn.

BLACKPOOL is probably Britain's liveliest and most popular resort. 1994 signified a major landmark in the history of this bustling seaside town, for its world famous 518 feet high **TOWER**, copied from Paris's scarcely more famous Eiffel, celebrated its centenary and in recognition of this was painted gold, making it an even more prominent feature!

It is hard then to believe that a little over 150 years ago, Blackpool was little more than a fishing village among sand dunes on the Irish Sea coast. In the early years, travel to and from the town involved considerable discomfort, taking two days from Yorkshire and a day from Manchester.

However, the arrival of the great Victorian railway companies who laid their tracks to the coast and built their stations, of which Blackpool had three, provided cheap excursions to Blackpool for day-trippers from Lancashire and Yorkshire and so this fishing village gradually transformed into the vibrant seaside resort you find today.

Blackpool Tower.

The famous **PLEASURE BEACH** boasts its own railway station and is an attraction that continues to be extended and improved. It is now home to the tallest (235ft high), fastest (85mph), and possibly most expensive (£12m) roller coaster ride in the world - not something to be undertaken by the fainthearted!

Nearby, **THE SANDCASTLE** provides all-weather fun, with waves, waterslides and flumes in a tropical indoor setting, and further down Blackpool's Golden Mile, **THE SEA LIFE CENTRE** proves popular with all ages, giving visitors a close-up view of the underwater world.

Of course, the one thing that Blackpool is perhaps best renowned for is its spectacular autumn **ILLUMINATIONS** which bring in thousands of visitors each year, all eager to witness the greatest free show on earth. As well as these modern attractions, Blackpool still retains more traditional and gentle diversions, such as tea-dances in the elegant **TOWER BALLROOM.**

This is all a far cry from Blackpool's first place of amusement, Uncle Tom's cabin, which perched precariously on the crumbling cliffs to the north of the town. Unfortunately the original building was lost to the sea in 1907.

The 1890s saw the development of many of the resort's now famous attractions. At that time it was estimated that Blackpool's 7,000 dwellings could accommodate 250,000 holidaymakers in addition to a permanent population of 35,000. Naturally these visitors would require entertainment and so the work began. In 1889 the original Opera House was built in the Winter Gardens complex and two years later a start was made on the "Eiffel Tower".

THE NORTH PIER was designed by Eugenius Birch and opened on 23rd May 1863. It soon became an exclusive promenade for 'quality' visitors and is now a Listed Building.

Despite its reputation as a vibrant and lively resort, Blackpool also has its quiet, romantic corners where you can escape the hustle of crowds. You only have to walk or take a tram along a few of the seven miles of its long promenade past North Shore and Bispham, or down to Squire's Gate or Lytham St. Anne's to find life moving at a much gentler pace, with much quieter beaches and promenades, rolling dunes, and pleasant town centres, yet still enjoying the bracing sea air for which Blackpool is renowned.

BLACKPOOL TRAMWAYS provide the most enjoyable way of exploring the quieter sides of Blackpool and Wyre. The world's first electric street tramway opened in Blackpool on 29th September 1885 and ran from Cocker Street to South Shore.

The route was extended along the Lytham road in 1895 and later connected with the system operated by the Blackpool, St. Annes and Lytham Tramway Company Limited. Following the opening of new bus services in the 1960s, the Promenade route was the only commercial electric tramway left in the country. Today, Blackpool's tram system is rivalled only by Manchester's Metrolink and the Sheffield Super Trams.

Many of Blackpool's unique 'streamline' trams date from the 1930s or 50s, and the Tramway Company has a fleet of vintage cars used for special occasions, such as the autumn Illuminations. But there are also comfortable modern vehicles which make a trip out to Cleveleys or Fleetwood - a delightful experience. It's possible to combine a tram ride with a walk along the foreshore to enjoy surprisingly fine coastline views, with excellent birdlife including a variety of seabirds, waders, and at certain times of the year, wild duck and geese.

LYTHAM ST. ANNES, further south along the coast, has a name synonymous with golf, for this peaceful resort boasts four magnificent championship courses attracting major tournaments each year.

What first strikes holiday-makers and visitors to Lytham St. Annes is the sensation of not knowing whether you are in one or two towns. There are in fact two towns here, Lytham and St. Annes-on-Sea, one is ancient and steeped in history while the other is relatively modern. Interestingly, St. Annes, whose array of mixed architectural styles belies its true age, was a forerunner of Britain's garden cities and was created from a wilderness of sand dunes inhabited mainly by rabbits.

The sandy beaches here are a sunbather's paradise, as well as being ideal for a variety of sports, with sand yachting proving one of the most popular.

THE QUEEN'S HOTEL holds a prominent position on Lytham St Anne's famous promenade facing the sea and also opposite the Lifeboat station.

Built during the mid 19th century, it is typical of the buildings in the area, with a grand facade. Inside the grandeur of the Victorian age has not been lost, though the hotel also offers the modern comforts of the late 20th century.

The Queen's Hotel

The Queen's Hotel has 9 en-suite cosy yet spacious bedrooms that would put many larger hotels to shame and the resident's lounge has wonderful views over the sea. The Victoria Restaurant, which features the rooms original flagstone floor, offers a good menu as well as a mouth-watering daily specials board. Open to non-residents every lunchtime and for dinner during the season.

The hotel was acquired by Pennine Inns in 1995 and as you would expect, there is a fine range of top class real ales and beers. Finally, The Queen's offers the best in hospitality and facilities and a visit here, for however long, will be memorable and enjoyable.

The Queen's Hotel, Central Beach, Lytham St Annes Tel: 01253 737316

Lytham is also renowned for its delightful parks, attractive gardens and beautiful floral displays. The atmosphere here is so relaxed that you can stroll unhurried, exploring the streets of the handsome town centre with its splendid shops, and pausing at one of the many quaint tearooms. You can even indulge in a little childhood reminiscence at the **TOY AND TEDDY BEAR MUSEUM.**

THE BEDFORD HOTEL, in the centre of St Annes, is a town hotel with a country house feel. Owned and run by Terri Baker and her son and daughter, Carl and Lyn, for the past 11 years, The Bedford is sophisticated yet homely with a comfortable and relaxing atmosphere. This hotel has plenty to offer its guests whether they are staying here on business or for pleasure.

All the 36 bedrooms are en suite, tastefully decorated and with all the little extras that you only expect in larger hotels. The delightful Coffee Shop, open all day, is the ideal place for a hot or cold snack, cake or pastry. The Memories Brasserie and Bar is a full á la carte restaurant serving a wide range of English and Continental dishes, from a succulent steak to a celebration dinner. To work off all that food The Bedford also has its own well equipped Health Club, where you can work out in the gym and follow up the exercise with a relaxing Jacuzzi, sauna or steam bath. In case the sun fails to shine there is always the solarium to top up the tan.

The Bedford Hotel, 307-311 Clifton Drive South, St Annes on Sea
Tel: 01253 724436

YORK HOUSE is an extremely attractive building situated within its own grounds in an excellent position on Clifton Drive South, close to both the beach and the local shops. Built in 1899 and formerly Oxford House School for Boys of the Gentry, in 1974 Marilyn and Antony Sykes bought the building and have, over a number of years, refurbished the house and produced 12 luxury apartments with every facility you could wish for included. All the apartments, which vary in size, are completely self contained with their own entrance and are all well up-to-date with all the latest modern equipment.

Marilyn and Antony live in the house themselves and are always happy to help, they have cots, highchairs and pushchairs available for hire and no problem is too small. An ideal place for a family holiday where you can be sure all your needs will be looked after by very caring owners.

York House, 261 Clifton Drive South, St Annes on Sea Tel: 01253 721701

WOODPLUMPTON and EAVES. Situated in the tiny hamlet of Eaves, with just a telephone box and a couple of farms, is **THE PLOUGH AT EAVES**.

The Plough at Eaves

Originally a 17th century coaching house, it is now home to a pub and restaurant run by Bob and Christine Bassinder. The pub has a very cosy feel and the oldest room has very low ceilings with exposed beams and horse brasses. Old shotguns hang over the fireplace which houses real, open log fires in Winter.

The restaurant and bar area are a more recent addition but still in keeping with the quaint country pub style. Excellent hand pulled beers are available and there is a good menu, for the restaurant and the bar, with daily specials. A wonderful secret hidden place for all to enjoy.

The Plough at Eaves, Eaves Lane, Eaves, Woodplumpton Tel: 01772 690233

PRESTON, Lancashire's administrative capital, makes a fine central point from which to explore the whole region. It is a town of ancient history, strategically situated on the highest navigable point of the River Ribble. It is still an active port, with cargo vessels and even an occasional special passenger boat, though most maritime activity nowadays comes from sailing and windsurfing in the Riversway Marina.

There is an impressive range of public buildings. The Parish Church occupies a site which has been in use for christian worship since the 7th century, and the present church has an elegant 205 foot high spire which soars above the town centre. **PRESTON TOWN HALL** was designed by Sir Giles Gilbert Scott in suitable Gothic style, whilst the fine **HARRIS ART GALLERY, MUSEUM** and **LIBRARY**, in equally impressive neo-classical style, provide a civic focal point close to the busy covered markets. The Harris Gallery has, incidentally, some of the most impressive collections of sculpture and paintings in the county.

Preston also has a number of covered shopping centres and pedestrianised areas, including the **GUILD HALL** and **CHARTER THEATRE COMPLEX** which host a wide variety of events from straight theatre to classical and pop music and sporting events.

A famous event which takes place here is the **PRESTON GUILD**, originally a celebration of restrictive practices which later became a fashionable bun-fight for the nobs and is now Britain's biggest carnival, celebrated every 20 years by an entire town. The Preston Guild merchant has an ancient and colourful tradition dating back more than 800 years.

The first Guilds were formed in Anglo-Saxon times as people grouped together for help and protection, but as trade and wealth increased, the "Guild Merchants" came into being. It is not known precisely when Preston's own Guild Merchant was established, but there is proof of a Preston Charter as early as 1179, and there may well have been a charter as early as 1100, 34 years after the Norman conquest.

Preston's merchants not only benefited from the exclusive trading rights they were granted and the freedom from tolls, but they also employed the Guild Merchant as a vehicle to ensure the quality control of Preston goods. Special Officers were appointed to see that cloth, for example, came up to a very exacting standard, that bread was baked to a specific size, and ale brewed to a given strength and sold at a prescribed price. Orders made under the Guild Merchant powers ensured that the cottagers could buy in the market before the larger buyers came in, and all merchandise had to be sold in the open and within sight of the market cross - no doubt a reminder of people's Christian duty to one another.

With all this good fortune the merchants and people of Preston had plenty of reasons to celebrate and they set about creating the first Preston Guild ceremonies. However, you have a long wait until the next one, it isn't until 2012!

FULWOOD PARK HOTEL, just a few minutes drive from the centre of Preston, is well worth finding in this quiet suburb of the town. The impressive Victorian building was originally two private houses but was converted into a hotel many years ago. Now owned and run by partners Frank McGrath and Veronica Afrin, this is a real home from home and as the hotel is not open to non residence you really get a chance to settle in.

There are 21 bedrooms of varying size, many with en suite facilities, and there is also a very well laid out disabled suite. The warm hospitality is matched by a licensed bar, lounge and TV room to relax in and a delicious menu prepared by the chef served in the restaurant.

Fulwood Park Hotel, 49 Watling Street Road, Fulwood, Preston
Tel: 01772 718067

It's only a short drive south of Preston to Worden Hall, Leyland. The **WORDEN ARTS AND CRAFTS CENTRE** is surrounded by 157 acres of parkland and can be found just off the B5243. Opened in 1984, the Centre occupies the remaining buildings of Worden Hall, home of the Farrington family until 1947. The Centre houses a fully equipped theatre, craft workshops and a coffee shop. It is fascinating to watch crafts such as Pyrography, Woodturning, Knitting, Ceramics, Photography, Landscape Painting, Stained Glass, Blacksmithying and Stencilling in the process of being worked on.

Adjacent to the Centre is the Lancashire branch of the Council for the Protection of Rural England, a registered charity which seeks to improve, protect and conserve the countryside. CPRE has a gift shop and an exhibition area, which features permanent displays of Worden Hall 'Then and Now'.

The main features of Worden Park include a 17th century ice house, a miniature railway, Victorian maze, a garden for the blind, an arboretum, miniature golf, a children's play area, and several picnic areas. There is ample parking which is free in the main car park, and in the Centre car park. Coach parties are also welcome, but prior notice is requested. In the winter months visitors are advised to telephone before visiting individual workshops.

Worden Arts and Crafts Centre, Worden Park, Leyland Tel: 01772 455908

Set in sixteen acres of beautiful, well tendered gardens, deep in the heart of the Lancashire countryside, yet close to Preston and the M6 motorway, **BARTLE HALL COUNTRY HOTEL** is a truly outstanding establishment. It was originally built in the 17th century as a private residence and is now run by the Howarth family as a hotel of exceptionally high quality.

Bartle Hall Country Hotel

As well as offering guests the very best in comfort and personal service the restaurant is renowned throughout the area for its imaginative dishes which will delight even the most critical diner. For many years Bartle Hall has also offered the most charming setting and facilities for small or large weddings and banquets. This is certainly an ideal setting for that special occasion.

Bartle Hall Country Hotel, Lea Lane, Bartle, Near Preston
Tel: 01772 690506

LEA. Close by the village of Lea, is the **SADDLE INN** which was originally a farmhouse in the early 1800's before becoming a Coaching Inn. Nowadays, the is a wonderful family place with David and Sue at the helm. The inn welcomes more visitors each year while providing a good local trade with top quality food and refreshment.

Sue is in charge of the catering and provides delicious food at very reasonable prices with special dishes for children. Additionally, the 'specials board' supplements the general menu, supported by a separate sweet board selection. David keeps excellent Thwaites ale including Fawkes Folly and Porter Ale - always in top condition. Well worth a visit. Ample parking.

The Saddle Inn, Lea, Preston, Lancashire.   Tel: 01722 726982

WALTON LE DALE, a few miles south of Preston, is where you will find the relatively new **VINEYARD HOTEL** built in the style of a Swiss Chalet. It is easily reached from the M6 and M61 Motorways and is ideally located for the old town of Preston, Blackpool and beyond.

This hotel has charm and character with very pleasing decor and furnishings. Sixteen en-suite bedrooms offer a good combination of accommodation and are very well appointed. Owned by Pennine Inns (Scottish and Newcastle), this hotel, as with others in the same ownership, place a lot of emphasis on catering for the family and offer very good value.

A two tier bar area serves a fine range of well kept ales and bar snacks while the attractive restaurant offers very good table d'hôte and a 'la carte menus. Weddings, Conferences and Special Events are catered for.

The Vineyard Hotel, Chorley Road, Walton-Le-Dale, Preston, Lancashire. Tel: 01772 254646 Fax: 01772 258967

BARTON. Alongside Barton Grange Hotel, on the A6 at Barton, is the outstanding **BARTON GRANGE GARDEN CENTRE**. When, in 1963, Eddie Topping set up his humble shop, 16 feet square and selling a limited choice of plants with a modest selection of seeds and tools, little did anyone think that it would, in thirty years, grow into the premier garden centre it is today.

Still owned and run by the Topping family, Barton Grange is the place to come for anyone with an interest in plants. The staff, some what larger than in the early years, are experts in their particular fields and always ready to help and offer advice. Everything you could possibly want for even the most modest garden can be found here and it is a pleasure to wander around the various greenhouses and outdoor grow-ing areas and take in the wide variety of shrubs, trees and indoor plants that are available.

Barton Grange Garden Centre, Garstang Lane, Barton Tel: 01772 864242

WHITESTAKE. Here, the unique **TURBARY HOUSE GARDEN CENTRE** has absolutely everything for the enthusiastic gardener in a landscaped setting, offering hours of interest and enjoyment for all the family.

In addition to an extensive display of indoor and outdoor plants to suit every home or garden, there is also a wide selection of garden accessories, tools, books and gifts, including basketware, ceramics, and fresh, dried and silk flowers. All of the aforementioned are attractively displayed in Turbary's well-stocked shop.

We cannot think of anywhere else that visitors can take a lakeside or woodland stroll and wander around hundreds of trees, shrubs and conifers whilst selecting their purchases, happy in the knowledge that the children are playing safely in the adventure playground. Every

Wednesday is Senior Citizen Day at Turbary House, with a special discount on most items.

The Centre offers a unique gardening advice service, and can arrange special displays, demonstrations and functions to suit club and party bookings.

They are happy to tailor events to suit the individual party, and it would be wise to enquire about the morning coffee, afternoon tea, hot pot suppers, barbeques or buffets which can be made available, in order to ensure a really special social event for all attending. Turbary House Garden Centre is open all year, with the exception of Christmas Day.

Turbary House Garden Centre, Chainhouse Lane, Whitestake, Preston
Tel: 01772 36664

LEYLAND is a small town, and it has seen a lot of changes in the last 20 years. In many ways, despite the demise of the commercial vehicle industry which previously dominated it, it has moved into a period of renewed prosperity and taken on a more leisurely and attractive character.

The town is proud of its past, and has a **BRITISH COMMERCIAL VEHICLE MUSEUM** to attract today's visitors. The museum is housed in the former Leyland South Works on King Street, where commercial vehicles were produced for many years. The museum is devoted to the history of British Commercial Vehicles and efforts are made to ensure that exhibits include representations of all major manufacturers.

The museum is the largest of its kind in Europe with exhibits ranging from the horse-drawn era through to steam wagons and early petrol vehicles up to the present day. The evolution of road vehicles can be traced as they developed to meet the vast growth in demand for passenger, goods and delivery vehicles.

THE BLACK BULL public house, lying on the outskirts of Leyland, really is an impressive establishment. Linda and Harold Dutton run the pub and, with a fair number of years experience in the trade and Linda's exceptional ability as a qualified chef, this is an wonderful place to dine. The decoration and furnishings are second to none and are equalled by the tremendous, friendly atmosphere.

The Black Bull is open all day, everyday serving a fine range of quality ales. The menu, supplemented by a mouth-watering selection of daily specials, offers a lovely range of tasty dishes for lunch and dinner. The traditional Sunday lunches, served all day on Sunday, are a must and there is a special children's menu for 'Little Bulls'.

The Black Bull, Dunkirk Lane, Leyland Tel: 01772 422899

ULNES WALTON. Set in 5 acres in the village of Ulnes Walton, **AULDENE GARDEN CENTRE** is the premier garden centre in the north west. When Cyril Iddon retired in the 1950s and bought the then Auldene Nurseries to potter about in little did anyone know what it would grow into! The centre is still owned and run by the Iddon family and it really is the place to come for both keen and occasional gardeners alike. There is a team of well trained, knowledgeable staff on hand to answer any questions and the centre runs a packed calendar of events throughout the year with talks, demonstrations and workshops. Whatever you need for your garden from a packet of seeds to a set of garden furniture this is the place to find it.

Auldene Garden Centre, 338 Southport Road, Ulnes Walton, Leyland
Tel: 01772 600271

This area south of the Ribble estuary has a strong agricultural and industrial heritage. Many villages also have fine churches. Visit **ST MICHAEL'S** in MUCH HOOLE. This church was erected in 1628 and is regarded as the home of the beginning of English astronomy. **ST MARY'S** in PENWORTHAM has a lovely setting on Penwortham Hill overlooking the Ribble. The site dates back to Roman times, and the church has a 14th century chancel and tower which is 'perpendicular period'. In Leyland itself, look out for St. Andrew's. It is a 900 year old parish church and has beautiful stained glass windows.

From here, we cross the Irish Sea to the Isle of Man for the next chapter.

CHAPTER SIX

The Isle of Man

Cregneish Cottages

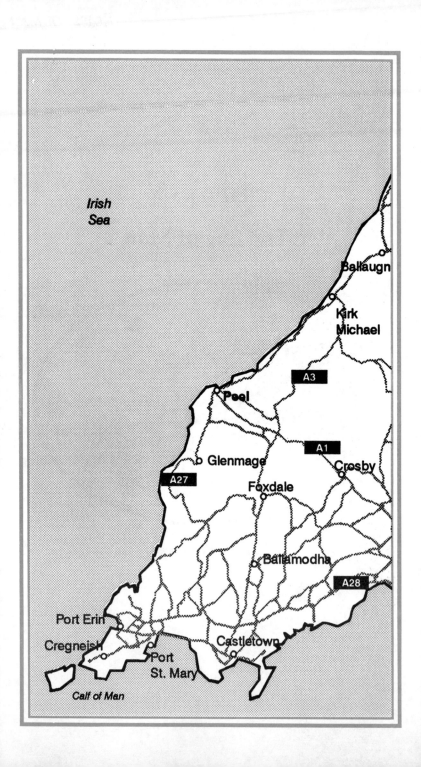

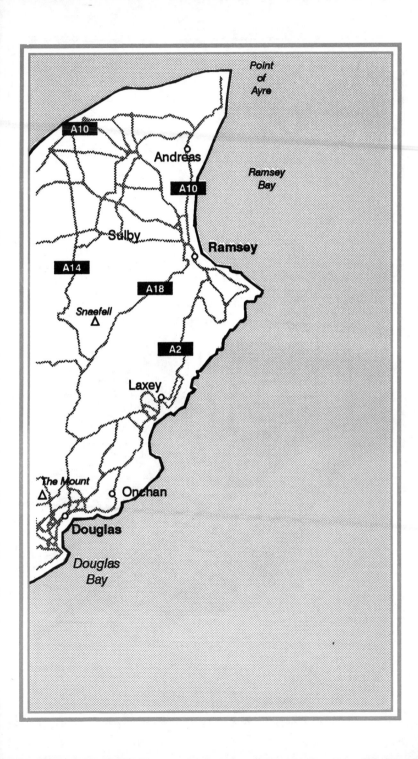

Snaefell Railway

CHAPTER SIX

The Isle of Man

The Isle of Man is perhaps best known for its annual T.T. motorcycle races, its tailless cat, Manx kippers and as a tax haven for the wealthy. However, there is much more to this beautiful island which, set in the heart of the Irish Sea, truly is a world apart.

There are around 100 miles of coastline, encompassing eight major resorts, each one with its own individual character and appeal.

Getting here is much easier than you would expect. The island has its own airline, Manx Airlines, which operates a regular daily service from most UK airports and there are ferry services from Liverpool, Heysham and Fleetwood, as well as Belfast, Dublin and Stranraer.

This magical Isle became an island around 10,000 years ago when the meltwater of the Ice Age raised the sea level. Soon after this, the first people came, working and developing the island into the landscape we see today. The distinctive influences of the various different cultures who have lived here still remain, leaving a land with a unique and colourful heritage.

Among the first arrivals here were the Vikings. Evidence of this era, from the earliest chieftains to the last Norse King, abounds throughout the island. Against the skyline on the seaward side of the road between Ballaugh and Bride some early hilltop Viking burial mounds can be seen.

At the ancient castle in Peel, an archaeological dig revealed many hidden Viking treasures which are now on display at the Manx Museum in the island's capital of Douglas, and at the Boathouse in Peel you can see a replica of the type of longship that brought the likes of Magnus Barefoot, Sigurd the Stout and Olaf the Dwarf.

Despite their reputation for plunder, rape and pillage, the Vikings also made some positive contributions to the island, not least of which was the establishment of the Manx governmental system, known as **TYNWALD**. The Manx name of the Tynwald Hill is "Cronk Keeill Eoin", Hill of St. John's church. There is no record to confirm the story that it contains earth from all of the seventeen parish churches, but it is not unlikely that token portions of soil were added to the mound in accordance with an old Norse custom.

The Tynwald ceremony continues to this day with an annual meeting of the Tynwald on Midsummer's Day at the ancient parliament field at St. Johns, where Manx citizens can petition parliament. Thus the Isle of Man is an independent country, with its own taxes, currency (British currency is also acceptable) and native language, although virtually everyone speaks English.

The famous three legged symbol seems to have been adopted in the 13th century as the amorial bearings of the native Kings of the Isle of Man, whose dominion also included the Hebrides. After 1266, when the native dynasty ended and control of the Island passed briefly to the Crown of Scotland and then permanently to the English Crown, the emblem was retained, and among the earliest survivng representations are those on the Manx Sword of State, thought to have been made in the year 1300 AD. The Three Legs also appeared on the Manx coinage of the seventeenth to nineteenth centuries, and are still seen in everyday use in the form of the official Manx flag.

Why the Three Legs were adopted as the Royal Arms of the Manx Kingdom is unknown. Many heraldic emblems had no meaning and were chosen merely because they were distinctive. This may have been the case with the Three Legs, though the emblem as such - like the cross and the swastika, to which it is related - has a long history reaching far back into pagan times. It was originally a symbol of the sun, the seat of Power and Life.

The motto incorporated with the Three Legs of Man on the official Coat of Arms is "Quocunque Jeceris Stabit", and means - "Whichever way you throw I shall stand".

DOUGLAS, the island's capital is the obvious place to begin your tour and not surprisingly perhaps, is the liveliest of the resorts, its two-mile promenade being the focus of the island's nightlife. Live entertainment is provided at the Gaiety Theatre, Villa Marina and Summerland indoor leisure centre and there are numerous pubs, discos, cinemas, restaurants and amusement parks to choose from.

From dawn to dusk you can enjoy a leisurely ride along the magnificent sweep of Douglas Promenade aboard the **DOUGLAS BAY HORSE TRAMWAY**, a remarkable and beautiful reminder of a bygone era. The history began when a civil engineer, Thomas Lightfoot, retired to the Isle of Man and, seeing the need for a public transport system along the promenade, designed the tramway. That the Douglas line has survived into the 1990s is remarkable. during the 1900s attempts were made to electrify the line and extend the Manx electric railway along the promenade - the plans were later dropped.

A story often told about the horses that pull the trams, concerns a parrot that lived in a cage in a hotel close to a tram stop. The bird learnt to mimic the sound of the tram's starting bell and used to practise this skill constantly. The tram horses would stop when they heard the bell and immediately start again before passengers could alight. Result, chaos!

Proudly standing in the centre of the Victorian promenade at Douglas is **THE EMPRESS HOTEL**. This 102 bedroom, white Victorian hotel was built in the heyday of the Isle of Man's holiday maker years, when wealthy businessmen and their families from the North of England came here for weeks at a time. The Empress Hotel was completely rebuilt

ISLE OF MAN TRANSPORT
Arraghey Ellan Vannin

The Isle of Man boasts many wonders of Victorian engineering, many of which are still in full working order. Among the most outstanding examples are its steam and electric railways, a network kept in beautiful condition and popular with old and young visitors alike.

THE VICTORIAN STEAM RAILWAY between Douglas and Port Erin provides a memorable journey along cliff tops, through bluebell woods and between steep sided rocky cuttings, and serves as a reminder of of a system that once served the whole island.

THE MANX ELECTRIC RAILWAY was one of the world's first when it first came into service in 1893. Today, the original electric tramcars still ply the 17 mile long route between Douglas and Ramsay. The tramcars grind their way through leafy glens and hollows, before emerging on top of precipitous cliffs, which provide spectacular views across the Irish Sea towards the Cumbrian coast.

THE SNAEFELL MOUNTAIN RAILWAY also dates from the 1890s and provides the only means of transport to the Island's highest summit. The views are truly spectacular and a trip to the summit is the ideal day out for the whole family.

Snaefell Mountain Tram No 4

Isle of Man Transport, Strathallan Crescent, Douglas.
Tel: 01624 663366 Fax: 01642 663637

internally in 1991. The comforts you would expect in a modern hotel are all here, bedrooms with en suite facilities, interior designed decor, satellite television and hospitality tray. Guests can enjoy a quiet drink in the Piano Bar with the gentle sound of music in the air. The conservatory, spanning the whole length of the front of the hotel, offers a sheltered place to sit whilst enjoying a panoramic view of the historic promenade and beyond to Douglas Bay.

The Empress Hotel, Central Promenade, Douglas Tel: 01624 661155

Also standing on Loch Promenade, overlooking Douglas Bay is the **SEABANK PRIVATE HOTEL**. Owned and run by Roger and Jenny Grossman, this is a charming small hotel that welcomes everyone, even the family pet! With 16 well furnished and delightfully decorated bedrooms, most are en suite and are all fitted with satellite television and hospitality trays, this is really a home from home. For honeymooners there is a special suite available, with panoramic views across the Bay, that will help to make your holiday memorable. A three course evening meal is available on request and there is a discount for children.

Seabank Private Hotel, 21 Loch Promenade, Douglas Tel: 01624 674815

Tucked up a little side street, close to the centre of Douglas you will discover an excellent place to eat called **SCOTTS BISTRO**. This is the oldest house in Douglas and first received mention as far back as 1750. Its age and character are immediately apparent, with stone flagged floors, oak beams and dark wooden furniture creating a cosy olde worlde atmosphere. there is a ground floor and cellar restaurant and two further rooms upstairs which are available for private functions.

In the summer months the small courtyard provides a lovely outdoor setting in which to enjoy your meal.

The bistro has a well deserved reputation for the quality and variety of its food and owner Donald Slee has created an extensive menu which caters to every palate, ranging from light bites for visitors who just fancy a snack, to a choice of full meals, all using the finest local produce, accompanied by a fine wine selection. This is definitely one of the Isle of Man's hidden gems.

Scott's Bistro, 7 John St, Douglas. Tel: 01624 623764

When you're in the heart of Douglas, look out for the **MANX CATTERY**. The Manx Cat, that has no tail, is probably the most famous export of the Isle of Man. One of the many delightful tales of how the cat lost its tail follows:

At the time that Noah built the Ark there were two Manx cats, both with tails. Noah sent for all the animals to come to the Ark two by two, but the Manx cats said "Oh, traa dy liooar" (which in Manx language means, time enough) and continued to play outside. Finally when they did decide to enter the Ark, Noah was just slamming the doors, and their tales were chopped off!

A variation on this story was that one cat reached the Ark safely but the other lost his tail when the door slammed shut. The tail-less one became the Manx cat, and the other became the infamous, grinning Cheshire Cat.

THE STAKIS HOTEL AND CASINO, on the Central Promenade in Douglas, overlooks the sandy beach and Douglas Bay. This prestigious hotel, part of the nationwide chain, has all you would expect in a top class establishment. All the 133 rooms are en suite, with bath and shower,

Eyreton Castle, Marown

and there are several lovely suites with panoramic views over the sea. The Renaissance Health club, open to all guests, has a fine indoor heated pool, spa pool and sauna and a great gym. If exercise is not quite your thing the club also has an expert beauty therapy salon and a fine hairdresser.

Casinos are great fun and all guests are invited to try their hand at the hotels casino. With roulette, blackjack, stud poker, Casino brag and slot machines this is not just for the big player, stakes range from 10p a slot so there is room for everyone.

With several restaurants to choose from and its central location the hotel makes an ideal base from which to explore this fascinating and historic island.

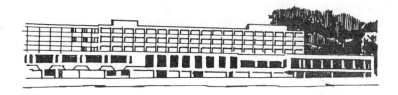

Stakis Hotel and Casino, Central Promenade, Douglas Tel: 01624 662662

The Rovers Return

Not far from Douglas town centre, on Church Street, in one of the oldest parts of the town, you will find the **ROVER'S RETURN**. a particularly cosy establishment with a very traditional feel, perhaps due to the fact that it is the oldest pub in Douglas. Visitors should look out for the firemen's memorabilia including two brass and copper hose nozzles on the hand pumps. Real ales are served here with good food and a friendly welcome.

The atmosphere is enhanced by the flagged floors and open fires. There is a courtyard beer garden to the rear. This pub, which incidentally is owned by Bushy's, the youngest brewery on the Isle of Man, is very popular with locals and visitors alike.

Rover's Return, 11 Church Street, Douglas, Isle of Man. Tel 01624 676459

One of the island's most famous landmarks is the **TOWER OF REFUGE** which lies on the east coast of the island in Douglas Bay. Sir William Hilary, founder of the R.N.L.I., lived in a mansion overlooking the bay and, following a near-disaster on 20th November 1830 when the Royal Mail Steam Packet "St. George" was driven onto rocks in high seas, Hilary launched the Douglas lifeboat. Miraculously, all 22 crewmembers of the "St. George" and the lifeboat crew were saved, despite the treacherous conditions. It was after this incident that Hilary decided some sort of refuge was needed on Conister Rock for any shipwrecked mariners to shelter in. Thus the Tower of Refuge was built, with Hilary laying the foundation stone, appropriately enough on St. George's Day 1832. Since then, for more than 150 years, it has been used, though fortunately not often for its intended purpose.

Situated on the main promenade in Douglas and overlooking the Bay and the Tower of Refuge is **ELLAN VANNIN** Private Hotel. Ellan Vannin is the Gaelic name for the Isle of Man and it is also the name of a passenger steamship that was sunk in Liverpool Bay by a freak wave in 1909. However be comforted, your hosts, Eddie and Margaret Collister, both Manx born and bred, offer a warm and friendly welcome and are justly proud of their reputation for being spotlessly clean. This small establishment also offers good old fashioned hospitality, excellent food and personal service in a homely atmosphere that makes it an ideal place for a relaxing holiday.

Ellan Vannin, 31 Loch Promenade, Douglas Tel: 01624 674824

Perched on a headland overlooking Douglas Bay is a Camera Obscura, known as the **GREAT UNION CAMERA**. The camera was originally situated on the old iron pier, but when this was demolished in the 1870s the camera was re-sited on Douglas Head.

In a Camera Obscura natural daylight is focussed onto a white panel through a simple system of a lens and angled mirror, providing a living representation of the scene outside. At first apparently still, you soon become aware that the pictures are moving. The detail is remarkable, and it is often a wafting blade of grass or passing seagull which shows that this is no ordinary slideshow.

Manx National Heritage has developed the **"STORY OF MAN"**. A dramatic and wide ranging portrayal of the unique history of the island. The journey of discovery begins at the **MANX MUSEUM** in Douglas, and a visit here is a must during your stay.

At the "Island's Treasure House" in Douglas you can see the highly acclaimed Story of Man film, which introduces visitors to ten thousand years of turbulent history. The exciting gallery presentations which precede the film include the superb National Art Gallery, and describe the Story from the time of the 'Great Deer' to the present day, including the famous T.T. races and the Manx finance sector.

This showcase of Manx heritage is an invitation to begin a journey of discovery that will take you the length and breadth of the island. The Manx Museum is open Monday to Saturday. Admission is free and there is also a tea room, library and Heritage Shop.

Around Douglas

Only two and a half miles north of Douglas is GROUNDLE GLEN. It is of a deep, and in places, rocky nature, with lively bubbling stream running through its length. Excellent specimens of beech grow in the upper section while lower done pines and larch are more abundant. A small water wheel is situated in the lower glen. An attraction in the Glen is the miniature railway run by enthusiasts, operating certain days only.

On the main road to Castletown, just three miles from Douglas, and set in 92 acres of fine grazing land is the **CHARITY HOME OF REST FOR OLD HORSES**. The Home came into being in 1950, when Mrs Mildred Royston and her sister, Miss Kermode, became dismayed at the number of perfectly fit, old working horses being shipped from the island to a doubtful future. From small beginnings, hard work, dedication and a lean income the Home progressed until 1955 when a fortunate legacy provided the means to purchase 'Bulrhenny' where the Home is now.

Since 1950, more that 270 animals have found happy retirement here and at present 46 horses and 8 donkeys are gently spending their days grazing in the fields. Of particular concern to the Home are the old tram horses and today it has a first option on all the animals as they are retired.

The Home is open Monday, Tuesday and Wednesday from the end of May to early September and all visitors are welcome. You can feed the

Groundle Glen

horses and donkeys from the Home's supply of pony nuts, wander around the courtyard to view the loose boxes and operating theatre, and there is also a souvenir shop, museum and café. The Home also runs an adopt a horse or donkey scheme that benefits everyone, particularly the animals. As a charity, many of the people working at the Home are volunteers.

Charity Home of Rest for Old Horses, Bulrhenny, Richmond Hill, Douglas
Tel: 01624 674594

Despite its relatively small size, the Isle of Man really is the ideal holiday island, with a range of superb amenities, activities and events to suit every age group and pocket. There are various events throughout the year, ranging from Viking long boat races and vintage transport weekends, to the world renowned TT Motor Cycle Races and less well known and very wet World Tin Bath Championship!

Sporting facilities here are excellent, with clear seas and indoor pools for swimming, gentle pony trekking rides, and for the golfing enthusiast several championship courses, with some clubs offering special competitions to visitors.

LAXEY, seven miles up the east coast from Douglas is set in a deep wooded glen. This is a village of interesting contrast. Tracing the river up from its mouth in a small tidal harbour and adjacent partially stoney beach, the route takes you past the woollen mill, tram terminus and on up to the Great Laxey Wheel marking the once thriving mining centre.

LAXEY GLEN is one of the Island's seventeen National Glens, maintained and preserved by the Forestry department of the Manx Government. There is no admission charge to any of the Glens, so be sure visit them, and enjoy the scenic beauty of the Manx countryside.

On the eastern coast of the island, set within the Agneash Valley between Douglas and Ramsey lies the village of Laxey. Here, standing proudly at the head of the Laxey Mines you will discover the famous **LADY ISABELLA WHEEL**, the largest water wheel of its kind in the world. The circumference is a staggering 228 feet, the diameter 72 feet and the top platform stands some 72 feet above the ground.

Lady Isabella Wheel, Laxey

It was Robert Casement, engineer to the mines, who constructed this mechanical wonder, designed to pump 250 gallons of water per minute from a depth of 200 fathoms. It was officially opened on 27th September 1854 and named Lady Isabella after the wife of the then Lieutenant Governor of the island.

Today, after considerable repairs and major reconstruction work, the Wheel functions exactly as it did over 100 years ago, creating a unique Victorian engineering feature and making this a centre for industrial archaeology. The viewing platform over the wheel is very popular with the more daring visitors, while others may enjoy the tranquility of the glen where the remains of one of the greatest lead mines can be seen. The wheel is open daily from Easter to the end of September and there is an admission charge.

The Laxey Wheel, Laxey, Isle of Man Tel: 01624 675522

Situated in a beautiful natural glen in the Manx hills, not far from Laxey, the **BALLALHEANAGH GARDENS** are given a star in the Best Gardens of Great Britain, which puts them among the top in the country . Any visitor who is interested in gardening or just in the beauty of nature will find these gardens a delight. Steep winding paths cling to the valley sides and crystal water cascades below carry the bells of pieris to the Irish Sea.

The valley is packed with rhododendrons, shrubs, bulbs and ferns as well as much more unusual species. The Ballalheannagh Gardens, created by the owners Clif and Maureen Dadd, are in effect gardens to visit with a nursery from which you can also buy. The Dadds maintain an extensive catalogue of unusual plants which can be seen growing in their natural habitat. The Gardens are in a very well hidden spot, but one which is worth seeking out.

Ballalheannagh Gardens, Glen Roy, Lonan Tel: 01624 781875

The island has a surprisingly varied and unspoilt landscape. From the northern lowlands with their seemingly endless sandy beaches to the delicate flora of the central moorlands, from mountainous and rugged fell country which rewards the stalwart walker with spectacular views, to the dramatic cliffs and coves of the southern seascape - a haven for a myriad of sea birds who make their nests here - the Isle of Man is a walker's paradise.

RAMSEY, the northernmost resort of the Isle of Man, is an attractive coastal town with a snug harbour which is highly regarded by visiting yachtsmen. Once ashore you will find a rich variety of bars, restaurants and fine shops in which to browse at your leisure. A short walk out of town will take you to the Mooragh Park and the Rural Life Museum, both of which are well worth a visit.

Just 1 mile north of Ramsey is the **GROVE RURAL LIFE MU-SEUM**. A pleasantly proportioned, time capsule Victorian house, the

Ballalheanagh Gardens

Grove Museum was developed as a summer retreat for Duncan Gibb, a Victorian shipping merchant from Liverpool and his family. The rooms, from drawing room to scullery, retain their period furnishings, augmented with displays of toys and costumes. The outbuildings house an interesting collection of vehicles and agricultural instruments appropriate to the larger Manx farms of the 19th century.

Take time to stroll through the beautifully maintained gardens, complete with ducks and Manx cats! The museum is open from Easter to the end of September and there is an admission charge.

Travelling inland from Ramsey, family members of all ages will enjoy a trip to **CURRAGH'S WILDLIFE PARK** which lies between SULBY and BALLAUGH. Officially opened in 1965, this magnificent park aims to educate, stimulate and entertain the thousands of visitors who come here each year. It also plays a crucial role in animal welfare and the conservation of endangered species.

Since it opened, the Park has succeeded in achieving its ultimate aim, that is, that all the animals are breeding. This is true of all species of mammals and most species of bird currently at the Park, including the only breeding colony of Scarlet Ibis in the British Isles. One of the major attractions has to be the magnificent walk through the aviary with birds of every colour and description. From the café you can enjoy the beautiful sight of the flamingo beach and main lake, where these beautiful pink birds offset perfectly the backdrop of the blue lake and green hills.

Another popular attraction is the 'Tantalising Ten', a group of ten Canadian and Small Clawed otters whose antics in their own private 'swimming pools' provide hours of amusement for visitors of all ages. Of course no visit here would be complete without witnessing feeding time, with penguins and pelicans being fed at 11.00am and 3.00pm and the sea-lions who put on quite an act for their audience, being fed at 11.30pm and 3.30pm.

Ginger Hall Hotel

In the heart of rural Isle of Man, just outside Sulby, lies the **GINGER HALL HOTEL**. The building dates back to the late 1800s and is ideally situated for easy access to good trout and salmon fishing in Sulby River and it also lies at the start of a ramblers walk to Laxey. Owned and run by Linda Thompson, this small hotel caters for the family, even the pet, in a relaxed and friendly atmosphere. With a recently refurbished restaurant, open fires in the bar and residents lounge, and swings and slides in the garden for the children this is a super place to make your holiday base.

Ginger Hall Hotel, Ballamamagh Road, Sulby Tel: 01624 897231

PEEL lies on the western side of the island. It is generally felt that Peel, renowned for its sometimes spectacular sunsets, typifies tthe unique character and atmosphere of the Isle of Man. Traditionally the centre of the Manx fishing industry, including the delicious oak smoked kippers and fresh shellfish, Peel has managed to avoid any large scale developments. Its narrow winding streets exude history and draw the visitor unfailingly down to the harbour, sandy beach and magnificent castle in local red sandstone.

PEEL CASTLE, one of the Isle of Man's principal historic monuments, occupies the important site of St. Patrick's Isle at Peel. The Castle's imposing Curtain Wall encircles the ruins of the many buildings, including St. Patrick's Church and the Round Tower from the 11th century, the 13th century Cathedral of St. German, and the later apartments of the Lords of Man.

In the 11th century the Castle became the ruling seat of the Norse Kingdom of Man and the Isles, first united by Godfred Crovan - the King Orry of Manx folklore.

Peel Castle

Recent archaeological excavation has discovered exciting new evidence relating to the long history of the site. One of the most dramatic finds was the Norse period grave of a lady of high social status buried in pagan splendour. The jewellery and effects buried with her can be seen on display with other excavation finds at the Manx Museum in Douglas, while a walk beneath the Castle's brooding walls will instil something of the strength and history of this great natural fortress.

The museum is open daily from Easter to the end of September and there is an admission charge.

There is a legend attached to the dungeons of Peel Castle, which are said to be haunted by The Black Dog, or to use its Manx name, Mauthe Dhoo. The people of Peel will tell you that on dark windy nights you can still hear howling across the harbour.

Peel Castle, Peel, Isle of Man Tel: 01624 675522

The current **MARINE HOTEL**, in the centre of Peel, is the third public house of this name in the town. Joseph 'The Diamond King' Mylchreest, who, as his name suggests, made his fortune prospecting for the stones in South Africa, constructed the present hotel in about 1890. Standing on the promenade, overlooking Peel Bay, this is an ideal place to stop for a quiet drink and watch the comings and goings of the local fishermen hard at work.

The Marine Hotel has been in the Faragher family since 1928 and Peter, along with his wife Sandra, are the current license holders. As well as offering a pleasant place to drink, the establishment also has a full menu available in its restaurant and, less formally, bar snacks throughout the day.

Marine Hotel, Shore Road, Peel Tel: 01624 842337

GLEN MAYE, south of Peel, has to be one of the most picturesque parts of the Isle of Man. A spectacular bridged gorge and waterfall dominate this glen, which is some 3 miles south of Peel. Comprising eleven and a half acres, its beautiful sheltered, fern-filled woodland includes some relics of the ancient forests that once covered Man. A feature of this glen is the "Mona Erin", another of the many water wheels which once provided power for the Manx lead mines.

PORT ERIN. If ever the words 'safe haven' applied they must surely belong to Port Erin's beach. Situated between magnificent headlands. The sand is soft and cleaned daily, there are rock pools to one side and a quay to the other. Sitting on the beach can be a day dreamers paradise, watching the world go by - maybe the RNLI lifeboat will indulge you in a practise launch whilst you are there. When the guilt born of inactivity overcomes you, a walk up to Bradda Glen and its licensed café bar with garden tables is recommended.

CREGNEASH, in the south of the island has a lot to offer the keen explorer. Perched right on the south western tip of the island, **CREGNEASH VILLAGE FOLK MUSEUM** offers a unique experience of Manx traditional life within a 19th century crofting village. Overlooking the small island and bird sanctuary known as the CALF OF MAN, Cregneash is isolated from the rest of the island and was one of the last strongholds of the traditional skills and customs which characterised the crofters' way of life.

Cregneash Village Folk Museum, Cregneash, Isle of Man
Tel: 01624 675522

By combining small scale farming with other occupations, a small community of Manx men and women have successfully prospered here since the middle of the 17th century and in the carefully preserved buildings at the southern end of the village you can see the conditions in which they lived and marvel at the tenacity of spirit which must have sustained them in their rugged lifestyle.

The centre-piece of the village is without doubt **HARRY KELLY'S COTTAGE**. Kelly was a renowned Cregneash crofter and fluent speaker who died in 1934. The cottage provided the starting point of the Museum when it opened to the public in 1938 and much of Harry's own furniture and other equipment is on display here.

There are various other buildings of interest, such as the Turner's Shed, The Smithy and The Karran Farm, all inviting exploration.

Cregneash is also one place on the island where you will see the unusual Manx Loaghtan four-horned sheep, a breed which, thanks to the development of two healthy flocks by Manx National Heritage, has been preserved for the foreseeable future.

The museum is open daily from Easter to the end of September and there is an admission charge.

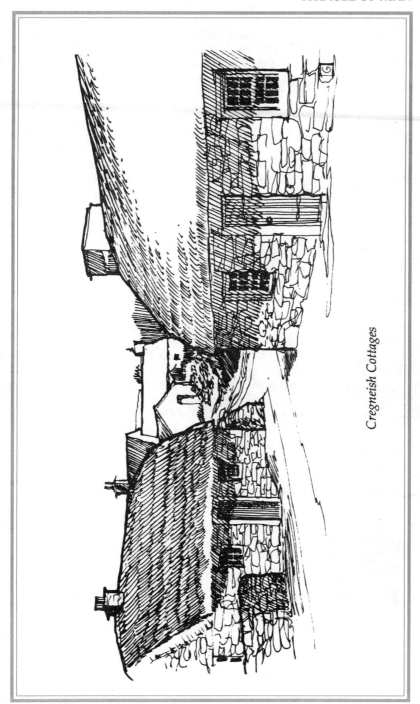

Cregneish Cottages

For those searching for the legend of King Arthur, the Isle of Man is a must. Many historians seek to establish the truth behind the legends and the island is believed, by some and in particular local historian Stephen Lewis Ingham Pettit, to be the most likely site of Avalon and probably also the castle stronghold of Korbenik.

After all that investigating, the **CALF SOUND CAFE** is the ideal place to stop and take refreshment. Built in 1899 and one mile from Cregnesh, the café is situated in an isolated spot overlooking the Calf of Man isle. Owned and run by Terry and Carol Jackson this has to be one of the most scenic locations in the country.

With delicious local crab a house speciality it is well worth taking the time to come out here. Years ago this was the site of a Bronze Age port and it was also Viking country. Kitter, a Viking Chieftain, raped and pillaged the Isle of Man over a long period of time until his longboat crashed upon the small island named Kitterlan, next to the Calf of Man, and he and his crew perished.

The Calf Sound has seen many ships come and go. The largest armada of Viking longships ever assembled in the British Isles congregated here before crossing the sea to invade Ireland. Men from Port St Mary were granted a medal for their gallantry by Napoleon, believed to be the only medal he presented to British subjects, when they came to the rescue of the crew of the St Charles Schooner from France which floundered on Thousla Rock in the Sound.

Today the Calf of Man is bird sanctuary owned by the National Trust but has in the past been owned by the Dukes of Athol, one of which requested that his tenants pickled puffins! In 1777, a stone was found on the isle in the garden of Jane's Cottage, though it was called the Mansion in those days. Called the Calf Crucifixion Cross, the stone is believed to date from the 8th century and is one of the earliest Christian finds in Europe. The Cross can be seen in the Manx Museum.

Calf Sound Café, Calf Sound Tel: 01624 834096

PORT ST MARY with its inner and outer harbour, two piers and with good anchorage for visiting yachts, is very much a small working port. The beach here, just along the scenic walkway from the harbour, is no more than two miles from Port Erin beach and yet faces in almost the opposite direction, so finding a sheltered bay in this part of the Island is easy.

For lovers of cliff walks and coastal scenery, one of the finest walks in the Isle of Man is the route from Port St. Mary to Port Erin along the **RAAD NY FOILLAN** (the road of the gull) - a long distance footpath around the perimeter of the island. The first part of the walk takes you to **THE CHASMS** - gigantic vertical rifts of varying width, descending in some places the whole height of the 400 feet high cliffs. Down below the Chasms is the **SUGAR LOAF ROCK**, a huge detached sea stack of horizontal slate. Sugar-loaf rock is teaming with bird life, so keen photographers should take a telephoto lens to get good pictures.

Castle Rushen, Castletown, Isle of Man Tel: 01624 675522

CASTLETOWN, to the east, is the original capital of the island, its harbour lying beneath the imposing battlements of the finely preserved **CASTLE RUSHEN**. Like Peel Castle, this too is said to be haunted, by a ghost known as The White Lady. Believed to be the ghost of Lady Jane Gray who travelled to the island from Scotland with her family over 100 years ago, she has been seen walking the battlements at night and occasionally walking through the closed Main Gate of the castle during the day.

The castle itself dates back to around 1153 when Norsemen began its construction. A series of fascinating displays bring the history and atmosphere of this great fortress vividly to life, presenting in authentic detail the sights, sounds and smells of a bygone era. Among its various points of interest is a unique one-fingered clock, which was presented by Queen Elizabeth I in 1597 and still keeps perfect time. Operated by a series of ropes and pulleys, it has to be wound daily, a task quite often undertaken by one of the castle's many visitors.

Another place worth visiting in Castletown is the **NAUTICAL MUSEUM** where a display centres on the late 18th century armed yacht 'Peggy' in her contemporary boathouse. Part of the original building is constructed as a cabin room of the Nelson period and the museum has various other displays of a nautical theme.

While you are driving around this corner of the Island, look out for the **FAIRY BRIDGE**. For centuries, people in the Isle of Man have taken no chances when it comes to the little people. Tales of the 'Bugganes' and the 'Mauthe Dhoo' live on in the minds of the Manx people, and the 'cross cern' fashioned from the branch of a Rowan tree still guards against evil spirits over each and every doorway. Few pagan customs seem to have such a hold as that of bidding Good Morning to the fairies that live under Ballalona Bridge, it is thought to bring you luck!

MOUNT MURRAY. Situated on on the A5 Douglas to Castletown road is **BUSHY'S BREWERY**, the newest brewery on The Isle of Man and a fascinating place to visit, for here visitors can observe the complete brewing process. the brewery even has its own hop garden so you really can see the initial raw fruit being made into beer. There is even provision for visitors to sample the finished product!

Next door to the brewery is a pub, called appropriately enough, **THE HOP GARDEN**. It is a traditional style of pub where visitors can enjoy good food with a good pint from Bushy's. There is a patio and beer garden offering splendid views of the island and makes a perfect place to while away a few hours.

Bushy's Brewery and The Hop Garden. Mount Murray, Braddan, I.O.M.
Tel: 01624 661244

The island's pace of life is so easy that you can't help but relax. For a short break or a longer stay, the Isle of Man is a unique and fascinating holiday destination.

CHAPTER SEVEN

West Lancashire and Merseyside

Speke Hall

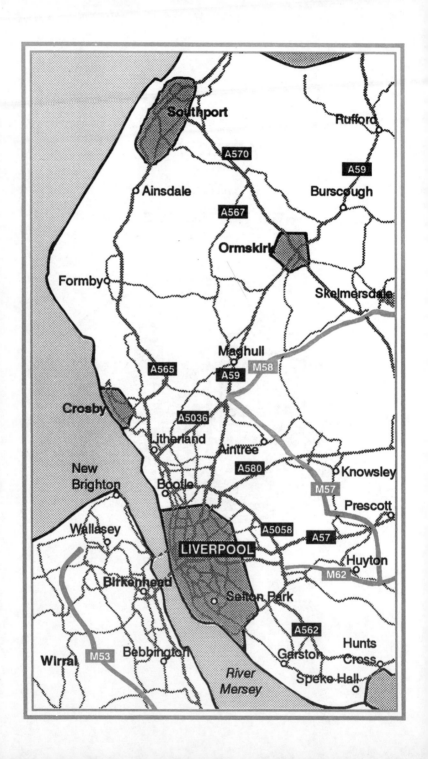

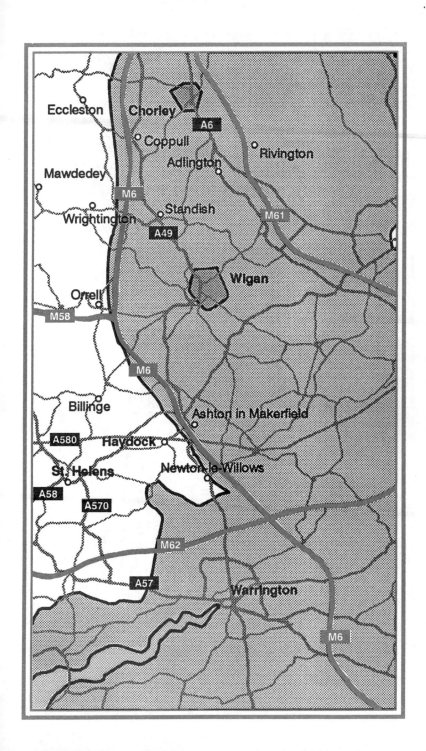

Astley Hall, Chorley

CHAPTER SEVEN

West Lancashire and Merseyside

CHORLEY, a bustling, friendly place, has always retained the friendly atmosphere of a market town, with its market dating back to 1498. Today there are two markets - the covered market and the open, 'Flat Iron' market.

History breathes through this intriguing name, which is derived from the ancient practice of trading by displaying goods on the ground without the use of stalls.

Momentous events in history have affected Chorley; the Civil War brought fighting close by with the Battle of Preston Moor and retreating Royalist troops were twice engaged in battle by Cromwell's soldiers. The outcome was not a happy one for the Royalist army, but it guaranteed Chorley a place in the history books.

Tangible evidence of Chorley's exciting and evocative past can be found in the wealth of architectural riches scattered throughout the borough.

Look for the **PARISH CHURCH OF ST LAURENCE** for example. It dates back to 1360 and the remains of St. Laurence are reputedly enshrined there.

Chorley also has strong associations with sugar, being the birth-place of Henry Tate in 1819. He was the founder of the world famous **TATE & LYLE** sugar refiners and benefactor of the art galleries across England that now bear his name, The Tate Galleries.

The jewel of Chorley is without doubt **ASTLEY HALL**. Built around 1580 and set within beautiful parkland, it is regarded as a fine Eliza-bethan mansion. Extended in 1666, and later in 1825, it is truly a house with a history. The rooms reflect the passage of centuries, containing fine furniture from 1600 to the Edwardian period.

The Hall was given to the Borough in 1922 by Reginald Tatton, and it was he who insisted that it should incorporate a memorial to those who died in World War I. So, there is a small room in Astley Hall which displays the names photographs, and Books of Remembrance and relatives still come to find the record and to remember.

The truly remarkable ceilings in the Great Hall and the drawing room, thought to be the best examples of their kind in England, display the skills of those who created masterpieces in plaster. Then, of course, there is the Cromwell mystery - and his boots. Did he stay here or not? The case can be argued both ways. Intriguing questions abound about Astley Hall. But one thing is certain. Many of those who visit often fall in love with its atmosphere.

So it comes across as a home, not as a static collection of things from the past. And that is exactly the effect the staff strive to achieve. Astley Hall, alive with bustle and people in 1580, lives on today and waits to welcome you.

Astley Hall, Astley Park, Chorley Tel: 01257 262166

Just a few minutes walk from Chorley town centre is the delightful **ASTLEY HOUSE PRIVATE HOTEL,** blending Victorian elegance with modern comforts and where the emphasis is on discreet friendly service and attention to detail.

The beautifully decorated hotel has six bedrooms which are centrally heated, have colour television and tea and coffee making facilities. Some rooms have en-suite bathrooms or shower rooms.

In the morning, a deliciously varied English breakfast is served in the elegant breakfast room. A very welcoming, friendly and family run hotel. ETB and A.A. registered.

Astley House, 3 Southport Road, Chorley, Lancashire. Tel: 01257 272315

COPPULL If you are looking for a home from home, in a charming rural setting, then **BRIDGE FARM GUEST HOUSE** is the place for you.

Situated just outside the village of Coppull, near Chorley, in the heart of Lancashire yet close to both the M6 and M61 motorways, Bridge Farm is a working dairy farm.

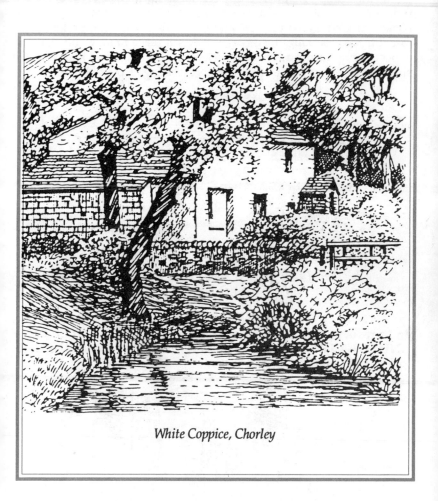

White Coppice, Chorley

Owned and run by Ralph and Joan Woodcock, the large modern farmhouse offers bed and breakfast accommodation in three well appointed bedrooms that are tastefully decorated and with tea and coffee making facilities.

The bright and spacious lounge, with views over the farmland and to the hills beyond, is an ideal room in which to relax after a hard day at work, travelling or sightseeing. The large farmhouse style breakfast room creates just the right mood in which to enjoy a superb English cooked breakfast or simply tea and toast, which ever you prefer. With safe, off road parking this is an wonderful place to stay and you can expect a very warm and friendly welcome from Ralph and Joan who are sure to make your stay as pleasant and relaxing as possible.

Bridge Farm Guest House, Coppull Moor Lane, Coppull, Chorley
Tel: 01257 792390

WHITTLE-LE-WOODS. Set amongst mature trees, lakes, streams and acres of well-manicured grassland lies **SHAW HILL HOTEL, GOLF AND COUNTRY CLUB,** a magnificent Georgian building and beautiful 'par 72' parkland golf course.

Shawhill Hotel, Golf and Country Club

This superbly appointed hotel offers a very high standard of comfort with its luxurious and stylish reception rooms and recently re-furbished bedrooms with en-suite facilities, colour television, direct dial telephone and chilled mini bar.

The Vardon a'la carte restaurant overlooks the course and is well respected for its very fine cuisine and extensive wine cellar; its glittering chandeliers and romantic candlelight creates a delightful dining experience. Your visit on a golf weekend guarantees one complimentary round per day, weather permitting, with others at a modest additional cost. A superb experience! ETB 4 Crown Highly Commended.

Shaw Hill Hotel, Golf & Country Club, Whittle-Le-Woods, Chorley, Lancashire.   Tel:01257 269221 Fax: 01257 261223

UPPER and LOWER WHEELTON are just outside of Chorley, on the other side of Junction 8 on the M61. Divided into two parts, this pleasantly laid out village is situated on the main Chorley-Blackburn road. Its tiny streets climb in slopes, giving an accurate impression of the surrounding hilly countryside. The locks on the Leeds Liverpool Canal are a fascinating reminder of the canal link that was once so vital.

WITHNELL FOLD VILLAGE, a little further towards Blackburn off the A674, was built to house the workforce of the nearby paper mill, by the Parke family. This idyllic little village of terraced cottages and tiny houses, stone-built mills and impressive village square is almost certainly one of the most attractive in the country. Withnell Fold was, in latterday times, a famous exporter of banknote paper to the world.

BRINDLE. In the pretty village of Brindle, on the B5256, you'll find **THE CAVENDISH ARMS** run by Peter and Alison. Set at right angles to each other, the church and the pub look pretty as a picture, as the saying goes. Their pasts are closely linked - indeed, there has been a pub on this site since the church was first built; behind this picturesque scene there are however, memories of bloody and historic events.

In 1530 the Gerrard Arms stood here. The present building, named after the Cavendish family who lived at Holker Hall, dates from the 17th century, and the history of the pub and the area are depicted in pictures hanging in the private function room upstairs.

The really distinguishing features here are stained-glass windows, which tell the story of the momentous Battle of Brunanburgh. It took place nearby in the year 937AD, and united England under one king for the first time. One of the scenes shows King Athelstan receiving a new sword to replace his broken one. In another, some surviving Vikings stop in their flight to bury a chest of treasure. This Cuerdale treasure was not re-discovered until 1840.

The framed account of the full story of the battle hangs in the bar. Here, there are many more features to admire - beams and brasses, open fires and low ceilings, and a 'duck or grouse' doorway to one of the rooms. The taproom contains a glass case displaying a stuffed hare. From the days before blood sports became controversial, the quaint inscription celebrates this valiant quarry, who eluded the hounds for 37 minutes on the 3rd. November 1875. Picturesque, historical, a garden for good weather - and good food, too! Trained as a chef, Peter offers attractively presented homemade bar food.

Cavendish Arms, Brindle, Nr. Chorley, Lancashire.   Tel: 01254 852912

RIVINGTON is a charming village, surrounded by moorland of outstanding natural beauty and interest. **RIVINGTON PIKE** is 1,191 feet above sea level and was originally the site of a signal beacon.

Lying on the western edge of the West Pennine Moors, south of Chorley and on the eastern side of the M61, is **LEVER PARK**. Situated on the lower slopes of Rivington Moor was made over as a gift to the general public in 1902, by William Hesketh Lever, later Lord Leverhulme and eventually Viscount Leverhulme. Lever Park comprises a awe-inspiring pot-pourri of ornamental, landscaped gardens, tree lined avenues, cruck framed barns, a Georgian Hall and a treasure trove of natural history exhibits extending to over 2,000 acres. Lever Park's moorland setting, elevated position and adoining reservoirs provide scenery on a grand scale which leaves a lasting impression.

Before returning to Chorley, the **LEAD MINES CLOUGH** on **ANGLEZARKE MOOR** shouldn't be missed.

CROSTON. A delightful, award-winning village to the west of Chorley across the M6 by the little River Yarrow, which is now a conservation area complete with some 17th century almshouses and a lovely 15th century church.

Strong links with agriculture and farming are still apparent in this area and the open farmlands actually extend right into the centre of the village.

This historic village in the heart of rural Lancashire, has been a centre for the local farmers since it was granted a weekly market charter in 1283. Overlooking the ancient village church, in the Conservation Area of the village, is **COCKFIGHT BARN.** This delightful and charming 250-year old brick built barn has recently been thoughtfully converted to provide excellent self-catering accommodation. The original beams and some more unusual and interesting features have been retained to maintain the character of the building and, from the first floor, there are wonderful views over the surrounding countryside.

Owned and run by Douglas and Diane McMillan, whose own home is adjacent to the barn, this is a wonderful place to make your base whilst visiting the area. On three floors the accommodation comprises three bedrooms, two bathrooms, a spacious living area with woodburning stove, a dining area and a fully equipped kitchen. Beautifully decorated and furnished throughout there is also a secluded garden and orchard for guests to use. The village's amenities are all within easy walking distance and access to the motorway network is only a few minutes drive away. This really is a home from home and the visitors book is living proof of the wonderful times that past guests have had here.

Cockfight Barn, Manor House Farm, Carr Lane, Croston, Preston .Tel: 01772 600222 & 01772 601222, Fax: 01772 601444

MUCH HOOLE. **THE ROSE AND CROWN** is an ideal stopping point for good food and refreshment on the A59 at Much Hoole.

The Rose and Crown, Much Hoole

Bill & Julie Sutton took on the business in 1988 when it was in a sorry state, since when they have transformed the Rose & Crown into a thriving and successful country inn and restaurant. There is plenty of character in this 18th century inn with its blazing open fire and exposed beams. The cosy dining area seats around eighty people who can enjoy a good selection of traditional home cooked food. The blackboard menus are varied and portions are well above normal. Good quality ales are kept and a visit to the Rose and Crown surely will not disappoint.

Rose and Crown, Liverpool Old Road, Much Hoole, Preston, Lancashire.
Tel: 01722 614084

RUFFORD, to the south, and just off the A59, is an attractive village of white walled houses notable for its church and its old and new halls. The church was built in 1869 and is a splendid example of the Gothic revival period with its modern coloured glass and tall spire that dominates the skyline.

The new village hall provides the venue for a host of community activities. There is also an annual May Fair held on the Village Green which celebrates a charter granted by Elizabeth I in 1573 and retains a charming medieval atmosphere.

Situated at the north end of the village, **RUFFORD OLD HALL** is without doubt one of the finest examples of 15th century architecture in Lancashire. Particularly noted for its magnificent Great Hall, this impressive black and white timbered building invites exploration. From the superb, intricately carved movable wooden screen to the solid oak chests and long refectory table, the atmosphere here is definitely one of wealth and position.

Rufford Old Hall

Within outbuildings, you will find the **PHILIP ASHCROFT MU-SEUM OF RURAL LIFE**, a National Trust property which houses a unique collection of items which illustrate fully village life in pre-industrial Lancashire. There is also a popular restaurant and a shop where you will find the perfect memento of your visit.

Rufford Old Hall, Rufford, Near Ormskirk Tel: 01704 821254

BISPHAM. The 16th Century **SPENCERS FARM BARN**, better known locally as 'owd barn', at the junction of Daub Lane and Rufford Road is unusual in having a pigeon loft in an upper floor at the north end of the building, accessible by stone steps. It seems likely that in the days when it was in use, the birds would be kept for their eggs and for the table rather than as a hobby. Below the loft is another floor which was used either for storage or as the sleeping quarters of occasional labourers at harvest time.

Today the barn is no longer used for agricultural purposes, it now houses the **OWD BARN CRAFT SHOP**, which is well worth a visit for there are so many delightful things to browse around. In addition, there is a large farm shop stocking the very best local produce, all grown on the adjacent farm.

Spencer's Farm Barn

Spencers Farm, Rufford Road, Bispham, Near Ormskirk. Tel: 01704 822659

MAWDESLEY is well worth a quick visit as it is a past winner of the 'Best Kept Village in Lancashire'. Again, this is a village devoted mainly to agricultural pursuits, but it was once associated with a thriving basket making industry, founded 150 years ago. **MAWDESLEY HALL**, thought to have been erected by William Mawdesley in 1625 is worthy of some architectural note, as is the school.

MAWDSLEY'S EATING HOUSE AND HOTEL, situated in this pretty village, was built in the 1830s as a shippon and stables with a carthouse and haystore. Converted into a restaurant and hotel in the early 1980s much of the building's original character and charm remains.

The Mawdsley family, who own and run the establishment, have been in this area for centuries; during the 12th century it is reputed that one of the Mawdsley family was made the Sheriff of Lancashire and lands in the surrounding area were given to him. To differentiate between his family name and that of the village they placed an extra 'e' in the village name.

Today, Mawdsley's Eating House and Hotel has much to offer. The restaurant is renowned for its inventive speciality dishes and convivial atmosphere; the hotel has 36 en suite bedrooms that have been designed to bring guests the very highest standards of comfort at realistic prices; there is a leisure club with an indoor heated swimming pool, spa bath and solarium in which guests can relax and, finally, the hotel takes pride in hosting conferences and other functions in its impressive Tudor Room.

Mawdsley's Eating House and Hotel, Hall Lane, Mawdesley, near Ormskirk, Lancashire Tel: 01704 822552/821874

WRIGHTINGTON. Although it is only three miles from the M6, **THE RIGBYE ARMS** at Wrightington nestles in the heart of rural Lancashire. Always a hostelry, the pub was built in the 1600s and named after Sir John Rigbye; it still retains all the character and distinct flavour of those by gone days.

The Rigbye Arms

The landlords, brothers David and Simon Jones, have, over the last few years, established a firm control at the helm of this fine inn. David, the chef, has brought to the Rigbye Arms all the experience gained while working at the Sharrow Bay Hotel in Ullswater and puts together an adventurous menu which is a joy to read and an even greater joy to try.

Simon, with experience in kitchen and hotel management, runs the pub in a quiet and efficient manner that ensures your visit will be exceedingly pleasant. There is a wealth of fine wines and traditional real ales to try; the Rigbye Arms is a member of CAMRA. A log-burning stove is a feature of the attractive lounge bar which is also warmed by open coal fires and includes a snug area where children are welcome. In the warmer weather, guests are encouraged to enjoy the bowling green, barbecue, garden and children's play area.

The Rigbye Arms, 2 Whittle Lane, Highmoor, Wrightington
Tel: 01257 462354

This area to the west of the M6 is full of surprises, yet unfortunately the nearest most people are to this part of the world is when they stop at Charnock Richard Services or are taking the family to the nearby Camelot Amusement Park.

THE HIGH MOOR INN AND BRASSERIE is one of the hidden treasures in the heart of rural Lancashire.

Situated on the outskirts of the village of Wrightington, close to the M6 motorway this really is a super place to find. Built in 1642 as a private house, this wonderful, renowned restaurant has been under the personal ownership of Jim Sines for the past thirteen years. The decorations and furnishings maintain the olde worlde feel and there are plenty of features including flagstone floors, a metal range and a lovely inglenook fireplace in the restaurant. Open seven days a week for lunch and dinner, it is advisable to book a table to avoid disappointment. The menu is mouth-watering and features many interesting and imaginative dishes. This certainly is one of the best places to eat in Lancashire.

The High Moor Inn and Brasserie, High Moor Lane, Wrightington, Near
Wigan Tel: 01257 252364

BURSCOUGH. If you are a keen birdwatcher and nature lover, then your next port of call should definitely be **MARTIN MERE**

WILDFOWL AND WETLAND CENTRE which lies north of Burscough. Set within 363 acres of marshland, this excellent nature reserve plays a vital role in the conservation of 120 different species of geese, ducks and swans, some of which are very rare and unusual, but tame enough to be fed from the hand. The excavation of a large lake and development of several ponds has created the ideal habitat for the 1600 resident birds. From the unique Norwegian log Visitor Centre with its turfed roof which blends in so well with the landscape, you can look out on the Swan Lake and Flamingo Pool from the viewing concourse or take time to browse through the Exhibition Hall and picture gallery. Outside, the acres of fine landscaped gardens are a joy to stroll around and a peaceful nature trail also links nine birdwatching hides, where you can see wild flower and plants, woodland birds, butterflies and other insects.

Added to all this is a café, shop and ample free parking and almost all of the Centre is accessible to wheelchairs and buggies, which makes Martin Mere an ideal place to spend a day out.

Travelling south along the A59 you will come to Burscough itself. A semi-urban area located between Ormskirk and Rufford. The village adorns the Leeds to Liverpool canal which passes through the parish. Burscough Parish Church was one of the Million, or Waterloo Churches, built as a thanks offering after the final defeat of Napolean in 1815. A later addition to the church was a memorial window to those who gave their lives in the First World War.

The crumbling ruins of **BURSCOUGH PRIORY** lie strewn along Abbey Lane, adjacent to the A59. Although scheduled as an ancient monument, only very small parts of some walls remain. It was founded for the Black Canons in the early 12th century and subsequently received such lavish endowments that it became one of the most important religious houses in Lancashire.

Also at Burscough, **THE MARTIN INN** is a traditional Lancashire Inn with super landlords. It is always a joy to come across a real family run hostelry with pleasant, friendly staff who aim to please their customers.

The Inn can found just four miles from Ormskirk and seven miles from Southport, and is easily reached from the M61, M58 and M6 along the B5242. This part of rural Lancashire is unspoilt and renowned for its hospitality and genuine friendliness to visitors.

John, Peter and Dianne who run The Martin Inn actually live on the premises, so guests are guaranteed that quality is maintained. The Mere bar is frequented by regulars who create an atmosphere of jovial hostpitality.

For lovers of real ales, the Inn provides a wide variety to choose from and has won numerous awards for their excellence. Accommodation is also available in the form of 12 comfortable en-suite bedrooms with extensive views of the surrounding countryside.

Anyone wishing to enjoy a quiet weekend in the country, with good food and good company at a price that won't break the bank, should not pass up the opportunity of visiting the Martin Inn. The surrounding area

Ormskirk Parish Church

has a wealth of leisure activities ranging from golf to water sports, and a little further afield is Liverpool's famous Albert Dock Village which is well worth a visit.

The Martin Inn, Martin Lane, Burscough Tel: 01704 892302

ORMSKIRK, a little further south, along the A59, is a pleasant market town which has some interesting 18th century and Victorian buildings - shops, inns and public buildings, as well as some attractive terraced houses of the same period.

There is an excellent shopping centre here, much of which is pedestrianised and on Thursdays and Saturdays is converted into an open air market. Dating back some 700 years, the market continues a tradition which owes its existence to the Burscough Priory Monks. It was during the reign of King Edward I (1272-1307) that a Charter was granted to the Monks to hold a weekly market which to this day is a browser's delight, with a wide range of stalls selling everything from fish, meat, and vegetables to clothing, china and bric-a-brac.

Keep an eye out for two houses on Greetby Hill, **BALACLAVA VILLA** and **INKERMAN LODGE** in rememberance of the Crimean War. Their gateposts are topped with real cannon balls!

ORMSKIRK PARISH CHURCH is an architectural gem and is almost unique among Parish Churches by having both a spire and a separate tower. Originally dating back to the 12th century there is evidence of Saxon, Celtic and Norman work. The building was used by the local nobility including the Stanleys, the Scarisbricks, the Earl of Derby and his step-son King Henry VII. All have left their mark on the chapel.

The new Church Walk Complex in the heart of the pedestrianised centre of Ormskirk is an ideal situation for **BRAMLEY'S COFFEE HOUSE**. Owned and personally run by Mark Gore with help from his super, friendly staff, this is the place to drop in and take refreshment in this old market town. The wooden floors and stylish decoration all add to the atmosphere and with the wonderful coffee aroma greeting you as you enter, who could resist at least one cup. Open all day Bramley's serves morning coffee, snacks and lunches and afternoon tea.

The daily specials make a mouth-watering list and there are plenty of homebaked cakes and pastries to satisfy those with a sweet tooth. Mark is planning to open the coffee house in the evening as a wine bar / bistro. We wish him every success!

Bramley's Coffee House, 6 Church Walk, Ormskirk Tel: 01695 518801

For some gentle relaxation in a peaceful setting, why not visit **BEACON COUNTRY PARK**, just outside Ormskirk. The Park boasts a superb Golf Course and driving range, walking trails, a pizzeria where you can indulge in the finest Sicilian pizzas, and a relaxing bar - all of which adds up to 360 acres of pure enjoyment.

SCARISBRICK, to the west of Southport along the A570, is made up of restaurants, shops and houses, all straddled along the main road. There are also some fine farm buildings dating back to the last century. Horse riding is a popular sport here, and the canal provides ample opportunity for fishing, boating and walking.

SCARISBRICK HALL is situated on the site of the ancestral home of the Scarisbrick family, which itself dated back to the time of King Stephen. The present building was completed in 1867 and is reputed to be the finest example of Gothic Revival Architecture in England. The turrets, gables and pinnacles are dwarfed by the slender, 100 foot tower, which bears a great resemblance to the clock tower of the Houses of Parliament. The last member of the family to live here was Sir Everard Scarisbrick who disposed of the Hall in 1945. It is now a boarding school.

SOUTHPORT, to the west, remains one of Lancashire's most popular resorts. If it doesn't have quite the bravura of Blackpool, it does have style, with **LORD STREET** and its arcades still being one of the region's most elegant shopping streets. Even though it is a seaside resort, you sometimes have to travel some distance across broad expanses of sand to reach the sea, and the pier is so long that a railway takes you out to the pier end, where at low tide the sea and the Mersey estuary can still be some way off. There is all that you would expect to find at a seaside resort: lots of sand (especially dunes), refreshments, funfairs, rides, walks, boating pools, toy trains and fine gardens, including superb herbaceous borders and dahlia beds in late summer. It is also worth travelling out from here to **HESKETH PARK** or to the delightful **BO-TANIC GARDENS** at **MEOLS HALL**.

Situated on Lord Street in Southport, is the delightful **ATKINSON ART GALLERY** with superb collections of British Art, English glass and Chinese porcelain. Admission is free.

On Derby Road you will find the **SOUTHPORT RAILWAY CENTRE** which has a large display of steam and diesel locomotives, housed in the old engine shed. Before leaving the area, the **BOTANIC GARDENS AND MUSEUM** in CHURCHTOWN are well worth a visit. The gardens are a delight at any time of year and contain an aviary, fernery, bowling greens and children's playground. The museum houses an interesting display of Victoriana. Admission is free.

Billinge Church, near Southport

FORMBY, further south along the coast, is of national importance for its nature conservation interest. Here too is BIRKDALE, famous for its golf course. Lying between the Mersey and Ribble estuaries, **FORMBY POINT** is an area of constant change where Man battles with the elements in an effort to prevent the merciless erosion of the coastline. The dunes protect the hinterland from flooding like a natural sea wall, but they also bring their own problems. Sand blown by storms has in the past threatened inland villages with engulfment and since around 1700, leaseholders in the area were required by law to plant marram grass to help stabilise the dunes. The woods were first planted at the beginning of this century for the same reason, and the intention was that an esplanade would be constructed along the coast if the sand could be held at bay.

The fact that Nature refuses to be so easily tamed has proved to be of great benefit to nature lovers who visit the area, as much of it is now a **NATIONAL NATURE RESERVE**. Almost 500 acres of Formby's dunes and woodlands were bought by the National Trust in 1967, and it now

The Bluecoat Chambers

Metropolitan Catherdral of Christ the King

provides a natural habitat for a wide range of animals and plants. Two animals in particular make Formby Point well known. The **Red Squirrel** colony descends from the variety introduced here from the Continent many years ago, and owes its success largely to being so well fed by visitors. The fact that so few trees grow on Formby's hinterland means that the colony is also well protected from its enemy, the grey squirrel, which is prevented access. The other animal which is eagerly looked for, but far more difficult to spot than the red squirrel due to its nocturnal habits, is the rare **Natterjack Toad**. Artificial freshwater pools have been dug to encourage this protected creature to breed. As you explore this fascinating area, please be careful to keep to the marked footpaths, as the erosion of the dunes is caused as much by the trampling of feet as by the natural forces of wind and waves.

St George's Hall, Liverpool

LIVERPOOL. The name alone immediately makes you think of Ferries across the Mersey, the Beatles, Red Rum, Shirley Valentine and two world famous football teams, but there is much more to this amazing city. Home to two outstanding Cathedrals, totally different in style and character they are reminders of the close links which the city has always had with Ireland, growing in importance while the much more established city of Chester declined as a port largely due to the silting up of the Dee estuary.

In the 19th century, the Port of Liverpool was the gateway to a new world with thousands of British and European emigrants making their way across the Atlantic to start a new life in America. Today the historic waterfront with its 1,000 Listed Buildings - including **ALBERT DOCK**, Britain's biggest and most popular heritage attraction - is as busy as ever, for this is a city which, like Manchester, is discovering itself as a major northern tourist centre.

The famous Mersey skyline is best viewed from a ferry with the magestic **ROYAL LIVER BUILDINGS** dominating the scene. Incidentally the clock faces are even bigger than those on Big Ben making them

The Albert Dock

the biggest in the country.

If you are exploring the centre of Liverpool look out for a magnificent building tucked away off Church Street on School Lane in the form of the **BLUECOAT CHAMBERS**. This is a superb example of Queen Anne architecture and was built originally as the Bluecoat School. The building occupies three sides of a cobbled courtyard and is today used for a variety of cultural purposes. To the rear is the **BLUECOAT GALLERY** and a delightful hidden garden which displays the work of many local artists and craftspeople and is a great place to pick up a gift or souvenir.

A short walk from here will take you to **MATTHEW STREET**, site of the rebuilt **CAVERN CLUB**, immortalised by the Beatles, and where there are some very good places to eat and drink.

If you have been to the Albert Dock then you will have already found plenty of places to eat and drink but in the city centre there are still more to choose from.

Prince among Pubs has to be the **PHILHARMONIC**, virtually opposite the concert hall of the same name on **HOPE STREET**, which is the road that runs between the two cathedrals. The splendid wrought iron gates are a clue to the opulence of the interior which is a riot of stained glass and wood panelling. Parties of tourists are frequently ushered in to see the brass and marble fittings in the Gentleman's toilets, so do be careful!

Liverpool's heyday as a port brought many cultures to the city along with their own types of cooking, and the city is very well served with ethnic restaurants. For Greek try **THE KEBAB HOUSE** around the corner from the Philharmonic, on Hardman Street, or further down the hill on the corner of Leece Street is the wonderful **ZORBAS**. We recommend the Greek banquet or Mezedes. Bookings on 0151 709 0190.

Opposite the restaurant at the top of Bold Street is an interesting church called **ST. LUKES**. The church was bombed during the war which destroyed all but the shell of the building which stands today as a memorial.

St Lukes Church

Past the church heading towards the Anglican cathedral there is a good Chinese restaurant on the corner of Duke Street. The **YUET BEN** has been here for many years and specialises in Peking style cooking.The ribs and duck are first class.

Many of the great merchant warehouses, banks and trading houses of this once mighty port survive along broad streets to give Liverpool a sense of grandeur which lives on. Behind the warehouses and newly pedestrianised areas run narrow streets and alleyways, some with old inns and restaurants which were once the haunt of mariners. Since the 1960s, these have been linked to the names of four young men who gave the city a new fame - the Beatles, whose music and 'Mersey Beat' in the Cavern Club became known worldwide. You can now take a daily **BEATLES TOUR** to visit the places that influenced their music, such as Penny Lane and Strawberry Fields - details are available from the Liverpool Information Centre on 0151 709 3631.

Liverpool is also a great cultural centre today. **THE ROYAL LIVERPOOL PHILHARMONIC ORCHESTRA** has an international reputation and is based in the **PHILHARMONIC HALL** in Hope Street. The **LIVERPOOL PLAYHOUSE** in Williamson Square is Britain's oldest repertory theatre, and the **EVERYMAN THEATRE** and **EMPIRE** also have an outstanding reputation. If you do decide to go to a show at the Everyman Theatre, the Bistro there is highly recommended.

The **WALKER ART GALLERY** has a splendid collection of Great Masters from early Flemish painters to the 20th century, including fine Rembrandts and Cézannes, while the **NORTHERN TATE GALLERY** at Albert Dock houses one of the most impressive collections of contemporary art outside London.

Albert Dock is also home to the **MERSEYSIDE MARITIME MUSEUM** where, among other fascinating exhibits, there is the reconstructed interior of a 19th century emigrants' ship which gives an impression of what it was like for so many people seeking a new life across the Atlantic.

Leaving the city, by keeping the Anglican Cathedral on your left, and heading out towards the airport you will soon be heading towards **SPEKE HALL.** If you are looking for a place to eat or stay outside the centre yet convenient for both the airport and the town centre you might consider stopping in the Sefton Park/Lark Lane area ,which is off the main A561 Aigburth Road.

SEFTON PARK was at one time *the* place to live in Liverpool, and all around the perimeter are houses which were once the homes of the mega rich merchants of the city. Most are, alas, now divided into flats and a couple now serve as hotels, such are their size. The park itself is still a wonderful facility for all to enjoy and is best explored on foot.

If you have worked up an appetite you should head for **LARK LANE** which runs off the park. This victorian suburb has a bohemian air about it and is home to a number of interesting pubs and eateries, the renaissance of this backwater being led many years ago by the local landmark of **KEITH'S WINE BAR.** Recently extended it still serves excellent food

Speke Hall

at reasonable prices and has a very good wine list.

Out of the park heading towards the airport there is a turning to the right down Jericho Lane which will take you to the waterfront and **OTTERSPOOL PARK**. Here there is a marvellous waterside promenade and park, which adjoins the site of the Garden festival which Liverpool hosted some years ago. Further along the main road again this t me on the left as you head out of town is a turning which has a discreet ign pointing you to th

GRANGE HOTEL, a good choice as a place to stay. Quiet and comfort able. Reservations on 0151 427 2950. Travelling along the A561 toward the southern end of the Mersey estuary, you will come to SPEKE, a name probably familiar because of its airport. However, it is also the home of **SPEKE HALL**, a beautiful half-timbered Elizabethan manor house whose grounds have a wealth of interesting features for the whole family to explore. When visiting the Hall you can discover the secrets behind the eavesdrop chamber, or find out what life was like below stairs in the servants' hall and kitchen. You may even bump into the tapestry ghost on your travels. The oldest parts of Speke Hall were built nearly 500 years ago by the Norris family. Over succeeding generations, the building developed around a cobbled courtyard which is dominated by two yew trees, known locally as Adam and Eve.

The Great Hall dates back to Tudor times, but has considerably altered over the years. The house as we see it today owes much to the refurbishments carried out in Victorian times, with many of the smaller panelled rooms containing fine furnishings from the arts and crafts movement, designed by William Morris. Outside, there are superb grounds and gardens. The moat which surrounded the house in the 17th century has now been drained and forms a feature of the grounds, which include a Victorian Rose Garden, a Croquet lawn, ancient woodland and the raised walk, which offers fine views across the Mersey.

To make a visit even more enjoyable, the National Trust has an on-site tea room, serving light lunches with home baking, teas and ices, and a shop where you can purchase books, stationery, souvenirs and gifts. For the disabled, much of the house, garden, woodland walk, and tea room is accessible; lavatories have been adapted to facilitate wheelchairs, and free use of a wheelchair is also available. Special events are arranged throughout the year and include music, drama and walks. Situated on the Northern bank of the Mersey, Speke Hall is just six miles east of Liverpool city centre and only thirty minutes from Chester.

Speke Hall, The Walk, Liverpool Tel: 0151 427 7231 Fax: 0151 427 9860

Outside of Liverpool, in the area to the east of the city, there are lots of interesting places to visit.

ST HELENS is home to the fascinating **PILKINGTON GLASS MUSEUM**, which traces the story of glass making. Whilst PRESCOT, has the equally interesting **PRESCOT MUSEUM OF CLOCK & WATCH-MAKING.**

KNOWSLEY,has something for all the family at **KNOWSLEY SAFARI PARK**. At one price per car, including all passengers, you can drive through the 450 acres of rolling countryside where many of the world's wildest animals roam free. You could see the largest herd of African elephants in Europe, lions, tigers, baboons, buffalo, rhion, zebra, camels and many more. In addition there is a pets corner for the children, sealion shows, reptile house, a miniature railway and an amusement park. The Park is open daily from March to October and visitors should arrive no later than 4pm.

Knowsley Safari Park

For those who want a day out that is that little bit more exciting, then why not have a day at the races. There are two racecourses here. AINTREE, home of the world's greatest steeplechase, the **GRAND NATIONAL**, hosts 2 race meetings each year - the National Festival in early April and the Bechers meeting in mid-November.

HAYDOCK PARK RACECOURSE offers 28 race days per year covering both the Flat and National Hunt calendars.

Leaving Merseyside behind us, the next chapter takes us across to the Wirral and on to the western half of Cheshire.

CHAPTER EIGHT

The Wirral
and West Cheshire

Church Farm, Bidston Village, Wirral

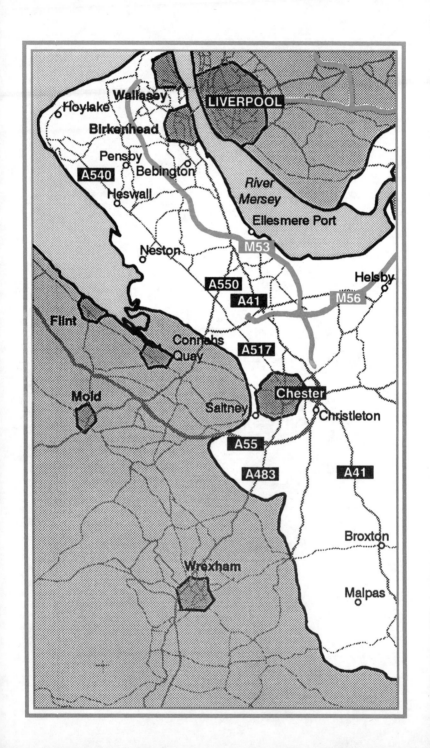

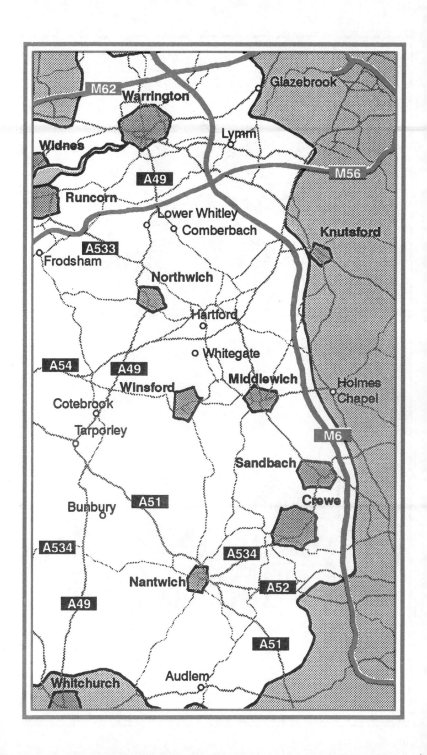

Bidston Windmill

The Bridge Inn, Port Sunlight

CHAPTER EIGHT

The Wirral and West Cheshire

For a real Merseyside experience, you have to take a Ferry 'Cross the Mersey. The services today continue in the tradition of Mersey river crossings that began in 1207. These powerful little vessels, strong enough to withstand the Mersey tides, have been refurbished in traditional style and provide a miniature cruise between the Pier Head at Liverpool, SEACOMBE and WOODSIDE in Birkenhead. The views from the ferry back down the estuary to the famous Liverpool waterfront, are truly memorable.

The Wirral is also readily accessible by road with a comprehensive motorway network giving access from Liverpool via one of the two road tunnels, or from Cheshire via the M53. Alternatively Merseyrail, the local rail network, serves the northern part of the Wirral extremely efficiently, with frequent services to Chester, Liverpool and towns across the peninsula.

The Wirral describes itself, with good reason, as the Leisure Peninsula. Though the once great industry of shipbuilding at Birkenhead has declined, much of the area has undergone a change, not only with the restoration and smartening up of ferry terminii, but with the creation of attractive walkways along the seafront.

BIRKENHEAD. If the elegant Hamilton Square no longer contains the smart town houses of sea captains, **BIRKENHEAD PRIORY**, the chapter house of a Benedictine monastery established in 1150 AD, now a church, has changed little and contains a Heritage Centre and Museum.

BIRKENHEAD PARK to the east of the town centre is a remarkable example of an early Victorian urban park, with lake, rockery, lawns, and formal gardens, which interestingly enough became the model for an even more famous park - Central Park in New York.

Near Birkenhead town centre on East Float Dock Road you will find a pair of historic warships, now museums. Both the frigate **HMS PLYMOUTH** and submarine **HMS ONYX** served during the Falklands conflict and are now preserved so you can discover for yourselves what life is like aboard a ship of the Royal Navy. Open from 10am daily you can get further details on 0151 650 1573.

BIDSTON has a hilltop observatory and windmill close by, and OXTON, a conservation area, is noted for its fine views.

THE WIRRAL WAY can be reached If you take the train from Liverpool Lime Street's Merseyrail Underground station to WEST KIRBY This is a 12 mile long walkway along the old West Kirby - Hooton railway line, leading into Wirral Country Park. The two adjoining towns of West Kirby and **HOYLAKE** take on a holiday air in the summer, and are popular with day trippers from Liverpool as well as locals enjoying a day at the seaside. Off the coast here is a bird sanctuary at **HILBRE ISLAND**, while the area has some outstanding links golf courses.

THURSTASTON is some three miles along the old railway line and just off the A540, there is a car park and an excellent **COUNTRYSIDE CENTRE** close by. Here you'll find a choice of walks and trails along the coast.

HESWALL. Further along the coast is a marvellous place for a detour off the A540 at Heswall. If you take the road down to the beach from the town centre there are outstanding views from an elevated position across the Dee estuary to the hills of Wales beyond.

The Dee is now heavily silted and the club house of the former Dee Sailing Club now serves as a restaurant. A walk down the beach will bring you to Parkgate where there are a couple of nice pubs .

PORT SUNLIGHT is a model garden village, founded in 1888 by William Hesketh Lever to house his soap factory workers. It was named after his most famous product, Sunlight Soap. The village is officially rated as a Conservation Area. In March of 1888, Mrs Lever cut the first sod of Port Sunlight, and thus helped to lay the foundations of a village which was to be appreciated by many generations to come.

It was the aim of her husband, who later became the first Viscount Leverhulme, to provide for his workers 'a new Arcadia, ventilated and drained on the most scientific principles'. He took great pleasure in helping to plan this most picturesque garden village, and he employed nearly 30 different architects to create its unique style.

Port Sunlight is now a conservation area, still within its original boundaries.

The Port Sunlight Heritage Centre

The history of this village and its community is explored in **PORT SUNLIGHT HERITAGE CENTRE**, where there is a scale model of the village and of a Victorian Port, Sunlight House, the original plans for the buildings, and displays of period advertising and soap packaging. The Village Trail shows you the Village's attractions, including the **LADY LEVER ART GALLERY**, which contains Lord Leverhulme's world famous collections of pre-Raphaelite paintings and Wedgwood.

Pre-booked guided tours of the Village are available from the Heritage Centre for parties and schools, and a Village Trail leaflet enables visitors to find their way around.

Port Sunlight Heritage Centre, 95 Greendale Road, Port Sunlight
Tel: 0151 644 6466

If you are looking for somewhere different to eat, then why not try the restaurant which is situated in the basement of the Lady Lever Art Gallery (pre-booking needed for large groups). It offers fine foods, a wonderful setting, and fascinating and beautiful treasures to appreciate.

EASTHAM, just off the busy A41 road from Birkenhead, is worth a detour to discover this little village which was mentioned in the Domesday book, and which has some very interesting buildings, including the local church which is reputed to have the oldest yew tree in England in its grounds.

There is a local pub, and a country park which is right on the river Mersey. Sometimes from the park, you are rewarded with wonderful views of the large tankers which glide upriver to the refinery at STANLOW

WILLASTON-IN-WIRRAL is another charming village which has a windmill, as well as a number of 17th century cottages and a village green.

ELLESMERE PORT. **THE BOAT MUSEUM** is a living museum with a unique collection of boats, exhibitions, engines and much more. Home to the world's largest collection of traditional canal boats, visitors can step aboard into some of the cabins and discover how canal people managed to live and raise families in a home no bigger than the hallway of a modern house. Situated in an historic dock complex where the Shropshire Union and Manchester Ship Canals meet, during the summer months visitors can enjoy leisurely boat trips and experience the flavour of a bygone age.

Ellesmere Port Boat Museum

GREAT SUTTON. Many people enjoy a day out at a garden centre which nowadays offer a lot more for the casual visitor.

On the main A41 Birkenhead to Chester road is one of the most popular attractions in the area **SYCAMORE PARK GARDEN CENTRE,** one of the family owned and run " Garden Centres of Cheshire "

A wide and varied selection of plants and shrubs are displayed in relaxed and friendly surroundings.

Of particular note is the excellent Aquatic Centre, which stocks a fascinating array of tropical and cold water fish together with all the equipment associated with keeping them.

Helpful expert staff are always on hand to help you make the right choice. Why not round your visit off with refreshments available from the centre's coffee shop.

Sycamore Park Garden Centre, 1024 Chester Road, Great Sutton, Sth Wirral
Tel : 0151 339 1289.

RUNCORN is one of Britain's best known post war new towns, built around a much older town bearing the same name. Here **NORTON PRIORY** is always a delightful and intriguing place for a family visit, whatever the weather. Despite being situated close to Junction 11 of the M56, it lies in a peaceful oasis just outside , with 16 acres of beautiful woodland gardens in which to wander and enjoy a picnic.

The Augustinian Priory was built as the prosperous abode for 12 canons in 1134. It was transformed into a Tudor and then a Georgian mansion before it was abandoned in 1921. Daily life for the canons was strictly disciplined and a typical day would consist of prayer, worship and work duties, with some time set aside for relaxation according to the rule of St Augustine.

The main activity would be worship, so the day was almost wholly taken up with attending the church services. The canons were known as 'Black Canons' because their outer garment was a cape of black woollen cloth, worn over a white linen surplice.

Life was not as spartan for them as one would imagine because they ate two meals a day in the refectory or dining room. We know they were allowed to eat meat because when excavations were carried out, many bones of animals were found. As well as a staple diet, beer was the drink that accompanied their meals.

Day-to-day life in 12th century Cheshire is reflected through the exhibitions which have been created in the prize winning **MUSEUM**.

Age old crafts and art forms such as tile making and sculpture are revived and celebrated in workshops and demonstrations which are held periodically throughout the year. Just a short walk away is Cheshire's best kept secret - the **WALLED GARDEN**, which received a special prize in the 1990 Britain in Bloom competition.

Norton Priory

DARESBURY, near Runcorn is a small village which is well worth a visit. Charles Lutwidge Dodson, more famously known as Lewis Carroll, was born here in 1932. Some of his best loved characters from *Alice in Wonderland* are commemorated in stained glass at the local church, All Saints.

HATTON. The impressive **HATTON ARMS** is situated in the picturesque village of Hatton, found between Stretton and Daresbury on the B5158 and close to the man A49 and A56 roads. Originally a series of cottages, the inn is everything a village pub should be and more. Inside, the inn consists of many small rooms, those of the former cottages, and all are beautifully decorated and furnished with plenty of style and character. As well as serving an excellent pint of ale and offering a warm and friendly welcome, the landlord and landlady, Peter and Sue Bradshaw, also run a wonderful restaurant from the Hatton Arms. Very popular and with a great reputation, the Hunters Restaurant serves a delicious menu of tasty and interesting dishes in a cosy and intimate setting. Finally, the Hatton Arms also has three superior letting rooms so that you can prolong your visit to this wonderful inn.

The Hatton Arms, Hatton Tel: 01925 730955

WIDNES is where you will find **CATALYST**, the Museum of the Chemical Industry. This fascinating museum is located close to the River Mersey and the Runcorn-Widnes Bridge, and explores various aspects of one of Cheshire's greatest industries, with an emphasis on 'hands-on' scientific exploration for the whole

The Hillcrest Hotel

For somewhere convenient to stay, **THE HILLCREST HOTEL**, has grown from its humble beginnings nearly 30 years ago as a five bedroomed house providing bed and breakfast for visitors, to being one of the North West's premier hotels providing excellence in every department.

Having recently undergone a total refurbishment, The Hillcrest has all the facilities required by today's busy executives. All of the 49 guest rooms are en suite and equipped for maximum comfort and yet, despite its size, this Four Crowns rated hotel still retains the very friendly, personal atmosphere of its early days.

From the nautically themed Nelson's Bar to the Palms Restaurant with its extensive and imaginative a la carte menu and interesting tropical island setting, everything about Hillcrest Hotel assures you of a relaxing and enjoyable stay.

The Hillcrest Hotel, Cronton Lane, Widnes Tel: 0151 424 1616

WARRINGTON, North East of Widnes, is North Cheshire's largest town and the main focus for industrial development in the region.

It lies both on an important bridging point of the River Mersey, midway between the huge conurbations and ports of Manchester and Liverpool, and on a nodal point of communications close to where the M6, M62 and M56 motorways intersect and where the electrified West Coast Main Line railway links London and Scotland. Not for nothing does Warrington, with its excellent communications, claim to enjoy Britain's most convenient location.

In past years Warrington was most famous for its heavy industry, including the manufacture of chemicals and the production of steel rope and wire for industry.

Today the town is also an important centre for brewing, soap manufacture and scientific research, but it still has several fine Georgian and Victorian buildings around the town centre and a pleasant central shopping centre around Horsemarket Street. **THE TOWN HALL** is a former country house built in 1750 for Lord Winmarleigh, before being acquired with its park by the Council in 1872. Some of the windows are framed in copper and the magnificent cast iron gates, which are 25 feet high and 54 feet broad, were given to the town in 1893.

Another good reason for visiting Warrington is its excellent **MU-SEUM AND ART GALLERY** in Bold Street, one of the earliest Municipal Museums in the country, dating from 1857, and a real Aladdin's Cave in the very best Victorian tradition. The museum collection dates from 1848 and contains everything from shrunken heads, a unique china teapot collection, a scold's bridle, Egyptian mummys, a rare Roman actor's mask and other Roman artefacts discovered in nearby Wilderspool.

There are some fine paintings as well, most of which are Victorian watercolours and oils, but also a rare Vanous still life.

THE ADELPHI VAULTS HOTEL, situated on Mersey Street in the centre of the town, is one of the oldest public houses in Warrington. dating back to the early 19th century as a licensed premises, it was formerly a blacksmith's with accommodation and stabling. Times have changed, but the hospitality you will find at the Adelphi is as good as ever. Pat and Derek McLellan, your hosts, came here in 1992 and they have over 50 years experience in the licensed trade between them. You could not be in better hands. Offering a warm welcome to all their guests, Pat and Derek have created a wonderful atmosphere where you can enjoy an excellent pint of real ale, delicious food, and interesting conversation. Add to this the four comfortable bedrooms and you have the perfect inn.

The Adelphi Vaults Hotel, Mersey St. Warrington.   Tel: 01925 635893

Around Warrington.

LATCHFORD. On Station Road in Latchford, just east of Warrington, you would be well advised to call in at **CANTILEVER GARDEN CENTRE**, one of four family-run businesses which form the group 'Garden Centres of Cheshire'. As with the other three members of the group, quality is the highest priority here and there is a large selection of plants and shrubs available all year round. Originally a station yard, this was the original Centre and has been here for over 25 years, enjoying a unique position overlooking the Manchester Ship Canal. The centre has a well deserved reputation for the service and high standards it offers its many customers and in addition to selling plants, offers a wide choice of garden furniture, equipment and accessories to cater to your every need. Having made your purchases, you can complete your visit by savouring the homemade snacks available in the Centre's well-run coffee shop.

Cantilever Garden Centre, Station Road, Latchford, Warrington
Tel: 01925 35799

WINWICK. The impressive **SWAN** is situated in the heart of the Cheshire village of Winwick, opposite its famous hospital, just a minute or two's drive from the M62 and M6.

Built at the very end of the 19th century to replace an earlier inn, this magnificent public house now offers the very best in food, ale and hospitality to visitors and locals alike. Lavishly decorated and furnished and full of character and charm, the Swan is very popular. Well known for its delicious food, which is available everyday from noon until 9.30pm, there is a varied and interesting menu supplemented by an ever-changing specials board. All well prepared and presented and very reasonably priced, there are traditional Sunday roasts and also a children's menu. For those who like their beer, there are always at least three real ales to choose from including Theakston's, Ruddles County and Webster's Yorkshire. A super place for all the family that is excellent in every department.

The Swan, Golborne Road, Winwick Tel: 01925 631416

CROFT. **COTTAGE GALLERY AND CRAFTS** is situated in the heart of the Cheshire village of Croft, next door to the Horseshoe Inn.

Housed within what was originally two 18th century cottages, the shop, owned and personally run by Anne Grice, is full of interesting and exciting arts and crafts. Anne is an accomplished artist herself and you will be able to admire some of her work here amongst the other stock. Everything in the gallery is individual, there is no mass production, and Anne certainly has a talent for finding unusual and beautiful items. Cottage Gallery and Crafts is a wonderful place to visit, where you will be sure to have an enjoyable and pleasurable time. Anne also offers a first class framing service and a comprehensive selection of prints and pictures. Open all day from 9 am to 5.30 pm except Mondays, Wednesdays and Sundays, (which are by appointment) so do drop in if you are in the area, you will not be disappointed.

Cottage Gallery and Crafts, 8 Lord Street, Croft Tel: 01925 764162

THE HORSESHOE INN, situated in the peaceful and picturesque Cheshire village of Croft, is a real gem of a place. Personally run by Elizabeth and Charles Monks for the past seven years, the inn offers the very best in warm hospitality, delicious food and excellent, well-kept ale. Though the Horseshoe's history is uncertain, it is known that there was a licensed premises here in the late 18th century and it is also thought to have been a blacksmith's where accommodation and stabling was available.

Renowned throughout the area for its cuisine, don't expect to be eating the usual pub grub at the Horseshoe Inn. The carefully selected menu would not be out of place in top class restaurant. Adventurous and exciting, you will be sure to revisit the Horseshoe time and time again.

The Horseshoe Inn, Smithy Lane, Croft, near Culcheth Tel: 01925 764464

GLAZEBROOK. Just yards off the main A57 at Glazebrook, you will discover a real gem at **MOUNT PLEASANT CRAFT CENTRE.** Housed within old converted barns, there is something here to appeal to all of the family.

A homely, friendly atmosphere is immediately apparent and this wonderful Centre houses an abundance of quality crafts, beginning on the ground floor in the craft shop with its rich variety of pottery, jewellery, walking sticks and much more besides.

The adjoining card boutique provides cards of every description to suit any occasion and between these two areas is the needlework stable which supplies everything that the needlework enthusiast could possibly need.

A passage leads from here to Conservatory Interiors which houses a stunning display of cane and wicker furniture. After all of this, it must be time for refreshment and the tea and coffee shop with its welcoming log fires caters for everything, from light snacks to full meals.

From here it's upstairs to an area offering embroidery classes and then through into the attractive dried flower display. As its name suggests, 'Something For Grandma to Buy' is a corner full of gifts for the grandchildren. Finally, take a look around the Fashion Loft before calling in at the Farmhouse Kitchen with its collection of quality pottery, china and kitchen utensils.

Mount Pleasant Farm Craft Centre, Glazebrook, near Warrington.
Tel: 0161 775 2004

For somewhere convenient to stay in the area, **THE RHINEWOOD INN AND HOTEL,** conveniently situated close to the motorway network, is a former Georgian rectory that has been tastefully renovated and extended into a traditional-style hotel.

There are 30 comfortable bedrooms, all with en-suite facilities, including two executive suites with lounges for business people or that special occasion. There are two restaurants; Bentleys Bar and Restaurant and The Copper Beech Restaurant where the choice of menus combine with an atmosphere of friendly hospitality and the wine lists suit all tastes.

The Rhinewood also has the Glazebrook Suite which can accommodate conferences, weddings and private functions. Whatever the event, you will find that we maintain a relaxed atmosphere that makes any stay enjoyable, be it for business or pleasure.

The Rhinewood Inn and Hotel, Glazebrook Lane, Glazebrook, Near Warrington Tel: 0161 775 5555.

Just south of Glazebrook lies **RISLEY MOSS NATURE PARK**, over 200 acres of scattered woodland, mossland, ponds and pools. Make time to call in at the visitor centre and climb the Observation Tower with its magnificent views of the Peak District fells nearly 30 miles away. Close by is Birchwood Forest Park, which lies about half a mile from the Birchwood/Warrington intersection of the M62.

LOWER WHITELEY. For visitors to the area looking for a place to stay, just two and a half miles south of junction 10 off the M56, **TALL TREES LODGE** makes an ideal base from which to explore the surrounding Cheshire countryside. Opened in October 1992 by owners Denise and Paul Garnett, the modern exterior of this hotel belies the warm, friendly atmosphere within which makes this far and above the run of the mill lodge. The twenty en suite guest rooms are attractively furnished and equipped to a high standard for maximum comfort and the newly opened bar provides the perfect setting in which to relax with a quiet drink and light snack. With the Little Chef situated next door, you have ready access to full meals throughout the day and travelling out a little way, you will find yourself within easy reach of many charming country pubs serving excellent food to suit all tastes.

Tall Trees Lodge, Tarporley Road, Lower Whitley, Near Warrington
Tel: 01928 790824

RIXTON. **HOLLY BANK CARAVAN PARK**, situated 2 miles east of Junction 21 (M6) on the A57 at Rixton, in open countryside between Warrington and Manchester, makes a super base for those who prefer the freedom of a camping holiday.

There has been a park on this site since 1978 and the current owner Jim Walsh took over in 1987, having returned to Britain after living in Australia for 20 years.

Probably one of the best caravan parks in Cheshire, Holly Bank carries a well-deserved Four Ticks rating under the ETB quality grading scheme. It is set in nine acres of lovely grounds and can accommodate up to 75 tourers and 10-15 tents.

Facilities include a well-stocked shop, hot showers, toilet block, 55 electric hook-ups, a games room, launderette, adventure play area and public telephone. The site is open all year round.

Holly Bank Caravan Park, Warburton Bridge Road, Rixton
Tel: 0161 775 2842

LYMM is a delightful village close to Warrington, bounded by the M6 and M56 motorways and also on the Bridgewater Canal, with half-timbered houses, a market cross and village stocks.

The Cross Antiques

At the top of the High Street opposite the Golden Fleece Pub is **THE CROSS ANTIQUES.** This small, traditional, old fashioned shop is a browser's delight. It is packed full of antiques and curios; a treasure trove that is well worth a visit. As well as general antiques, Bob Entwistle, the enthusiastic proprietor, has a host of stripped pine traditional furniture, a collection of old French stoves and a wealth of metal jugs, buckets and containers all painted in the vibrant colours and designs associated with canal barges. Stepping inside you can easily be forgiven for thinking you have stepped back in time. Open every day except Monday and Wednesday, this is an ideal place to come looking for that special gift for somebody who deserves something unusual, different and special. From old brass kitchen ware to pottery birds and waterfowl, from Royal

Dux figures to fine china display plates there is something for everyone.

The Cross Antiques, 28 The Cross, Lymm Tel: 01925 753585

For lovers of fine food, **THE LYMM BISTRO** in Bridgewater Street can be found in an attractive 200-year old building and has been run for the past eight years by Jo Shenton and Michael Venning.

The Lymm Bistro

Since opening the Bistro, Jo and Michael have earned themselves an excellent reputation for providing first class food and wines. Michael is the chef, and he has obviously gone to great lengths to ensure that his diners receive only the very best and freshest of produce. Meals are cooked to order and served in the cosy, friendly atmosphere which the Bistro exudes.

Michael's speciality is fish, and this can be anything from a simple but exquisite whole Dover Sole, to really exotic and exciting dishes. For example, it is not unknown for Michael to offer amongst his daily specials such unusual dishes as giant Australian Snow Crab, Fresh Lobster, or Parrot Fish.

As one can imagine, offering dishes such as these makes the Lymm Bistro very popular, and it is not surprising that diners travel from far and wide to sample such excellent cuisine. Jo and Michael are on hand every evening to look after the personal requirements of their diners; the Bistro also caters for special tastes including vegetarian meals and private parties. In order to do justice to the menu which Michael has so thoughtfully put together, we feel we must enlarge upon the dishes which are offered.

Blackboard specials are always popular, and a selection of starters may consist of Avocado filled with Smoked Salmon and topped with a tomato vinaigrette, fresh Squid cooked with tomato and red wine, or perhaps plump Frogs Legs sautéed with onions and garlic and flamed in Brandy.

The main courses are just as mouthwatering. We particularly liked the sound of fresh Marlin Fish, sautéed with various Shellfish, served in a cream sauce. We were just as impressed with the Wild Boar - a roast saddle of Wild Boar served in a sauce made from its own juices, Juniper Berries and Port.

By now we are quite sure that we will have whetted your appetite, and can only conclude by suggesting that prior to visiting, you telephone and reserve your table. As you can imagine, the Lymm Bistro does become extremely busy and with a Table d'hôte menu available during the week as well, represents superb value for money.

Lymm Bistro, 16 Bridgewater Street, Lymm Tel: 01925 754852.

Standing beside the Bridgewater Canal in the heart of the village is the wonderful **BULLS HEAD INN.** In earlier days the inn stood level with the road but towards the end of the 18th century Lymm Bridge was completed leaving the inn below road level on its approach. With over twenty years experience in the trade, mostly in Cheshire, Denis and Kath took over the Bulls Head five years ago and have kept it the way it has always been, the old village inn.

It has a charm that has largely disappeared from many inns these days. An ideal place to meet the regular locals and join in with the chat. A warm welcome, Good ale and bar snacks at lunchtimes.

The Bulls Head Inn, 32 The Cross, Lymm, Cheshire.   Tel: 01925 752831

Lymm developed as an important centre for the fustian cloth trade in the 19th century. Lymm Dam is a large man-made lake in a lovely woodland centre which is linked to surrounding countryside and to the canal towpath by a network of footpaths and bridleways. The Dam is popular for angling and birdwatching.

THE CROWN INN, is situated on the main A56 in Lymm. Dating back to the mid 19th century, The Crown has obviously undergone major renovation and refurbishment over the years but still retains the charm and character of an old coaching inn.

Now owned by Whitbread breweries and one of the Brewer's Fayre chain, you can be sure of a warm welcome. Well known for its outstanding food and excellent range of well kept beers, The Crown is sure to be popular with all the family. There is an excellent menu containing a wide variety of dishes that will suit everyone; tasty and well presented they are all reasonable priced. With plenty of comfortable chairs and tables, a small patio area and a beer garden this is a real family pub.

The Crown, Lymm Tel: 01925 752485

Situated on Burford Lane at Lymm is **WILLOW POOL GARDEN CENTRE AND NURSERY.** The five acre site has been a garden centre and nursery for the past 50 years and offers a full range of plants including majestic magnolias, ivy, evergreens, spring flowers and bedding plants. In addition, many species are brought in from Holland, Wales and Scotland.

Willow Pool Garden Centre and Nursery

Willow Pool also specialises in antiques and antique garden furniture; they boast a success rate of over 90% in being able to find that special item whether it is a wrought iron pergola or an ornate table and chairs. This might have something to do with the owner's 25 years' experience in the antique business.

The Nursery and Garden Centre takes its name from the willow pool which is in a lovely large wooded area. Here visitors can spend a few moments in reflective mood before sampling the delights of the Tea Shop which can tempt even the most fastidious of tastes.

Willow Pool Garden Centre and Nursery, 25 Burford Lane, Lymm
Tel: 01925 757827

The canal is obviously a focal point for visitors and locals alike and the area is particularly well served by navigable waterways. A perfect way to spend a summers day is at one of the pubs which stand overlooking the canal.

The Bridgewater Canal

THE ADMIRAL BENBOW, just five minutes drive from Lymm and next to the Bridgewater Canal, has a picturesque and scenic position overlooking some beautiful Cheshire countryside. Built in 1994, the inn stands on the former premises of The Wharfage Boat Company which was owned by Norma and Ben Faulkner, who now run the pub.

The Admiral Benbow

Experienced in business, the couple have created a wonderful inn, full of character and charm, and in doing so have retained many old fashioned values of hospitality and service. The interior of the pub has been attractively designed with exposed brick walls and an eye-catching wooden bar area. There is a varied menu both at lunchtime and in the evening with delicious, reasonably priced dishes.

Moored adjacent to the Admiral Benbow is **THE CHESHIRE LADY** narrowboat, owned by the Faulkner family, which parties can hire for trips or to take a meal on or both. So whether, individually, as a party or even as a company, everyone can come and enjoy the Admiral Benbow and The Cheshire Lady.

The Admiral Benbow, Agden Wharf, Warrington Lane, Lymm
Tel: 01925 754900

Travelling out of Lymm on the B5160 Lymm road towards Altrincham, you will discover **DUNHAM MASSEY HALL**, one of Cheshire's most outstanding National Trust properties. It was built in 1732 for George Booth, the 2nd Earl of Warrington, who commissioned the little known architect, John Norris who perceived the idea of encasing an earlier Tudor building. The 2nd Earl was also responsible for laying out the park, and purchasing the collection of furnishings and Huguenot silver.

The house and estate subsequently became the principal home to the 9th Earl of Stamford in 1905. It was he who commissioned another architect by the name of Compton Hall to undertake the alterations to the south front of the house, which we see today.

The interior of the house and its refurbishment owes much to the sensitivity of Percy Macquoid, who handled the redecoration of the state rooms. He is acknowledged as being one of the finest and most distinguished furniture historians. The house was bequeathed to the National Trust in 1976 by Roger the 10th Earl of Stamford. Many of the paintings, prints and photographs are of the prominent Booth and Grey families, who through their association with Dunham Massey have left their mark for future generations to appreciate.

As visitors wander through the house, they can catch a glimpse of personal possessions such as documents and books which formerly belonged to members of the Booth and Grey families. One cannot fail to be impressed by the craftsmanship, richness and elegance of such a magnificent house with such fine furnishings.

In sympathy with the house, the garden is being restored by the Trust, and broadly speaking is in the character of the late-Victorian Pleasure Ground. The Trust has managed to retain modified parts of the Edwardian scheme such as the parterre, and the notable remnants of earlier schemes.

Organised events such as midsummer music evenings are staged throughout the year. Visitors are encouraged to visit the licensed restaurant for refreshments and the National Trust shop for souvenirs.

Dunham Massey Hall, Altrincham, Cheshire Tel: 0161 941 1025

Dunham Massey Hall

High Legh Garden Centre

Time for refreshment and what a change to see an Old English Pub renovated, extended and updated in a style which enhances its age and character without loss of the traditional atmosphere. **THE NAGS HEAD** is just such a pub which forms part of Whitbread's 'Brewers Fayre' chain. It is in a partially hidden position situated in Little Bollington on the A556 a quarter of a mile from junction 7 of the M56. The interior is eye-catching with its open fires and interior windows and wall which once formed part of the exterior. The separate rooms are, to an extent, reminiscent of old-fashioned front rooms. Food is served all day and every day with Roast Lunch available on Sundays.

The Menu offers plenty of selection including Vegetarian and children's dishes. Excellent ales with plenty of variety and very reasonable wine list. Children are well catered for and there are baby changing facilities. Well worth a diversion.

The Nags Head, Chester Road, Little Bollington, Cheshire.
Tel: 01565 830486

GRAPPENHALL, just west of Lymm is a village of Cheshire thatched cottages, with its church standing by the banks of the Bridgewater Canal.

If you look carefully above the west window of the church tower, you'll find the carved figure of a cat with a grin. This is thought to have been the original Cheshire Cat which featured in Lewis Carroll's 'Alice in Wonderland', and which has become a symbol of the County of Cheshire.

THE RAM'S HEAD, situated in the village of Grappenhall, is well known in the area and is probably one of the best inns in Cheshire. The pub is run by Austin Woolvine, a retired professional Rugby League player, and his lovely wife Judy. The couple have really worked hard to gain and maintain the Ram's Head's excellent reputation. A real picture to look at, with a host of hanging baskets and window boxes adding a splash of colour in the summer, inside you will find open fireplaces and lots of interesting memorabilia displayed around the walls. Cosy, warm and welcoming, Austin looks after the bar whilst Judy provides the most delicious and tasty meals. With several first class en-suite letting rooms available all year round, this is a truly wonderful pub.

The Ram's Head, Church Lane, Grappenhall Tel: 01925 262814

HIGH LEGH, East of Grappenhall on the A50, is definitely the place to visit if you are a keen gardener. **HIGH LEGH GARDEN CENTRE** was opened in 1987 and is truly a garden centre of excellence. With its huge range of plants, shrubs, tools and accessories, it is a mecca for any gardening enthusiast. A large car park gives immediate access to the many trees and shrubs on display. Huge polytunnels have been erected to ensure that all plant material goes on sale, and remains, in tip top condition.

High Legh Garden Centre

The primary aim of High Legh Garden Centre is that quality and service remain at all times a top priority. A wide selection of top quality outdoor plants are on view, and undercover areas protect the more vulnerable species. There is a large range of speciality house plants which include Bonsai, Cacti and Airplants, as well as an Aquatics Centre with numerous aquaria, fish, plants and other accessories. The fish tank, a recent addition, is fascinating to watch, stocked full with colourful and dazzling fish of all shapes and sizes.

One of the highlights of the Centre is the well-established gift shop which prides itself on the constantly changing selection of gifts. Many new and original items are to be found here and ideas range from china, glassware, ornaments and prints, to toiletries, men's gifts, confectionery, stationery, toys, books, pet supplies, fireworks and all items relating to the Christmas season. The Centre also supplies a top range of green-houses, conservatories and garden furniture. Their range of French furniture was recently awarded the 'Best Display' in the North West. There are also many demonstrations and events held during the year, but particularly around Christmas time, when the children's Grotto is always original and popular. Also on site is a bird of prey and wildlife sanctuary where you will see at close quarters owls, kestrels and falcons. Children are well catered for and there is a very safe and well-equipped play area set aside for them. To complete your visit enjoy a relaxing break in our fern-filled cafe which provides a full range of home-cooked meals and snacks.

High Legh Garden Centre, High Legh, near Knutsford Tel: 01925 756991

APPLETON THORN, to the west, is a charming village where every year the locals celebrate 'Bauming' the thorn. This unique custom owes its origin to a Norman knight, Adam de Dutton, who according to tradition returned in the 12th century from the Crusades with a cutting from the Glasonbury Thorn to plant at Appleton as a thanksgiving for his safe return. The present tree outside the church was planted in 1967 and is meant to be a direct descendant of the original.

The ceremony takes place on the third Saturday in June, when young children decorate the tree and sing the 'Bauming song', written by the 19th century Cheshire Poet, R.E Egerton-Warburton.

About three miles south east of Appleton Thorn, the former estate village of the Egerton-Warburton family, lies **ARLEY HALL.** The Hall and gardens have been in the Egerton-Warburton family for over 500 years and it is one of the few estates surviving in Cheshire as a family home with resident owners, now Lord and Lady Ashbrook. An agricultural estate deep in the North Cheshire countryside, Arley is only five miles from the M6 and M56.

The Hall, which is set in 12 acres of award winning gardens, contains excellent examples of panelling, plasterwork, furniture and family portraits.

Marriage connections tie the Ashbrook family with other great estates of Cheshire, Oulton, Tatton, Lyme and Norton Priory to name just four. Rowland Egerton-Warburton was renowned as a poet and visitors to nearby Great Budworth are able to read his works. His grandson, Piers Egerton-Warburton was a talented watercolourist and several of his charming paintings are displayed at the Hall. The Dowager Lady Ashbrook, an octogenarian, also exhibits her paintings on plant studies.

Also on the estate is the family Chapel, gift shop, garden nursery owned by Lord Ashbrook's sister selling specialist herbaceous plants, and a tea room serving delicious home-made selections in the former Tudor Barn.

The gardens, which have won several awards, offer great variety and interest and can be explored with the use of a guide book written by The Dowager Lady Ashbrook. The guide describes the historical background of the gardens and is a personal account as she has known the gardens intimately all her life. Carrying on family traditions, the present owners have reinstated the Grove, an area of ever-changing colour, beyond the Chapel and have planted hundreds of rhododendrons and azaleas to gladden the eye.

The Hall is now host to corporate events, functions, weddings, garden festivals and concerts but the owners welcome all visitors and are keen to meet specialist horticultural groups.

The entrance to the Hall is quite splendid and is like walking into a bygone age as you pass over the cobbled courtyard and under the famous clock tower by the 15th century cruck barn. With a variety of rooms available, all exceedingly well decorated and of differing size, there is somewhere for receptions of over 200 guests and for small seminars of under ten. Most importantly, Arley Hall staff provide friendly, professional support and advice in all the stages of preparation and execution of your event, including the catering, to ensure that it is a great success.

The Hall and gardens offer a delightful day out and during the summer months special events are held on the estate.

Arley Hall and Gardens, Near Northwich Tel: 01565 777353

GREAT BUDWORTH is not far from here and is notable for its charming red brick and timber framed cottages with twisted chimneys, all clustered round a green hill and the handsome parish church of St Mary and All Saints.

Great Budworth was once the largest ecclesiastical parish in Cheshire, encompassing 35 individual townships, most of which are now independent.

COMBERBACH. Dating back to the early 19th century, THE DRUM

AND MONKEY stands in the heart of the picturesque village of Comberbach. Previously named The Avenue, it was renamed in recognition of an old 'Organ Grinder' who entertained locals and visitors at weekends for many years. It is a traditional village pub with excellent well kept ales and renowned in the area for delicious home cooked food at lunchtimes. The inn is cosy and snug and the atmosphere is very conducive to taking up friendly chat with the 'regulars', in addition a quiz is held every Monday night and a live rock group plays on Wednesday evenings. Hosts Yvonne and John took over the Drum and Monkey six months ago and have rapidly made it a success.

The Drum & Monkey, The Avenue, Comberbach, Nr. Northwich, Cheshire.
Tel: 01606 891417

THE SPINNER AND BERGAMOT also stands in the heart of this lovely village. In case you were wondering about the unusual name, both Spinner and Bergamot were race horses owned by the Honourable James Smith Barry of Marbury Hall. Spinner was a grey filly who ran in the early 1760s and Bergamot, a bay colt, who won for his owner in the 1790s. This inn has, for many years, been one of the most popular in Cheshire.

The Spinner and Bergamot Inn

Nigel and Carol Ross moved here 12 months ago and has continued its success. Inside the Spinner and Bergamot is full of character, style and charm with a wonderful, friendly atmosphere and is renowned for both its delicious food and well kept ales. Except for Sunday evenings in winter, food is available at lunchtime and during the evening with a tantalising choice to be made from either the menu or the daily specials board. The Greenalls ale is often joined by guest beers. There is a lovely garden area for families. It is advisable to book a table for meals at the weekend.

The Spinner and Bergamot Inn, Warrington Road, Comberbach, Northwich
Tel: 01606 891307

MARBURY PARK. Situated between Anderton and Comberbach, next to Marbury Park and Budworth Mere, is **MARBURY HALL NURSERIES**. Owned and run by Eric and June Tomlinson, keen gardeners themselves, the Nursery is in fact in the 200 year old kitchen garden of Marbury Hall. The original, 15 foot high brick wall shelters many of the more delicate plants from the elements and adds to the old fashioned feel of the nursery, where the service and advice on offer is second to none. Whether you are a beginner or an expert there is always somebody pleasant and knowledgeable on hand to pass on advice and experience. Specialising in the unusual this is the place to come if you are particularly looking for hibiscus, oranges, bay trees and palms, alpines or fernsland don't forget to take a look at the mature vine that produces a heavy harvest of dark red grapes each year.

Marbury Hall Nurseries, The Old Wall Gardens, Marbury Park, Marbury,
near Northwich Tel: 01606 74168

LOSTOCK GRALAM, to the south, is where you will find **WINCHAM WHARF**, a working boatyard on the banks of the Trent and Mersey Canal. Opened in 1777, the canal provided a link between the industrial midlands and the Mersey Basin and it was at Wincham Wharf that goods were received and the horses were changed, fed and farriered. Today, Wincham Wharf is home to a bar and restaurant. Full of character, with exposed beams and brickwork, this is one place not to be missed.

Wincham Wharf, 216/220 Manchester Road, Lostock Gralam, Northwich
Tel: 01606 48581

Situated on the A559 just south of Warrington, in the village of Wincham, lies the **WINCHAM HALL HOTEL**. Standing among trees on a hill, the hotel overlooks the brook that is known locally as Peover Eye. An historic establishment dating back to the beginning of the 12th century, the present hall has recently undergone an extensive refurbishment that ensures that the accommodation is second to none. The proprietors, Richard and Jane Clemetson can be justly proud of their establishment: they have won the Cheshire Life Small Hotel of the Year Award and come Highly Recommended by Egon Ronay.

The restaurant offers an interesting a la carte and menu of the day for both lunch and dinner with such delights as Chicken with Asparagus and Pink Grapefruit in a Chervil and Lemon Sauce and Fillet of Sea Bass on Braised Fennel in a Cardamom and Ginger scented juice. Shell fish and in particular lobster from the hotel's own tank is a house speciality. Though in a rural setting, the hotel is conveniently placed for both the M6 and M56 motorways which make it the ideal place for wedding receptions and other family celebrations as well as conferences and corporate events.

Wincham Hall Hotel, Hall Lane, Wincham Tel: 01606 43453

PICKMERE lies just north of here, and is a delightful village commanding superb views of the Cheshire Plain from the Dee Estuary to the Pennine foothills. Not only is it ideally situated for exploring Cheshire's peaks, plains, parks and waterways, but it is readily accessible, being close to Manchester Airport and only two miles from junction 19 of the M6 motorway. This makes it an ideal stopover point for both northbound and southbound travellers. Chester, Manchester and Liverpool can all be reached within 40 minutes. Leisure activities in the area include golf, riding and watersports.

WEAVERHAM. At the crossroads in Weaverham stands the large black and white building that is **THE HANGING GATE INN.** Originally a farmhouse with its outbuildings dating back to 1680, it has also been a coaching inn on what was once the main route between Chester and south of England.

The age of days gone by is maintained in this pleasant and well kept establishment with exposed beams adding to the air of nostalgia. Owned and run by Alan, Sheila and Victoria Doleman, an experienced team, this is an ideal place to stop and enjoy liquid refreshment. Many locals do! The spacious dining room also serves an excellent menu of tasty bar snacks as well as delicious three course meals. With a large car park and swings and slides for the children this is a real family pub.

The Hanging Gate Inn, Sandy Lane, Weaverham Tel: 01606 852146

CHAPELS almost opposite the Weaver Gallery on the High Street, is an attractive wine bar and restaurant owned and personally run by Chris and Doug Carney. The building has had many functions over the years but none quite as excellent and special as today.

Chapels Restaurant

This is much more than just any wine bar serving food. The interior is stylish yet cosy and intimate. Doug does all the cooking and the dishes are very varied and absolutely delicious, a blend of French and English cuisine. It is also refreshing to find a restaurant that really caters for vegetarians without resorting to the usual standards. If, however, you are just here for a drink you will be made most welcome and there is an outstanding array of wines as well as Tetley ale, Kilkenny and guest beers. Chris and Doug also offer bed and breakfast accommodation in four en suite bedrooms that match the excellent standard of the rest of the establishment.

Chapels Restaurant, 15-17 High Street, Weaverham Tel: 01606 854485

HARTFORD. **THE HARTFORD HALL HOTEL** offers a luxurious, relaxed life-style of days gone by. This delightful 16th century building set amidst beautiful gardens has been tastefully and sympathetically restored to its original period splendour. The bedrooms at Hartford Hall are lavishly furnished and provide every modern amenity.

Each has a private bathroom and shower, colour television, radio, trouser press, direct dial telephone, baby listening service, and hospitality tray. The lounge bar serves light lunches, and excellent wines and spirits as well as morning coffee and afternoon tea.

For those wishing to dine, the standard of cuisine is comparable with some of the finest in England. Open to non-residents too, it is popular for both social entertaining and business meetings.

Visitors seeking peace and tranquillity combined with personal service, sumptuous surroundings and excellent restaurant facilities will not be disappointed. ETB 4 Crown & AA & RAC 3 Star.

Hartford Hall Hotel, 81 School Lane, Hartford, Northwich, Cheshire.
Tel: 01606 75711 Fax: 01606 782285

DAVENHAM. **RESTAURANT 913**, situated on Church Street, Davenham, is a delightful, secluded establishment owned and personally run by Sarah and Neil Robinson.

With experience in hotel management and catering, the couple opened the restaurant in 1994 after totally refurbishing the premises and giving the interior a very continental feel. Sarah, the chef, has put together an interesting and exciting a la carte menu with a variety of dishes that different tastes and textures to favourite foods. There is also a special dishes board which offers seasonal dishes, again all freshly prepared and cooked on the premises. Neil looks after the front of house and has a fine wine list that beautifully compliments the menus. Open Tuesday to Friday for lunch and dinner and over the weekend for dinner you can be sure of an outstanding meal at anytime.

Restaurant 913, 9-13 Church Street, Davenham, Northwich
Tel: 01606 330913

ANTROBUS. Situated alongside the main A559 between Warrington and Northwich at Antrobus, set in one and a half acres of land and surrounded by scenic countryside is the Antrobus Arms.

The Antrobus Arms

This impressive building was first licensed in 1760 and ever since has been a popular spot for visitors and locals to partake of real ale and fine food. The interior is beautifully decorated and furnished, there is even a play area for the children. The pub also has easy access for wheelchair users. Ron and Sue, the tenants are proud of the friendly and lively atmosphere that the pub has. The food is excellent and entertainment is provided most nights of the week, so why not make a point of calling in, you will not be disappointed.

The Antrobus Arms, Antrobus, Warrington Road, Nr Northwich.
Tel: 01606 891333

NORTHWICH, lies on the confluence of the Rivers Weaver and Dane. Its name derives from 'wych', meaning salt town. Salt has been extracted from Cheshire since before Roman times. In 1670 rock salt was discovered in nearby Marston, and Northwich developed as a major salt producer. In the 19th century, Brunner and Mond set up their salt works at WINNINGTON to manufacture alkali products based on brine.

Extensive pumping of brine has, however, caused subsidence and large holes often used to appear, even swallowing up buildings. Salt extraction is now carefully controlled, but you can still see flooded areas, or flashes, around the town and on Witton Street, the **WHITE LION INN** has sunk an entire storey! The subsidence led to the design of a new type of timber framed building in the area which can be jacked up as required.

Situated in the Northwich Workhouse building on London Road is Britain's only **SALT MUSEUM** With its unique collection of traditional working tools and lively displays which include working models and videos, the Salt Museum tells the fascinating story of Cheshire's oldest industry. Not only can ancient remains such as Roman evaporating pans and medieval salt rakes be seen, but there is much to remind visitors of the vital part that salt plays in the modern chemical industry.

Northwich Salt Museum

In the centre of Northwich, close to the Brunner Public Library, is the recently opened **CAFE D.** Owned and personally run by Dianne Travis, this stylish coffee house is in the pedestrianised shopping area of the town and offers a taste of the continent in the heart of old England.

Open all day, every day except Sundays, the café serves a vast range of hot and cold snacks and light meals as well as a hearty English breakfast. Ranging from hot chicken and club style sandwiches to freshly made omelettes and salad bowls; with hot waffles, Cheshire ice cream and a mouthwatering array of home baked cakes and pastries there is something for everyone and children even have their own specially designed dishes.

In fine weather there are tables and comfortable chairs outside on the pavement where you can watch the world go by whilst relaxing with a delicious cup of freshly ground coffee. With no vehicles in this area of the town the experience is particularly pleasurable. Inside, on either the ground or first floor, there is plenty of room, in peaceful and stylish surroundings, to take the weight off your feet.

Café D, 82 Witton Street, Northwich Tel: 01606 42097

THE BLUE BARREL INN is situated at Castle, just two minutes walk from Northwich Town Centre. One of the oldest buildings in the town, the Owen family, Ann and David with son Gary and his wife Rachel, came here three years ago and have turned it into one of the best pubs in the area.

The Blue Barrel Inn

Beautifully decorated and furnished throughout, with the bonus of low, beamed ceilings, this is a real, family run, friendly inn. There are

237

four, equally well decorated, guest bedrooms which offer the best in home comforts. Downstairs, the bar serves a range of real ales so is a must for real ale fans. Unfortunately, no food is available, except, of course, breakfast for overnight guests.

Blue Barrel, 69 Chester Road, Castle, Northwich Tel: 01606 74805

WINNINGTON LODGE public house is situated on the edge of Northwich town centre close to Northwich Hospital. Built in the late 19th century as a private dwelling house for a successful Northwich businessman's daughter, it is distinctive and eye-catching from the road.

As impressive inside and it is outside, the pub has retains the feel of a grand house with wonderful decoration and furnishings as well as plenty of memorabilia on the walls and shelves. Now one of the Miller's Kitchen chain of pub/restaurants owned by Greenalls, you can be sure of a well cooked and presented meal as well as an excellent pint of beer.

With a daily specials board and the Captain Coconut's Treasure Island menu for children, the whole family will be happily catered for in warm and friendly surroundings.

Winnington Lodge, Winnington Lane, Northwich Tel: 01606 74217

Also situated on Winnington Lane in Northwich, you will discover **WEAVER VALE GARDEN CENTRE**, one of four family-run businesses that come under the title 'Garden Centres of Cheshire'. This is the most recent addition to the group and as well as providing a wide and varied selection of plants and shrubs, also has its own machinery department complete with fully equipped workshop where customers are welcome to visit.

The Centre is set within beautiful lawned grounds and has everything you could need for the garden from Garden Furniture and Barbecues to ponds and liners and all the relevant accessories, from ornamental garden pots to fencing, walling and paving. The Centre's large gift shop sells numerous items including attractive dried flowers, preserves, chocolates and books, while in the coffee shop you can enjoy tasty cakes, snacks and meals.

Weaver Vale Garden Centre, Winnington Lane, Northwich Tel: 01606 79965

Taking a boat trip on an old Dutch Sailing Barge, run by **SOVER-EIGN CRUISES**, along the Weaver Navigation is a superb way to see the sights of Vale Royal. Setting out from Northwich, there are a variety of cruises available which gently take you passed the Anderton Boat Lift, through the Barnton Cut or down the deep river valley where Vale Royal Abbey once stood.

Sovereign Cruises, 'River View' Leighs Brow, Barnton, Northwich Tel: 01606 76204

ACTON BRIDGE. On the main street of Acton Bridge, close to the Maypole pub, stands **ACTON LODGE FARMHOUSE**, built in the 1720s. This is the home of Mr and Mrs Holland who offer bed and breakfast accommodation in 4 bedrooms.

Acton Lodge Farmhouse

The farmhouse, still displaying the original oak beams, is tastefully decorated and furnished with antique and period furniture all in keeping with the building to give a relax and homely atmosphere. Guests also have their own lounge with tea and coffee making facilities.

Ideal for business people and travellers, unfortunately the accommodation is not suitable for children. Set in the spacious farm gardens this is a peaceful spot to relax in after a hard day on the road.

Acton Lodge, Hill Top Road, Acton Bridge, Near Northwich
Tel: 01606 853178

THE HORNS INN, public house, in the village of Acton Bridge, is owned and run by Moira and Steve Redfern. Situated close to the banks of the River Weaver, this charming white washed, rambling building also offers bed and breakfast accommodation in five guest rooms.

A delightful establishment the bar is comfortable and there is also a large restaurant area with many nautical artefacts decorating the walls.

The daily specials are chalked up on a board and offer a range of tasty dishes. Steve was grew up in the pub and it certainly has a warm and friendly feel about it. Used by regulars and travellers alike this is an ideal place to stop for a pint and meal.

The Horns Inn, Warrington Road, Acton Bridge, Little Leight
Tel: 01606 852192

ASH HOUSE FARM lies at the bottom of quiet Chapel Lane in Acton Bridge. Originally owned by the last living relative of the Styal Mill family, Alec Greg, the house was built in the beginning of the 19th century. \

Ash House Farm

Now a working dairy farm, Sue Schofield and her family offer bed and breakfast accommodation in two rooms, one of which is a large family room equipped with a washbasin, the other a twin room with en suite facilities. The house is full of character and charm, reflecting its obviously Georgian exterior.

The entrance hall is original with open beams and a large dresser. The warm and friendly lounge has large French windows which open out into the gardens and orchard. Families are welcomed to this delightful establishment in the heart of rural Cheshire.

Ash House Farm, Chapel Lane, Acton Bridge, Northwich Tel: 01606 852717

FRODSHAM is an attractive town with a broad High Street lined with thatched cottages and spacious Georgian and Victorian houses. It was once an important coaching town during the 18th and 19th centuries and there are several fine coaching inns.

While in the area of Frodsham, a visit to **THE COTTAGE TEA SHOP** in the Main Street is a must. Louise and her Mum, Ruth took over the business a year ago and have already built up a good reputation. The Tea Shop has an attractive half-timbered frontage and dates from the early 19th century. It has a very warm and cosy atmosphere and only the best home-cooked and prepared food is available, ranging from freshly prepared soup, sandwiches, hot savouries and light meals. Ruth bakes delicious home made cakes and the menu and daily specials offer an excellent selection. In the summer additional tables are set outside. Open 10 - 4.30 Monday to Saturday throughout the Summer, closed all day Wednesday.

The Cottage Tea Shop, 121 Main Street, Frodsham, Cheshire.
Tel: 01928 733673

The outstanding **SQUIRES RESTAURANT** stands on the main street in the beautiful Cheshire village of Frodsham. Housed on the first floor of this Grade II listed building the restaurant is beautifully decorated in rich, warm colours that create a relaxed and peaceful atmosphere.

Michael Whalley, who has much experience of the catering business, opened Squires five years ago and has gained an excellent reputation for his glorious food. Open everyday except Sundays, the restaurant is well known throughout the area. During the day, between 10 am and 2 pm, there is a tasty menu of snacks and light lunches that make this a super meeting place. Come evening and the mood changes. The menu is extensive and there are a host of special gourmet evenings throughout the year. Thursday night is 'Fish Night', incorporated with the a la carte menu. There is a choice of at least eight different varieties of fish fresh from the market that morning, pluds a selection of ten sauces for you to choose from to accompany the fish of your choice.

In intimate and cosy surroundings you can enjoy the very best of English, French and Italian cuisine, with all the dishes prepared to order. When you book your table it is yours for the evening, a final touch that makes a meal here the perfect dining experience.

Squires Restaurant, 4A High Street, Frodsham Tel: 01928 735246

THE OLD HALL HOTEL is a lovely 16th century building situated right in the heart of Frodsham, opposite the Mersey Estuary. Within the grounds there are two commemorative stones dated 1862 which mark the level reached by flood waters at that time and in the gardens there is a large stone bath or well with a stepped access.

The Old Hall Hotel

The interior of the building is beautifully decorated and rather unusual, but of particular interest are the two areas of wattle and daub which have been left exposed. There are also lovely open fireplaces for added warmth in the winter.

The bedrooms are extremely spacious and decorated to a high standard. All are en-suite and have colour television, telephone, and tea and coffee facilities. As well as eight single rooms, 11 doubles, and one family room, there is also a suite available. The restaurant serves breakfast, luncheon and dinner, with á la carte and table d'hôte always proving to be popular with residents. The bar is well stocked and has a friendly, welcoming atmosphere.

Mr and Mrs Winfield have run the hotel for the past 20 years and like to provide their guests with first class standards and efficient staff. We thoroughly enjoyed our visit to The Old Hall Hotel and were delighted to have met with such friendly service.

The Old Hall Hotel, Main Street, Frodsham Tel: 01928 732052

HELSBY. Has a pleasant walk, albeit rather steep. The climb out of village along pretty woodland paths to the red sandstone summit of Helsby Hill, is where you'll find the site of an Iron Age fort. The hill is now owned and protected by the National Trust.

DELAMERE FOREST is a rambler's delight, its 4,000 acres of woodland incorporating a wealth of lovely walks and various picnic sites for a peaceful family day out in the country. In Norman times the word 'forest' meant a protected hunting ground for royalty or nobility. Delamere was originally used by the Earls of Chester and it became a Royal Forest in the 14th century, with James I being the last king to hunt deer here. Large areas of oak were cleared from the Forest in Tudor times for ship building and boat construction. Since the early 20th century, Delamere Forest has been under the control of the Forestry Commission, who undertook an intensive programme of tree planting and woodland management.

NORLEY. **THE TIGER'S HEAD** is a wonderful pub in the picturesque village of Norley found just off the B5152 and close to the main A556 and A49 roads.

Beginning life as a farmhouse in the late 17th century, this striking black and white building was once a coaching inn of great renown. As to its unusual name, this remains somewhat a mystery, it may have something to do with the original tiger's head that is mounted inside the pub but no-one is sure.

For the past two and a half years or so the Tiger's Head has been run by Barbara and Howard Lancaster and they have maintained the old English inn feel.

This makes the pub a popular place for locals and visitors alike. Open everyday all day between Easter and the end of September and during normal licensing hours the rest of the year, whenever you arrive you will receive a warm and friendly welcome from the charming hosts.

There is a delicious menu of home-cooked food available at lunchtime and every evening except Sundays and the bar stocks a range of excellent ales including Burtonwood Bitter and Top Hat.

The Tiger's Head, Pytchleys Hollow, Norley, Warrington Tel: 01928 788309

THE VALE ROYAL is an area of some 150 square miles, incorporating some of the most beautiful Cheshire countryside. Within this vast area there is a wealth of historic sites revealing the rich heritage of this lovely rural county. The name originated when Prince Edward, eighth Earl of Chester declared it to be "The Vale Royal of England" because he felt it was so beautiful. Among the many places to visit there is the **ANDERTON BOAT LIFT**, an impressive structure recently restored to its former glory. The lift was conceived and designed by Edward Leader Williams who later found fame for designing the Manchester Ship Canal, and it played a major part in the industrial development of the area. Using amazing hydraulics this cast iron construction was a marvel of the era, literally "lifting" boats and transferring them from the river to the canal.

The Anderton Boat Lift

For the sporting enthusiast, The Vale Royal has a wide range of facilities, including **RUDHEATH LEISURE CENTRE**, complete with sports hall, village room and fitness suite, **NORTHWICH SWIMMING POOL, WINSFORD INDOOR SPORTS COMPLEX** with amenities for all kinds of sporting activities and **KNIGHTS GRANGE SPORTS COMPLEX** which caters for a wide variety of sports ranging from golf to indoor bowls and crazy golf.

The abundance of countryside walks, meres, canals and rivers for the nature enthusiast, ensures that within this wonderful area there is something to appeal to everyone.

Vale Royal Borough Council, Wyvern House, The Drumber, Winsford
Tel: 01606 862862

WHITEGATE. **THE PLOUGH** is a very special 'hidden place' tucked away down a No Through road on top of Beauty Bank in the tiny hamlet of Foxtwist Green near Whitegate. Surrounded by fields and dating back to 1910, this charming, unspoilt pub is run by Mavis and Doug Hughes, who, until recently managed a pub in Comberbach. Locals and visitors mix easily here, in a homely atmosphere where fine ales and homecooked food are the order of the day. In the short time that they have been here, Mavis has established herself as a cook of excellent reputation, with a varied menu of delicious dishes that make the mouth water. Formerly a farm, The Plough was once part of the Delamere estate and the rear bar still features the original stoneflagged floor, making it popular with muddy-booted walkers who call for a refreshing drink.

The Plough Inn, Beauty Bank, Whitegate Tel: 01606 889455

LITTLE BUDWORTH, west of Winsford, is an attractive village with views over the Budworth Pool which gives the village its name - 'bode worth', or dwelling by the water.

Close by is **LITTLE BUDWORTH COUNTRY PARK**, consisting mainly of ancient heathland, with a mixture of heather, gorse, bracken and silver birch trees growing on sandy soil - much as they did thousands of years ago, though oaks and rowan trees are now appearing. This is an attractive area to sit or stroll in, with car parking and picnic areas.

The re-introduction of herbs is due to people such as Libby and Ted Riddell, who own and run a specialist herb nursery called **CHESHIRE HERBS** in Forest Road, Little Budworth. The main thrust of the company is the growing and selling of retail and wholesale herb pot plants, producing over 180 different varieties. The nursery boasts a herb garden where customers can see the plants in situ so as to be able to appreciate the individual stature of the plant they wish to buy. There is also a small yet comprehensive shop selling herb-related products. The company have won gold medals for exhibiting at the Horticultural Society and a variety of county shows.

Cheshire Herbs, Forest Road, Little Budworth Tel: 01829 760578

Vale Royal has given its name to the modern district of Cheshire in which it lies and it incorporates the Whitegate Way, a footpath that runs from Winsford to CUDDINGTON, using the old railway line that carried salt from the Winsford Mines.

Not far from here lies the site of the **ABBEY OF VALE ROYAL**, founded by Edward I in 1277, who, according to the story, did so in fulfilment of a vow he made as Earl of Chester when crossing the Dee in a storm. As he came ashore the ship sank, but the future king was safe. It was a Cistercian monastery and once had the longest Cistercian Abbey Church in England, and after the Dissolution in the 16th century it became a country house. It is now a special school.

WINSFORD is a town which, despite its growth in recent years with housing development, still retains several features of historic interest, including some timber framed pubs in the centre and an unusual timber framed church built for bargees travelling on the River Weaver.

Winsford is actually formed from two older townships, Over and Wharton on either side of the River Weaver. **WINSFORD BOTTOM FLASH** is a popular area for angling, canoeing and pleasure boating.

DARNHALL, **THE RAVEN INN** in the village of Darnhall lies just outside Winsford on the B5074 road to Nantwich. Known locally as the Old Crow, the inn was built in the late 19th century is an outstanding position with the rolling Cheshire countryside visible in every direction. A warm welcome awaits all visitors to the pub from managers Pamela and Stephen Duffy-Turner and their staff. As well as serving a well kept pint or two of traditional beer there is a wonderful menu of mouth-watering dishes, supplemented by a daily specials board. With a tremendous children's play area, The Raven Inn has something for all the family though it is advisable to book it you wish to eat here at the weekend.

The Raven Inn, Swanlow Lane, Darnhall, Winsford Tel: 01606 592680

WHARTON. On Station Road in Wharton, near Winsford, stands the **ODDFELLOWS ARMS** a charming pub run by friendly hosts Norman and Samantha Temple.

One of the first properties to be built in this area, the building housing the Oddfellows Arms has stood for well over 250 years and was, for a long time, a lodging house until it became a pub towards the beginning of the 19th century. The somewhat unusual exterior is matched by a magical interior full of character where a cheerful, welcoming atmosphere prevails.

The pub is tastefully furnished in keeping with the period and provides a relaxing setting where locals and visitors mix easily, enjoying a pint of fine ale and friendly conversation.

Oddfellows Arms, Station Road, Wharton, Winsford Tel: 01606 593643

MIDDLEWICH, another salt town, was also the site of two Civil War battles. It also lies on King Street, a Roman Road which is now the A530. In the church, dedicated to St. Michael, there are some old carvings and the coat of arms of the Kinderton family of nearby Kinderton Hall. The crest shows a dragon eating a child and this somewhat gruesome emblem related to a legend of how a member of the family, Baron Kinderton, killed a local dragon as it was devouring a child - presumably too late to save the unfortunate youngster. A lane at Moston near Sandbach, where the incident is supposed to have taken place, is still called Dragon Lane.

THE KING'S LOCK INN, sits alongside the Trent and Mersey Canal in Middlewich just a hundred yards from the junction with the Middlewich branch of the Grand Union Canal. Over 200 years old, the building has been, in its time, a shop, stables and an inn.

Since becoming a public house, there have only been four previous landlords and for the fifth, Belinda Foden, coming here has been a dream come true. In a wonderful position, opposite one of the canal's many locks, this is a really super place to visit. As well as serving well kept beers and ales, there is a delicious menu of home-cooked food available. During the winter the roaring fires keep the cold at bay and in the summer there is plenty of room to sit outside and watch the life of the waterway.

The King's Lock Inn, 1 Booth Lane, Middlewich Tel: 01606 833537

SANDBACH, lying on the Trent and Mersey Canal, which forms part of the Cheshire Ring, is an ideal stopping-off point for the canal traveller. It is also readily accessible by road, situated barely a mile from the M6 motorway. In its Market Place you will find a link with Cheshire's pre-Conquest history - two richly carved Anglo-Saxon sandstone crosses, dating from between the 8th and 9th centuries and making a focal point in this attractive town.

The crosses date back to 653AD, when Peada, son of King Penda was baptised in Sandbach after an ultimatum by Oswy, King of Northumbria, saying you will not marry my daughter unless you embrace the Christian faith.

Peada duly accepted the requirements and St. Chad and other holy missionaries came down from Northumbria to convert the ancient pagan

Saxon Crosses, Sandbach

kingdom of Mercia, which included what later became Cheshire, to Christianity.

The crosses were damaged by the Puritans but restored by a local historian, George Ormerod, in the last century and placed in their present position.

THE CROWN HOTEL stands right in the centre of the oldest part of Sandbach, next to the town's famous Saxon Crosses.

A typical Cheshire black and white building, it dates from the mid 17th century, this is a wonderful place for the visitor and local alike. Open everyday of the year, your hosts, Anita and Roy Batchelor, are always ready with a warm and friendly welcome and an glass or two of excellent ale.

From Wednesday to Sunday lunchtimes Anita and Roy also offer a varied and delicious menu for diners. The Crown Hotel is also well known in the area for its folk music and the folk club, with a number of well known artists, meet here every Tuesday evening.

The Crown Hotel, 10 Market Square, Sandbach Tel: 01270 762161

Just a few yards from the Market Square is **THE LOWER CHEQUER**, reputed to be the oldest building in the town and dating back as far as 1570.

Sandbach has some other interesting half-timbered buildings, including a fine old 17th century inn with its thatched roof.

The town's popular market, held every Thursday, brings people in from all over the area. It is held on **SCOT'S COMMON**, so called because it is the place where some of the followers of Bonny Prince Charlie were killed and buried after the battle of Worcester.

Sandbach is also celebrated as the place where Edwin Foden established his world famous **FODEN MOTOR COMPANY** - when he died in 1964, his coffin was carried to its final resting place in the little church at nearby Elsworth on a steam lorry known as Pride of Edwin, which had been made in his factory at Sandbach in 1916.

HASLINGTON to the east of Crewe has some interesting old cottages and a small 19th century church. The old timber hall in the village was originally built by Admiral Sir Francis Vernon, one of Drake's admirals who helped defeat the Spanish Armada in 1588.

At the junction of Waterloo Road with the main road, there was until quite recently, a working blacksmith. The last horse was shod at the old smithy in 1974.

THE HAWK INN situated on the old Sandbach to Crewe road in Haslington now bypassed by the A534, is a treat not to be missed. Built in 1510, probably from the timbers of ships from the Spanish Armada and from the Old Hall in Haslington, it was a coaching inn with stabling for about eight horses.

One of the more notable visitors thought to have rested at the inn is the famous highwayman Dick Turpin along with his faithful horse Black Bess. Whether the story is true or not, it is apparent that the inn has seen many things over the years. Though much altered and extended over the centuries, the original building still remains as does the now derelict thatched roof, under the more recent tiled roof, in the loft space over the dining room, lounge and games room.

Today, you will find the Hawk Inn a maze of little rooms, all different and all full of character. In particular, the Oak Room, so named after its spectacular oak panelling, is a real delight with its leaded windows.

Since 1986, Wilf and Joyce Batchelor have been landlord and landlady of the Hawk Inn. They offer a warm welcome to all visitors as well as a range of excellent real ales and an outstanding menu of delicious dishes. The licensing trade must be in the blood as the couple's youngest son is the landlord of the Crown Hotel in Sandbach, also featured in this book.

The Hawk Inn, 137 Crewe Road, Haslington Tel: 01270 582181

CREWE. For visitors to the area one of Cheshire's premier attractions, **THE RAILWAY AGE** at Crewe, has something to interest the whole family. Mention the word 'trains' and you immediately think of Crewe, indeed Crewe would not be on the map had it not been for trains.

At one time, seven out of every ten men in Crewe worked on the railways, for trains did not only pass through this busy town, but they were built here. At The Railway Age, you will find yourself stepping back in time to the bygone era of steam, with weekend rides available in an authentic brake van pulled by a steam locomotive on the Centre's own running line. In the North Junction signal box, one of three original boxes, visitors can enjoy some 'hands-on' exhibits and there are further activities available for younger members of the family in the indoor Children's Corner and yearly model railway exhibitions.

Although it seems sad in some ways that these giant steam engines are no more than exhibition pieces, we should nevertheless be grateful that someone had the foresight to preserve this important part of history for everyone to enjoy.

The Railway Age, Vernon Way, Crewe. 01270 258923

BARTHOMLEY, to the east of Crewe and close to the M6 motorway, is a beautiful little village, typical of so many in Cheshire with its black and white half-timbered cottages. It has a unique church dedicated to St. Bertoline, an 8th century Saxon prince who became a hermit on an island in the little River Sow in Staffordshire. It was here that a terrible massacre took place in 1643 during the Civil War, when a band of Royalist soldiers arrived in the village. The residents took refuge in the church tower, but the soldiers smoked them out with fire by burning the pews and rush mats. When the villagers surrendered, they were stripped and brutally murdered.

NANTWICH is definitely the focal point of this part of Cheshire. This lovely old town was once second only in importance to Chester in the county, being used by the Romans as a supplier of salt for their garrisons at Chester and Stoke. It remained a salt producing town from Saxon times onwards, but production declined in the 18th century as other centres with better communications on the canal system such as Northwich increased in importance. However, a brine spring still supplies the town's outdoor swimming pool.

In 1583, the town was devastated by a disastrous fire which raged across the half-timbered and thatched buildings and lasted for 20 days, leaving only a few buildings standing. It is recorded that during the fire the bears kept behind the Crown Hotel were let loose and the towns-women were afraid to help with fighting the fire for fear of the beasts. Four bears from Nantwich are mentioned in Shakespeare's comedy 'The Merry Wives of Windsor'.

Fortunately a few fine old buildings did survive the fire, such as the moated half-timbered mansion in Hospital Street belonging to Nantwich merchant Rychard Churche, which was built in 1577. It is now open to the public as a small museum and is well worth a visit. Another important Nantwich building to escape fire damage was the fine 14th century Parish Church, sometimes called the 'Cathedral of South Cheshire'. It dates from a great period of Nantwich's prosperity as a salt town and trading centre, and is richly decorated with an unusual octagonal tower. Of exceptional interest is the magnificent chancel and the wonderful carving in the choir. On the misericords (tip-up seats) are mermaids, foxes (some dressed as monks - an interesting social comment), pigs and the legendary Wyvern - half dragon, half bird, whose name is linked with the River Weaver, 'wyvern' being an old pronunciation of Weaver.

An amusing tale about the building of the church concerns an old woman who brought ale and food each day from a local inn to the masons working on site. Unfortunately the masons discovered that the woman was cheating them by keeping some of the money they put 'in the pot' for their refreshment. They dismissed her and sought revenge by carving her image in the church, being carried away by the Devil himself with her hand still in the pot.

When you are in the town, be sure to pop into **MAGPIE CRAFTS** at 44 Hospital Street. It is a charming little shop with the doorway and windows attractively surrounded by hanging baskets and window boxes, all jammed full of the most colourful flowers and plants.

Magpie Crafts

Sue Adams, the proprietor, has been in business for twelve years and is constantly on the look out for well crafted British made goods. The exterior has a charming Victorian shop front, and immediately prior to Sue purchasing the building, the rooms at the front of the property were used as living accommodation.

The interior of the shop is attractively decorated and has lovely low beamed ceilings which add to the atmosphere of the premises. Sue tries to seek out that something different, whether in gifts or cards, handmade cards are a speciality. Stock is constantly changing and ranges from jewellery to teddy bears; from collectables to bridal gifts.

Any purchase will be gift wrapped free of charge if required. We spent a very enjoyable half hour admiring the many items she has for sale, and of course could not leave without buying a little memento of our visit to Nantwich.

Magpie Crafts, 44 Hospital Street, Nantwich Tel: 01270 629808

During the Civil War, Nantwich was the only town in Cheshire to support Cromwell's Parliamentary army. After several weeks of fighting, the Royalist forces were finally defeated on 25th January 1644 and the people of Nantwich celebrated by wearing sprigs of holly in their hair and hats. As a result, the day became known as 'Holly Holy Day' and every year the Saturday closest to 25th January, the town welcomes Cromwellian pikemen, and battle scenes are re-enacted by members of the Sealed Knot. There are records of the Civil War and exhibitions in the Nantwich Museum in Pillory Street which also has material about the town and its dairy and cheese-making industry.

Kiltearn House

Situated conveniently close to the centre of Nantwich, **KILTEARN HOUSE** is one of the town's historic houses. There has been a dwelling on this site since 1100 and the front of the current building dates from the 18th century. This is a comfortable and charming with antique furnishings, roaring log fires, spacious living rooms, comfortable bedrooms and a pretty walled garden. Owned and personally run by Jean and Terry Pearson you can expect to enjoy good home cooking with fresh ingredients including stoneground wholemeal bread, farm butter and free range eggs. Always ready with a warm and friendly welcome this is a wonderful house with a lot of character.

Kiltearn House, 33 Hospital Street, Nantwich Tel: 01270 628892, Fax: 01270 626646

Situated mid way along Pepper Street is a veritable 'Aladdin's cave' of treasures gathered from the four corners of the world; **GRAPEVINE!** This is a family run business that provides a real alternative to mass production. Various family members spend time abroad searching out the unusual in gifts, jewellery and clothes. Buying this way cuts out the middlemen and makes individuality affordable without having to compromise on quality.

An extensive range of jewellery, fashioned in silver and studded with semi-precious stones by craftsmen of Jaipur, lie glittering in glass cabinets. Shelves are brimming with exotic textiles hand printed and dyed in indigo and other natural colours, musical instruments and a myriad of hand crafted artifacts.

Walls are decorated with paintings on silk and hand woven 'hangings' in Ikat and other rare weaves. Clothing made from natural fibres in easy to wear styles compliments this cornucopia of arts and crafts.

Dave and Chris Hogg, the owners strive to make shopping a pleasurable experience; so browse in Grapevine and visit the world, from the lofty peaks of the Himalayas to the burning plains of Africa.

Grapevine, 14 Pepper Street, Nantwich. Tel: 01270 610751

Around Nantwich

WRENBURY is a typical example of a pretty Cheshire village, with an old church by the village green which has a corner tower that carries stairs to the top of it. The village green was used for bear baiting and it is recorded that on at least one occasion the vicar stopped the Sunday morning service when a travelling bear arrived and went outside with the congregation to see the bear being paraded around the green.

WYBUNBURY lies to the east, it is situated off the A51 can be reached easily by car. A village long before Norman times, its name derives from 'Wigbeorns Fort' (early Anglo Saxon) and in the Domesday Book it is listed as 'Wineberie', an administrative and religious centre for ten surrounding townships. However, this small village has the misfortune to be sinking, due to the natural seepage of water dissolving the saltbeds deep underground, causing the whole area to subside. The church, famous for its leaning tower and medieval monuments, has had to be entirely rebuilt nearby on firmer terrain.

ACTON, an attractive village two miles or so west of Nantwich, means 'township among the oak woods' - a reference to Delamere Forest which once stretched this far. The church, with its large tower, was restored after the Civil War, but a Norman font survives from the earlier church, as well as an impressive tomb of William Mainwaring, a local nobleman, dating from 1399.

Close by **DORFOLD HALL** is said to stand on the site of a hunting lodge and deer park used by Leofric, Earl of Mercia, and his wife, who is better known as Lady Godiva. The present Hall is a magnificent Jacobean country house, built in mature brick with a beautiful cobbled courtyard, with richly decorated plaster ceilings and panelling. One of the upstairs rooms has been described as one of the finest in England Another room, prepared for a visit by James I, has coat-of-arms in plasterwork and a secret cupboard for his personal possessions. Sadly, the visit of the King never took place and the expense was in vain. The gardens have lawns, woodlands and a fine avenue of old limes. An ancient oak tree in the grounds is reputed to have been the southern-most point of Delamere Forest.

BARBRIDGE. THE BARBRIDGE INN lies on the banks of the Shropshire Union Canal in the village of Barbridge, just off the A51 road to Chester and only a few miles out of Nantwich.

The Barbridge Inn

The pub built when the canal first opened back in the mid-18th century. Today, Mo and Bill Eyre, the pub's managers, still welcome canal boats, and 24 hour mooring is provided right outside. The bar serves hand-pulled cask ales and guest beers are available in the summer. There is a separate dining area too, overlooking the canal, where you can enjoy an excellent meal taken from the interesting and diverse menu. The canalside garden is large and has a children's play area, and in the summer there are often barbeques. The towpath that runs past the pub is ideal for a gentle stroll after your meal.

The Barbridge Inn, Old Chester Road, Barbridge, Nantwich
Tel: 01270 528443

BUNBURY, between Barbridge and Tarporley, with its twisting streets and mixture of styles and periods, might be called a typical Cheshire village. With everything from timber-frame Tudor to Georgian brick it is certainly a pleasant place to stroll around. The village grew around the church with expansion in Tudor times and when the common land of Bunbury Heath was enclosed.

The village church certainly has a very interesting history. In the 14th century, Sir Hugh Calveley established a college in the church, some two hundred years later the tower was added to, together with battlements and the Ridley family chapel. Restored in Victorian times it suffered during World War II when a stray German bomb removed the roof. Luckily the church's two most important monuments escaped unscathed: one to Sir Hugh Calveley and the other to Sir George Beeston. Sir George lived over a hundred years, fighting in the army of Henry VIII in France and sixty years later commanding the warship Dreadnought in the battle against the Spanish Armada at the ripe old age of 89!

TARPORLEY, to the northwest of Nantwich, was an old forest town where the ancient foresters or forest wardens lived. In Utkington, just north of the village, is an old farmhouse and a Hall which has a column formed by an ancient forest tree, its roots still in the ground. The Hunting Horn of Delamere was once hung on this column as a symbol of authority for the foresters. It is now kept at the Grosvenor Museum in Chester.

Home of the Tarporley Hunt, the oldest Hunting Club in the country, **THE SWAN HOTEL** can be found on the main street of the town. The hotel is one of only two buildings officially permitted to use the heraldic insignia originated by Queen Margaret of Anjou, consort to King Henry VI and worn as a token of loyalty by the Cheshire gentry of the Lancastrian forces at the battle near Market Drayton in 1459. The oldest part of the hotel, the Kitchen Bar, dates from 1565 and features the insignia of the Fettered White Swan. Sadly destroyed by fire in 1735, this important staging post on the London-Chester-Holyhead route was rebuilt and the Georgian facade added in 1789. The Swan is still a very popular stopping-off point.

If you find yourselves on the main A49 at Cotebrook, near Tarporley, do make time to stop off at the **ALVANLEY ARMS**. This charming red sandstone building is run by Doreen and Joe White and their three children Stuart, Sally and Chris, who have gained the pub a very well deserved reputation for a warm welcome and really good food.

The building dates back to the mid 17th century and it is particularly attractive in Summer with a profusion of creepers and hanging baskets. Inside it is no less impressive with low ceilings and a log fire in winter. Here you will find everything from a quick sandwich to a full meal, all freshly prepared, and as the menu and daily specials would fill a page of this book, you can be sure of finding something to suit you. The beer here is very good too, and if you are not familiar with Robinson's Ales we can say that they are excellent. A pub not to miss. One final point to note is that they have two lovely en suite rooms available if you want to break you journey.

Alvanley Arms, Forest Road, Cotebrook, Tarporley Tel: 01829 760200

The western side of Cheshire approaching Wales begins to have the feel of border country, where ancient tribal feuds and wars between Saxon and Celt have their memory in the great castles of the Warlords of the Marches, which were designed to defend disputed territory. Positioned on a craggy cliff towering over the Cheshire Plain, **BEESTON CASTLE** just south of Tarporley is a major landmark. It is reputedly the site of some buried treasure left there by King Richard II, although no gold or jewels have ever been discovered. The castle's fascinating history spans 2,500 years and the present fortress goes back to 1220, when it was built by Earl Randle, Seventh Earl of Chester, as protection against the army of the Welsh Prince, Llewellyn the Great. Now in the care of English Heritage, it is open to the public and its hilltop location provides the most spectacular views of the surrounding countryside.

PECKFORTON CASTLE, visible from Beeston, has a very different history, its purposes being far from military. It is a grand Victorian mansion, occupying a three and a half acre hilltop site. It was built between 1844 and 1851 in exact Norman style to the designs of the architect Anthony Salvin, for Lord Tollemarch, Member of Parliament

Beeston Castle Gatehouse

for Cheshire between 1841 and 1872.

Described by the Victorian architect Sir George Gilbert Scott as 'the largest and most carefully and learnedly executed Gothic mansion of the present', Peckforton Castle with its 60 foot high towers is a fantasy in stone. It has been superbly restored and is now open to the public with guided tours, refreshments and a speciality shop.

CHOLMONDLEY CASTLE, is a beautiful 19th century castle. The castle is not open to the public, but the grounds are, and visitors can enjoy superb ornamental gardens, a lakeside area, a home farm with rare breed animals and an ancient private chapel. The grounds are open on Sunday afternoons in the summer months and refreshments are available.

The A41 leads from Whitworth to Chester and it is worth deviating from the main road every so often in order to explore the various little villages in this attractive corner of West Cheshire.

MALPAS is one of the most delightful old villages in Cheshire, though its Norman French name implies that it once lay in difficult border terrain - 'mal passage'. There was once a castle in the town, the seat of one of the Norman barons, the site of which can be seen behind the red sandstone church as a grassy green mound. There is an ancient village cross on steps, and some charming black and white cottages as well as elegant Georgian houses. In the 18th century, the village belonged to the Cholmondeleys, who built the town's almshouses.

STRETTON, close to Tilston, is where you will discover **STRETTON MILL**, a beautiful little water mill that has been carefully restored and is now open to the public. The wooden mill machinery dates back to the 18th century and is the oldest in Cheshire. Visitors can enjoy guided tours of the mill where they will be given demonstrations of how grain is ground, and in the nearby stable block, fascinating displays and models reveal the mill's history and workings. The mill is open Tuesdays to Sundays from 2pm till 6pm, from 1st March to 31st October. There is a shop and picnic area, and group visits are most welcome if booked in advance.

Stretton Mill

BURWARDSLEY. Lying east of the A41, **THE CHESHIRE CANDLE WORKSHOPS** in Burwardsley is easy to find and provides a very enjoyable and interesting day out for both adults and youngsters alike.

The owner of this thriving craft centre is Mr.James, and he has succeeded in creating a flourishing business of no small means.

The buildings have been on the site since 1830 and are situated right in the heart of the Cheshire countryside in a setting surrounded by medieval castles. The popularity of the place will be evident by our telling you that during the last year, over 2000 coach parties visited the premises. A visit here is a unique experience steeped in history, and proves to be exciting for all the family. If the children's attention should stray a little while Mum and Dad are watching the candles being made, there is a large play area for them to amuse themselves in.

Jacqueline is responsible for making the candles for special occasions to the client's specification. We thought that this was a super idea for personal presents, birthdays, anniversaries and weddings.

As well as the art of Candlemaking, there is also a Glass Studio. Rod Beckhurst runs this craft shop, and he has been making glass ornaments of every description for the past 37 years. Like Jacqueline, Rod will also happily accept private commisions for special gifts, and when you are buying a gift for someone special, it is always rather a nice touch actually to watch the article being made.

Exquisitely made jewellery can also be purchased, and although we were unable to meet Beverley Edwards who makes it, we were delighted with what we saw set out on her stall.

Cheshire Workshops, Burwardsley, Near Chester. 01829 70401

THE FARNDON ARMS INN and **RESTAURANT** is a pleasant 16th century coaching inn on the old London to Anglesey route, indeed, just a short distance down the village High Street is one of the country's oldest Roman bridges which crosses the River Dee into Wales. It is run by the Bouchier Family who have been in the hospitality trade for 35 years. The hotel is set in the village of Farndon which is on the outskirts of Chester and close to the market town of Wrexham. It is open every day and freshly prepared meals are served in the bar area or in the superb restaurant on the first floor at lunchtimes and evenings: a traditional lunch is available on Sunday. The comfortable en-suite bedrooms have colour TV and tea and coffee making facilities. This is a wonderful location for sightseeing or enjoying a relaxing holiday. Children are welcome. ETB 3 Crowns.

The Farndon Arms, High Street, Farndon, Cheshire. Tel/fax: 01829 270570

CHESTER. The ancient Walled City of Chester lies on the border with North Wales and has been welcoming visitors since Roman times. This is a city with a rich and colourful heritage and a wealth of historic buildings and great treasures from the past.

This is where mighty Roman armies built the Fortress Deva and surrounded it with the famous **CITY WALLS** to defend it against attacks by ferocious Welsh tribes. Today, thousands of visitors to Chester walk the two-mile circuit of the walls, taking in the splendid views of the city's illustrious past which is etched in the architecture of each building.

Your tour of the walls will take you past the largest **ROMAN AMPHITHEATRE** ever uncovered in Britain, the site of extravagant festivals watched by 7,000 spectators and a training ground for Roman legionaries.

Another beautiful sight is the city's **CATHEDRAL** which celebrated 900 years of history in 1992 with various events including a production of the Chester Cycle of Mystery Plays.

Within the city walls there are plentiful treasures to discover. The unique world famous two-tiered galleries of shops known as **THE ROWS**, line both sides of the main street and date from the Middle Ages. Here you will find a wide range of high class shops, restaurants and cafés, all inviting exploration.

Situated in the Grosvenor Precinct, close to the Pepper Street escalator, is **THE GALLERY**, a charming coffee shop and tea room.

Although sited in the centre of the city, surrounded by busy shops,

The Rows, Chester

entering The Gallery is like entering another world. This pretty tea room, with its large bow fronted window, is a step back in time to a delightful olde worlde cottage setting.

The British characteristic of drinking tea is one that is recognised all over the world and the custom of taking afternoon tea is probably one of the country's best known culinary traditions.

This tradition is faithfully carried out in The Gallery which has a fine selection of leaf and blended teas to taste. If tea is not your usual pick-me-up, there is also a delicious range of freshly ground coffees from which to choose.

This delightful tea room is open all day, everyday, and also serves a wide range of light meals and snacks not forgetting a mouth-watering array of cakes, biscuits and pastries. Being so close to the shops, this is an ideal place to stop and refresh yourself whilst out and about in the city.

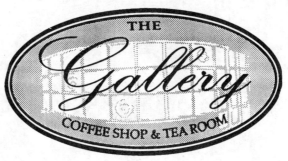

The Gallery, 24 Paddock Row, Grosvenor Precinct, Chester
Tel: 01244 347202

The beautifully ornate **EASTGATE CLOCK** has been watching over Chester since 1897 and apart from Big Ben in London, is probably the most photographed timepiece in the world.

If your own timing is right, you might be lucky enough to witness the **TOWN CRIER** giving a resounding message to everyone within earshot! If your ears can stand it, you can also join the city's resident loudspeaker for a leisurely stroll through the streets.

There is much to see and do in Chester and an ideal way to make the most of your visit is to join one of the many sightseeing tours given by a Blue Badge guide, which depart daily from the Tourist Information Centre, the Town Hall (even on Christmas Day!) and regularly from **CHESTER VISITOR CENTRE** which can be found opposite the Amphitheatre.

During summer months you can witness Caius Julius Quartus, a **ROMAN LEGIONARY** in shining armour escorting a Wall Patrol around the Fortress of Deva and recreating the life and times of a front-line defender of the great Roman empire.

Gamul House, on Lower Bridge Street, Chester, is a beautifully restored fine Jacobean Hall dating from 1620 when it was thought to have been built for Sir Francis Gamul, a wealthy city merchant and mayor of Chester. During the Civil War siege of the city in 1645 King Charles I, as a guest of Sir Francis, is believed to have stayed here. The building has had a chequered career over the years and has been used for storage, as an organ-builder's workshop and as an architect's studio. Following extensive restoration, which uncovered some fine medieval decorated floor times that are now mounted as a permanent display in the hall, the building has found further use as the home of **BENSON"S**. Owned and run by Chris and Anita Murphy, this restaurant and bistro is a real gastronomic delight serving excellent, freshly prepared food and fine wines in a wonderful, historic setting.

Benson's, 52 Lower Bridge Street, Chester Tel: 01244 319811

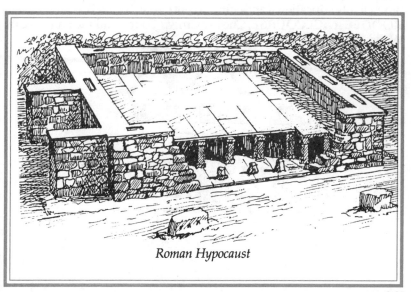

Roman Hypocaust

After the sun has set, if your nerves can stand it, you can join in the **GHOSTHUNTER TRAIL**, a night-time journey around the eerie haunts of Chester, exploring its mysterious and murky past and revisiting scenes of macabre events and spine-chilling happenings!

Among the many places worth visiting is **THE GROSVENOR MUSEUM** which houses exhibitions chronicling the Roman occupation of Chester, as well as outstanding collections of paintings and silver. You can discover more about the city's fascinating past through exciting audio-visual shows at **CHESTER HERITAGE CENTRE**, while for a taste of nostalgia, the **TOY MUSEUM** in Lower Bridge Street is a veritable treasurehouse of antique playthings from every age, including the largest collection of Lesney vehicles in the world.

After visiting **CHESTER CASTLE** and the **MILITARY MUSEUM**, with stirring displays of uniforms, weapons, medals and memorabilia associated with the famous local regiment, why not quench your thirst at **THE GOLDEN EAGLE** pub, just a short walk away in Castle Street in the medieval portion of this ancient city.

An impressive, symmetrical building, delighfully decorated during the summer months with an abundance of window boxes and hanging baskets, the inn has been offering hospitality to travellers for many, many years.

Today's tourist can be sure of a warm welcome and a relaxing rest in these peaceful surroundings. The bar is stocked with a wide selection of hand pulled ales and there is a delicious menu of home cooked bar snacks, along with daily specials, all freshly prepared and imaginatively served.

Open all day, every day the pub is also handy for **ST MARY"S CHURCH**, a beautifully restored 15th century place of worship that is now a lively educational and cultural centre, the **RIVER DEE**, the ancient **ROODEE RACECOURSE**, Chester Crown Courts and the famous City Walls.

Golden Eagle, 18 Castle Street, Chester Tel: 01244 325523

The River Dee

As you wander through the city streets, you will soon see why Chester is renowned for its shopping, with many shops retaining the magnificent architecture and elegance of a bygone era. However, there are more than just familiar High Street names here; Chester also has a great number of specialist and antique shops to appeal to the habitual browser looking for something a little different.

On Lower Bridge Street, Chester, **LABELS FOR LESS** have their showroom where a new concept is offered in affordable designer womens' wear and accessories; it's ideal place for the ladies to search for designer labels at substantially reduced prices, often 50 -75% of their original retail price. The policy of Labels for Less is to offer traditional service based on personal attention, providing quality and excellent value for money. Their special selection could provide that special outfit for the wedding day, a dinner dance or perhaps a day at the races. Whether your need is for professional, business or 'play clothes', Labels for Less have a special matching service where colour, sizing and lifestyle are entered into a client bank and an ideal ensemble can be sourced to meet your identified requirements. There is a   professional alteration team to look after personalised fittings.

Labels for Less, 62, Lower Bridge Street, Chester.   Tel: 01244 348818

Just off Bridge Street, alongside Liberty's shop, is Commonhall Street, called after the first Commonhall, a place of public assembly in Chester. In medieval times Friars took over the area and the Commonhall became a hospital and some time during the eighteenth century a row of warehouses was built nearby. Nothing of the ancient Commonhall remains today, but one of the old warehouses, restored and retaining its loading doors on the third floor, now houses **THE ARC**, a shop-cum-gallery devoted to the best of contemporary British Crafts.

The Arc stocks a wide range of ceramics, with a good representation of contemporary glass, wood, silks and woven textiles (including scarves, rugs and ties) and one-off affordable jewellery. Hand made crafts are a speciality and the whole stock is selected with an eye to good, unusual presents.

During the Summer an Exhibition programme focuses on one or two craftsmen of special merit or interest each month and occasional Exhibitions are held at other times of the year. It is also possible to commission work or order from certain well established makers. A celebration of British crafts that is well worth a visit.

The Arc, 4 Commonhall Street, off Bridge Street, Chester Tel: 01244 348379

As with its shops, Chester offers a cosmopolitan choice of food, ranging from traditional half-timbered English inns, to Cantonese, French and Cajun restaurants and chic wine bars, all of which offer cuisine of the highest standard. For a real taste of Chester, look out for Cheshire Cheese and fresh Dee salmon.

Situated in Lower Bridge Street, is **PIERRE VICTOIRE**. Part of a national franchise, the first Pierre Victoire restaurant was opened in Edinburgh and the outlets have established a good reputation for high quality, imaginative French food with a matching informal, continental atmosphere at a price that is just right.

The restaurant is staffed by a team of young and enthusiastic people which adds to the bustling, yet relaxed, air of the establishment.

The rustic style furnishings and continental pictures and decorations could easily belong in any number of cafés and restaurants the length and breadth of France.

The food is excellent, all cooked to order, and there are special three course, set price lunches and an à la carte menu for the evening. As you might imagine, wine is taken seriously but the emphasis is on enjoyment and the list is well worth reading. Naturally, this is a real find, but its success is no secret so booking is necessary at the popular times.

Pierre Victoire, 17/19 Lower Bridge Street, Chester Tel: 01224 310425

On the heart of the medieval alleyways and lanes of Chester, in Rufus Court, is the delightful and charming **HATTIES**. Run by Jan Asbridge, this olde worlde tea shop, in an unhurried and secluded setting, is surrounded by speciality shops with interesting and unusual window displays. An ideal place to stop and meet friends the tea shop has a friendly and cosy atmosphere. Tradition is followed in a reassuring manner with starched white table cloths and bowls of sugar-cubes complete with tongs.

Whether you sit outside at one of the courtyard tables or in the peaceful and relaxing shop itself you will be offered the same generous servings of tasty cakes, chocolate and coffee gâteaux are the most popular, together with high quality speciality teas. Also on the menu to tempt are succulent home-made scones, soups such as carrot and coriander all based on the freshest of the daily market's produce, and an interesting choice of daily freshly prepared light meals. The tea shop is open all day Monday to Saturday and occasionally Sunday, but check first. This lovely 'hidden place' is a real must for those out and about discovering all that the city has to offer, but take care, it would be too easy to linger so long that you run out of time!

Hatties, 5 Rufus Court, off Northgate, Chester Tel: 01244 345173

The **GARDEN HOUSE RESTAURANT** is situated close to the city walls in the peaceful and relaxed surroundings of, the originally medieval, Rufus Court. This secluded backwater lies just off one of the major streets in the city but, on entering the courtyard, all the bustle is left well and truly behind. Rufus Court is home to several speciality shops and Garden House is well suited to its surroundings. The building was originally the Arch Deacon's residence and dates back to the early 1800s. Inside the restaurant the atmosphere is one of excellence and grace in a charming and elegant Georgian setting.

Open Monday to Saturday for both lunch and dinner this intimate restaurant is an ideal place to come to for that special occasion. Small parties and individual functions can easily be catered for in the Garden House's usual professional manner. The menu is international and features gourmet dishes based on fish, meat and game. With a host of special dishes at the weekend there is sure to be something to tempt everyone. An extensive wine list compliments the menu. A popular and well recommended restaurant, it is essential to book your table to avoid disappointment.

Garden House Restaurant, 1 Rufus Court, off Northgate Street, Chester
Tel: 01244 320004

Ideally situated in the heart of the city of Chester, **HOTEL ROMANO** is an excellent base from which to discover the medieval city and the delights of the picturesque River Dee.

Hotel Romano

First opened as a hotel in 1981, this fine Georgian building is one of the more imposing buildings on Lower Bridge Street. The family run estabishment offers twenty nine ensuite bedrooms, all decorated and furnished to a high standard and including satellite television, and residents carparking to the rear of the building. To add extra romance to your stay, some of the rooms have four poster beds.

The hotel has two restaurants on the premises both serving traditional Italian cuisine in charming surroundings. The a la Carte Resaurant offers an excellent choice from home-made pasta and succulent steaks to fresh fish and imaginative vegetarian options, all in a candlelit, elegant dining room. If you prefer something more informal, Dino's, also part of the hotel, offers freshly cooked pizzas and pasta all made with true Italian flair in a dining room overflowing with continental atmosphere. The Hotel Romano is a taste of authentic Italy in the midst of one of England's oldest cities.

Hotel Romano, 51 Lower Bridge Street, Chester Tel: 01244 320841

Despite its long and varied history, Chester is by no means left behind in the Dark Ages, for in addition to its rich heritage and many ancient features, it also provides many modern attractions, including multi-screen cinemas, theatre and cabaret, plus concerts, ten-pin bowling and a leisure centre for the sporting enthusiast.

Of course, no visit to Chester would be complete without a trip to **CHESTER ZOO**. Lying outside the city and signposted off the A41 at Upton, this is Britain's largest garden zoo, set in 110 acres of landscaped grounds. Open all year round, except Christmas Day, this is definitely the place to come for a fun family day out. The mono-rail system gives visitors an exciting ride across the zoo and an alternative view of the residents and to make life even easier, you can hire wheelchairs, pushchairs and child reins should you wish.

Rhino at Chester Zoo

CHAPTER NINE

Cheshire Peaks and Plains

Marton Church

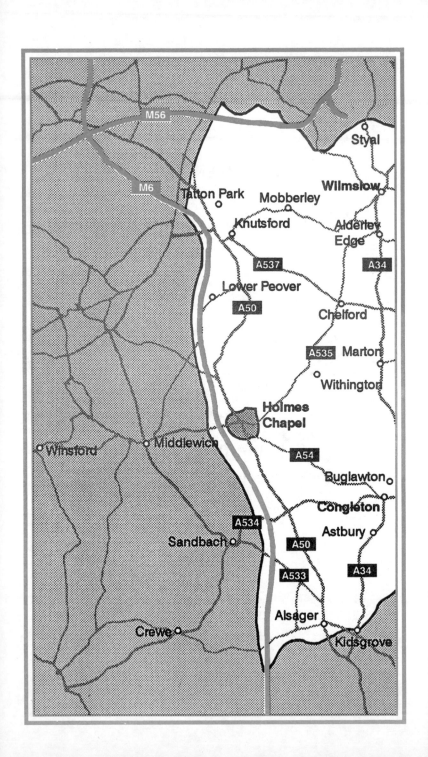

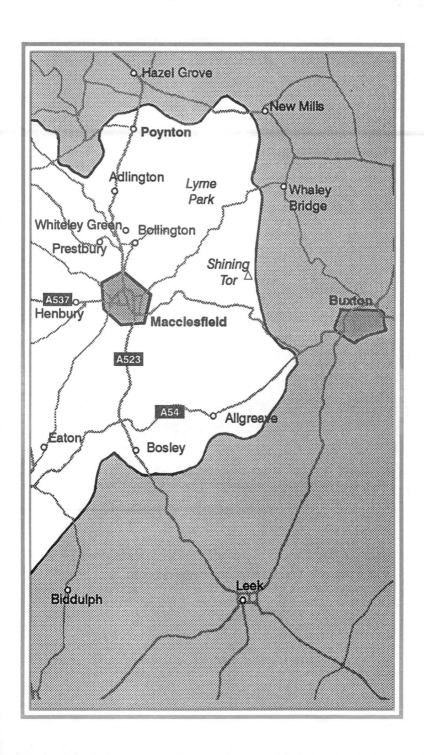

Mow Cop

CHAPTER NINE

Cheshire Peaks and Plains

East Cheshire is often referred to as 'Cheshire Peaks and Plains' to indicate the contrast between the high hills to the east and the gently undulating pastures and woods on the edge of the Cheshire Plain to the west.

The contrast is sudden. Within half a mile you can find yourself travelling out of lowland Cheshire into some of the highest and wildest countryside of the Peak District - acres of lonely moorland and gritstone crags through which steep valleys and moorland streams wind their way. On the summits of the bare and empty uplands you can enjoy a sense of grandeur and wide open space almost without equal in England.

This is part of Cheshire which has a magic of its own, especially for the rambler. You can cross an expanse of open moorland to drop suddenly down quiet hillsides into intimate valleys, or climb steep ridges and summits from where you can enjoy breathtaking views back across lowland Cheshire and across to the Shropshire hills. It was here, in the deeply cut valleys on the edge of the Peak, in towns like Bollington and Macclesfield, that the early textile mills, powered by fast flowing moorland streams and serviced by the new Macclesfield Canal, heralded a new industrial world. You'll find villages of weavers' cottages and industrial terraces close to the mills they served.

CONGLETON, south of Macclesfield is an historic town, known locally as 'the Bear Town.' It is thought to have its origins in Neolithic times and Stone Age people probably built the chambered tomb known as **THE BRIDESTONES**, the remains of which can be seen on the hill road to Leek.

There is a story that when the town bear died, the Elizabethan townsfolk lent 16 shillings to the Bear Warden for the purchase of a new one. The money had originally been collected to buy a town bible, hence the ditty: "Congleton rare, Congleton rare, sold the bible to buy a bear." Congleton was in fact one of the last towns in England to end the cruel practice of bear baiting.

Bear baiting apart, Congleton has a fascinating history. It was once an important medieval market town. It is also one of the few towns in Cheshire to keep its original medieval street pattern.

The oldest building is the **THE LION AND SWAN HOTEL.** This 16th century coaching inn, on the old Manchester to London route, has been offering travellers excellent accommodation and refreshment for centuries. Fully restored to its former Tudor glory, the Lion and Swan has plenty of exposed, dark oak beams and elaborately carved fireplaces as well as the oldest window in the town, dating from 1596. The intimate and sophisticated Candlesticks Restaurant has exciting á la carte and table d'hôte menus and an extensive wine list. There is a choice of two relaxing bars in which to enjoy a pre-dinner drink and all the twenty one bedrooms are sumptuously decorated. An ideal place to stay on business or for pleasure.

Lion and Swan Hotel, Swan Bank, Congleton Tel: 01260 273115

There is also an impressive Venetian Gothic style **TOWN HALL** built in 1866, which contains some interesting exhibits including a bridle for nagging wives that could be fastened to a wall in the market place!

Congleton Town Hall

The **BULL'S HEAD HOTEL**, in the centre of this delightful market town, is probably one of the oldest licensed premises in Congleton. Dating back to the mid 17th century, this former coaching inn has been in the Cropper family for the past 36 years and their experience and knowledge is very apparent in the level of service and facilities they offer their guests. A traditional hotel in many ways, all guests receive a warm welcome and this is a true 'home from home'. All the ten en-suite bedrooms are tastefully decorated and comfortably furnished and incorporate many of the conveniences of large hotels. Dining in the Tyrolean styled restaurant is a pleasant and relaxing experience. Decorated and furnished in pine, with many of the tables in their own booths, you can expect delicious, expertly cooked wholesome English roasts and grills that are sure to please. The hotel's watchwords, 'Your service is our pleasure', are taken seriously by all the staff and you can be sure of a very happy time here.

The Bull's Head Hotel, Mill Street, Congleton Tel: 01260 273388/275172

Hidden away in Little Street, in one of the town's oldest parts, is the wonderful **LITTLE'S WINE BISTRO.** Parts of the attractive old timber frame building date from the late 15th century; many old beams remain adding to the character of the place.

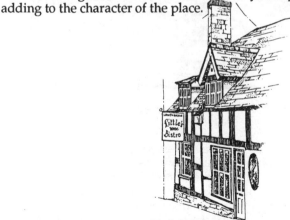

Little's Wine Bistro

The Bistro is run by Jo and Mandy (Mother & Daughter), Jo having been involved in the licensing and catering trade for 25 years and Mandy having been born into it! Jo is still involved with the cooking, along with her Chef Mike Piper while Mandy looks after 'front of house'. The ground floor has a welcoming log fire and exposed brickwork and further intimate dining extends to the first floor. The food is good quality and typically there's lots of variety with light meals, blackboard specials and table d'hôte menus. Closed Sunday & Monday.

Little's Bistro, Little Street, Congleton, Cheshire. Tel: 01260 273251

Pay a visit, too, to **CONGLETON PARK**, venue for the famous Congleton Carnival and renowned for its floral plaques.

Congleton developed as an important textile town in the 18th century with many of the mills involved in silk manufacture, cotton spinning and ribbon weaving. You can still see part of Congleton's oldest silk mill at Mill Green near the River Dane.

EATON is a neat little village close to Congleton, and set back from the A536 across the colourful little green is **THE PLOUGH INN.** Clive and Christine Winkle, the owners, will welcome you to this half-timbered freehouse originally built as a coaching inn during the 17th century. The elegant, traditional furnishings, oak beams and blazing log fires in winter, reflect the warmth and friendly atmosphere of its peaceful, rural setting.

The Plough Inn

The heart of The Plough is the kitchen, where the owners and their staff work hard to make your meal both tasty and memorable with intriguing combinations of flavour and texture to satisfy the most discerning palate. There is a comfortable bar where residents and guests can choose from an inspiring selection of fine beers and wines. The Plough is open seven days a week for lunch and dinner, including a traditional carvery all day Sunday. The converted stable block has been transformed into eight very individual bedrooms, each with a delightful character named and decorated in the style of famous Royal Doulton pottery ranges. The carefully co-ordinated colour schemes and furnishings are truly impressive. All rooms have spacious private bathrooms complete with every modern facility, generous wardrobes, colour TV, direct-line telephone, hair dryer, garment press and hospitality tray to ensure your stay is comfortable and relaxing. Impressive in every way. ETB Three Crowns Highly Commended.

The Plough at Eaton, Macclesfield Road, Eaton, Nr. Congleton, Cheshire.
Tel: 01260 280207 Fax: 01260 298377

BUGLAWTON. The magnificent **CHURCH HOUSE INN** stands back off the main A54 at Buglawton, just a mile outside Congleton in the direction of Macclesfield. At first glance you could easily mistake this for an 18th or 19th century property, in fact, the inn was built in 1941 on spare land near to St John's Church. Impressive both outside and inside; there are plenty of hanging baskets and window boxes and the grassed area at the front of the building is laid out with tables and chairs as well as the odd piece of farm machinery from a bygone age. Step inside and stroll up to the long bar where you can order a pint of excellent well kept ale such as Robinson's Best Bitter or Frederick's Premium. Open all day Sunday, there is also a mouth-watering menu of delicious home-cooked dishes from which to choose. Run by Lynn and Steve Frost, this is a super place where everyone will enjoy themselves. Families are made welcome.

Church House Inn, Buglawton, Congleton Tel: 01260 272466

SWETTENHAM. **THE SWETTENHAM ARMS**, in the quiet of the Dane Valley, is completely hidden for the road tucked away behind the parish church in Swettenham village. Once a nunnery and thought to be as old as the church, parts of the building date back to the 13th century. For many years, the Swettenham Arms has been providing the traveller with food, drink and a bed for the night. In days gone by this was pretty rudimentary, those days are over for now the Arms offers the very best in hospitality that larger places would find hard to equal. Food is served everyday at lunchtime and in the evening and it is advisable to book to avoid disappointment.

The Swettenham Arms, Swettenham Village, Congleton Tel: 01477 571284

ASTBURY is a small village just south of Congleton. Its redbrick and black and white cottages grouped round the village green are quite a contrast from the grey-brown villages of the Peak.

In Spring the green sports a thick carpet of daffodils. The splendid recessed spire of **ST MARY'S CHURCH**, that dominates the village, is considered one of the most striking in Cheshire. As you approach the church, you see that the spire is in actual fact detached from the nave. Though the church dates from pre-Norman times, the present building was erected between the 13th and 15th centuries and the spire was only added towards the end of construction. Beautiful timber work inside the building has made the church justifiably famous. A richly carved ceiling complements the intricate tracery on the rood screen and the lovely Jacobean font cover.

The **EGERTON ARMS HOTEL** is situated in the picturesque Cheshire village of Astbury adjacent to St Mary's Church. Although the hotel is only a couple of hundred yards off the main A34 this is quiet and peaceful spot.

Named after the local Lord of the Manor, Lord Egerton, the building dates back to the 14th century and it still retains the air of an old English inn. A friendly pub for friendly people, the Egerton Arms is run by Grace and Allen Smith who, though they only arrived here in the summer of 1995, have really made their mark. Keeping traditional licensing hours on Sunday, and open 11am to 11pm from Monday to Saturday, the Egerton Arms has a stylish lounge bar with a roaring log fire to greet you and the intimate restaurant, with candlelit tables, that can seat up to 50. A popular place for dining, the inn's reputation for excellent cuisine has spread far and wide in the area and it is advisable to book a table at the weekends so as not to be disappointed. Similarly, the cask conditioned ales and beers are equally excellent. The Egerton Arms has the added advantage of having six guest bedrooms, all of which will be en-suite by

1997. Children are not forgotten either and there is a wonderful outdoor play area where they will be safe.

The Egerton Arms Hotel, Astbury Village, Congleton Tel: 01260 273946

While in the picturesque village of Astbury it is well worth calling in at **ASTBURY MEADOW GARDEN CENTRE**, one of four 'Garden Centres of Cheshire', which can be found on Newcastle Road. Situated in the heart of beautiful Cheshire countryside, great care has been taken in the design and layout of the Centre which is set around the original shippons of a dairy farm and offers visitors a wealth of indoor and outdoor plants to choose from throughout the year. There is a wide choice of competitively priced garden and patio furniture, plus gardening equipment and tools, and for the browser there is a comprehensive gift and bookshop. On fine days you can relax beside one of the natural ponds and if you feel like some refreshment, the coffee shop serves a large selection of tasty homemade snacks.

Astbury Meadow Garden Centre, Newcastle Road, Astbury
Tel: 01206 276466

LITTLE MORETON HALL lies approximately three miles south of Astbury, just off the A34 and is undoubtedly one of the finest black and white timbered and moated Manor Houses in England.

Ralph Morton began its construction in 1480 and the fabric of this magnificent house has changed little since the 16th century. Huge carved overhanging gables and distorted panels create a kaleidoscope of black and white patterns. A richly panelled Great Hall, parlour and chapel show off superb Elizabethan plaster and wood work. There is also a beautifully reconstructed Elizabethan knot garden with clipped box hedges and a period herb garden.

It is only a short drive from here to the Staffordshire border and the National Trust property of **MOW COP**, a mock castle ruin. The location, on a hill 1100 feet above sea level, marks the beginning of the Staffordshire Way footpath. On a clear day the views are fantastic, you can see to Alderley Edge and beyond to Manchester to the north, north-east to the Peak District, south to Cannock Chase and Shropshire and west to Wales and the Berwyn Mountains.

For a day trip with a difference, pay a visit to the Steamer Pier at Damhead which lies to the east and just over the border in Staffordshire. A steamboat makes regular daily tours of **RUDYARD LAKE**, a picturesque lake which was artificially created in 1797 to feed both the Caldon and the Trent & Mersey canals. Known as the Windermere of the Midlands, it is thought that the parents of Rudyard Kipling met on a picnic outing here and that is why they later gave their son his unusual Christian name.

HOLMES CHAPEL is a small town which has an interesting village street and a church that dates from the 15th century.

A popular stopping off point, nestling in the midst of the rolling Cheshire countryside between Knutsford and Holmes Chapel, is **THE COTTAGE RESTAURANT AND LODGE**. Although its situation is on the main A50, nothing could be further from crowds and traffic for an enjoyable and secluded visit to this area.

The Cottage Restaurant and Lodge

As the name suggests, the cottage was originally an old Cheshire cottage that has been tastefully renovated and extended to give a delightful blend of new and old. The cottage is under the personal management of the owners, Chis Lowe and Fred Fletcher, who will be pleased to welcome guests, either for simple bar snack lunch, a gourmet dinner or

Little Moreton Hall

Mow Cop

even longer stay. All food is prepared on the premises by well renowned chefs, using only the best fresh ingredients and the cottage has recently been awarded an AA Red Rosette for its food. The ambience of the candle lit dining room does full justice to the dinner, as does the conservatory to the Summer luncheon. An excellent wine list is available, catering for all tastes and pockets. For the traveller, the 12 rooms are all extremely well fitted and appointed, with certain accommodation being specially adapted for ease of use by those who need to use wheelchairs.

Cottage Restaurant and Lodge, London Road, Allostock, Knutsford.
Tel: 01565 722470

About three miles from here you will find the award-winning **JODRELL BANK SCIENCE CENTRE** and **TREE PARK**, whose two vast radio telescopes dominate the skyline creating a major Cheshire landmark. **THE LOVELL RADIO TELESCOPE** is the second largest, fully steerable telescope of its kind in the world. The same size as the dome of St. Paul's, it receives radio waves from space 24 hours a day.

Being both exciting and educational, a trip to Jodrell Bank provides hours of fascinating fun for the whole family. You can take a tour of the Universe with Sir Isaac Newton, or enjoy an in-depth look at the Solar System in the darkened Planetarium, discover what electro-magnetic waves can do, or send the Earth around the Sun in the Gravity Hollow. Outside in the 35 acre Arboretum you can follow the various trails and see numerous wonders of nature, before perhaps stopping to enjoy a picnic within these attractive wooded surroundings.

Travelling northwards the A50 to Knutsford is a delightful road, taking you through some beautiful countryside. Just off to the east is **PEOVER HALL**, a Tudor manor house dating from 1585. The stables have some remarkable plaster-work ceilings and are worth a visit.

LOWER PEOVER is really two separate villages a half a mile apart. Pronounced 'Peever' the village consists of a clutch of thatched, half-timbered cottages around a green, and another group along a cobbled lane to the south. The second group includes the church, inn and two school buildings, and a sign on the green proclaims it to be the centre of the village. The original School is now a private house and carries a plaque in latin proclaiming it was built for humble scholars and dedicated to God and the church in 1780, it also retains the bell on the roof which would ring to call the children to their lessons.

THE CHURCH OF ST OSWALD dates back to 1269 and was built using a massive timber frame with complex cross-bracing, the stone tower was added some three hundred years later. It is one of the few remaining timber-framed churches in England. The interior has a some wonderful examples of carved wood and a rather unusual medieval chest, hewn from a single oak trunk. Local legend has it that girls who wished to marry local farmers would have to lift the heavy lid with one hand to show they were strong enough to make worthy farmers wives.

The Lovell Radio Telescope, Jodrell Bank

THE BELLS OF PEOVER is probably one of the most famous pubs in the country. In parts it dates back some 700 years and in bygone days it was a small village inn called the Warren de Tabley Arms. Situated next to St Oswald's church, in the beautiful Cheshire village of Lower Peover, it does not get its present name from the church bells but from the Bell family who came to live here. It was this family that brought fame to the inn when they started to brew beer here and, such was it wonderful taste, that in 1871 George Bell was requested to go to Hillsborough Castle in Ireland to make a special beer for the birth of the Sixth Marquis of Downshire.

Today, you can still enjoy a good pint of ale, along with a delicious meal from the bar or the a la carte menu. A charming pub to which people travel from far and wide, with plenty of history attached to it, and a real credit to the owners Christine and Keith Jones.

The Bells of Peover, The Cobbles, Lower Peover, near Knutsford
Tel: 01565 722269

THE CROWN public house is also situated in this charming village on the B5081. This magnificent 17th century inn has been owned and run by Lesley and Bert Flint for over 20 years and you can be sure of a warm and friendly welcome at any time.

The Crown

Well renowned in the area for the excellent food and well kept real ales, it is popular with locals and visitors alike. Whether you just want a light snack or a three course meal, it is easy to see why The Crown is so popular when you tuck in to your choice. The dishes are delicious, well presented and reasonably priced. If good food and drink are not enough for you, the interior of the pub is decorated with a wide variety of artefacts and memorabilia that represent Lesley and Bert's lifetime collection.

The Crown, Crown Lane, Lower Peover Tel: 01565 722074

OVER PEOVER. **THE DOG INN** nestles in the heart of the Cheshire countryside, at the village of Over Peover, its 18th century beauty enhanced summer and winter by colourful hanging baskets. The inn is highly acclaimed, with recommendations from the AA, RAC, English Tourist Board, Michelin, Egon Ronay and Camra. It has, most recently been Highly Commended as 'Free House of the Year 1995'. Quite an array of awards and, not surprisingly, the legendary cuisine of The Dog Inn draws food lovers from far and wide. The inn is also conveniently situated for the major northwest motorways and, with three en-suite bedrooms providing comfort and tranquility, it is also a popular place to stay.

The Dog Inn, Well Bank Lane, Over Peover Tel: 01625 861421

KNUTSFORD, an attractive market town, lies on the edge of gentle lowland countryside off the A556. Dating from medieval times it retains a certain quaintness and olde worlde charm, its narrow streets lined with a variety of fine shops, pubs, restaurants, and splendid Georgian houses.

THE RED COW, situated in the heart of historic Knutsford, is an inn of outstanding class and quality that has been recently refurbished. Dating back to the late 18th century, this former coaching inn retains many of its original features including the exposed brickwork. The splendid wooden floor and the pillars all add together to create a wonderful atmosphere. The traditional pub menu also includes more adventurous dishes as does the excellent daily special board. With a fine range of top quality real ales and a good wine list this is a fine place to eat and drink. Very much an inn for all ages, visitors are welcomed along with the regular locals.

The Red Cow, Knutsford Tel: 01565 633408

One of the best known of the restaurants is **LA BELLE EPOQUE** which offers outstanding French cuisine. The charming building in which it is housed has an Art Nouveau interior and is the work of Richard Harding Watt who admired the Mediterranean architecture which he saw in his travels. The building was originally named the King's Coffee House, and was an idealistic social endeavour to ween the working man away from the pub by providing concerts, debates and even 'a warm bath at any hour' for sixpence. A walk along Moorside will reveal more Watt architecture together with recent interpretations of Watt's style.

JANE'S COFFEE SHOP, on King Street, is a well established and popular business in the heart of historic Knutsford. Owned and run by Vivien Hammond, this is a warm and friendly place with an old fashioned feel that serves a range of delicious home-made snacks and light meals. The cakes are mouth-watering and absolutely wicked!

Jane's Coffee Shop, 117A King Street, Knutsford Tel: 01565 651898

KNUTSFORD WINE BAR, on the town's main shopping street, is a magnificent restaurant housed in a fine old building dating back to the 18th century. In its time this building has been many things including a fire station and a car show room but since early 1992 it has been a wine bar and restaurant.

Each day, except Sunday, Knutsford Wine Bar opens at 12.00pm for lunch/snacks and welcomes people just for coffee or drinks. Bucks Fizz Breakfast is served on Sunday mornings from 11.00am and proves to be extremely popular. Closing mid afternoon, it opens again in the evening. The menu is very imaginative and interesting using a wealth of ingredients from home and abroad. All the dishes are freshly prepared and delightfully garnished. The interior decor of the wine bar mirrors the classy, unpretentious exterior. On two levels with exposed brick walls, wooden floors and high ceilings there is a wonderful spindled balustrade leading upstairs. With stylish, live music two nights a week this is a wonderful place for lunch, an intimate dinner, or special party celebrations.

Knutsford Wine Bar, 41A King Street, Knutsford Tel: 01565 750459

THE WHITE LION in Knutsford dates from the early 18th century when Kings Street was the main coaching route through the town. The character and style of this inn with its roaring log fires, low beams, old prints and memorabilia , is such that you could imagine yourself back in that bygone era. The furnishings and decor are outstanding although they have been kept in character with the inn. Home made food is available every day at lunchtime when you can 'let go' on a Giant Yorkshire Pudding with delicious fillings or a selection of many satisfying down-to-earth lunches or daily specials. With a Beer Festival held on the premises twice a year you can rely on a good regular selection of ales. Numerous attractions and offers during the year. Open all day throughout the week.

The White Lion, 94 King Street, Knutsford, Cheshire. Tel: 01565 632018

Housed in one of the charming black and white buildings, on the main shopping street in Knutsford, is **CROMWELLS**. This exclusive chocolate shop, with is mouth-watering window display and large window awning, could easily have been lifted straight from the elegant shopping streets of Paris or Brussels. Inside, the air conditioned shop is dedicated to the enjoyment of chocolate.

Owned and run by Janet Layfield, all the sweet delicacies are specially prepared, by hand, from natural ingredients. Whether you like milk, plain or white chocolate, hard or soft centres, truffles, cream filled or fruit flavoured centres there is something to tempt everyone. These luxury items are a pleasure to give and receive for anniversary's, birthday's or at the end of a hard working day.

Cromwells, 15 King Street, Knutsford Tel: 01565 654832

Housed in one of Knutsford's oldest buildings, which dates back to the 16th century, is **THE CROOKED WALL**, so named because of the mis-shaped wall leading to its entrance.

The Crooked Wall

In the centre of the town this restaurant and coffee house, owned and run by Ian Ordish, has breathed a refreshing blast of fresh air and relax continental flair into the heart of this old market town. The intimate

King Street, Knutsford

restaurant serves a wide range of set evening meals on Friday and Saturday evenings with the menu including steaks, fish and vegetarian dishes and a ever changing list of specials that make the most of the fresh seasonal produce available from the market.

As well as serving evening meals and a hearty Sunday lunch the Crooked Wall is also open to serve morning coffee and afternoon tea with a wide selection of cakes and pastries all made on the premises by the restaurant chef. The lunchtime menu includes light snacks and mouth-watering succulent sandwiches and the a specialised list of herbal teas. With its relaxed and friendly atmosphere this is the place to stop and enjoy a leisurely cup of coffee.

The Crooked Wall, 48 King Street, Knutsford Tel: 01565 633211

THE CROSS KEYS, in the heart of Knutsford, is probably one of the oldest inns in the town though its exact age is difficult to pinpoint. It may well have been one of the 42 inns listed in the records of 1642 and it certainly appeared on a town map of 1786. Formerly a thatched inn, The Cross Keys was rebuilt in 1909 shortly after the Gaskell Memorial Tower was built next door by Richard Harding Watt. Recent conversion of the stables and coach house into 12 luxury en suite bedrooms means that the inn is once again providing a full service for travellers. Owned and personally run by Pat and John Burke, their son Andrew and his wife Rachel this is a an ideal base for business or pleasure which retains the atmosphere of an 18th century coaching inn though all the facilities are modern. The Cross Keys also has a long standing reputation for excellent food and drink. In the Cellar restaurant, guests can choose from the extensive a la carte menu of traditional, continental and vegetarian dishes, make a selection from the daily specials board or simply opt for a light snack. With a full range of fine wines from around the world there will be something to complement you meal perfectly. A superb hotel where you will be sure to enjoy your stay.

The Cross Keys, King Street, Knutsford Tel: 01565 750404

Just off bustling King Street, down one of Knutsford's many

narrow alleys, is **THE COURTYARD COFFEE HOUSE**. This old, quaint, one storey brick built cottage overlooks a charming cobbled courtyard that provides a delightful olde worlde setting in which to sit and relax. Owned and run by Mrs Watts, the coffee house offers a mouth-watering menu of delicious and original dishes. The house speciality, Welsh rarebit, made to an old recipe using brown ale and a little egg, is well worth tasting. The home made soups, based on seasonal produce, are aromatic and refreshing and include such delights as fennel and courgette, parsnip and orange and apple, mushroom and celery. With fourteen different speciality teas on offer and a wealth of home made cakes, scones and ice cream this is a superb place to stop.

Housed in the same building as the coffee house is one of the first Penny Farthing museums. For barely two decades, at the end of the 19th century, these giants flourished and these Ordinaries, as Penny Far-things were then known, adorn the walls and hang from the ceiling along with other cycling memorabilia and old photographs. The collection also includes a replica of the largest ever such cycle made, the Starley Giant, with a front wheel 7 feet in diameter! A fascinating place to visit there is also a splendid model of an American train which runs around a track high up on the walls, just below the ceiling.

The Courtyard Coffee House, Rear 92 King Street, Knutsford
Tel: 01565 653974

During the 18th century Knutsford rapidly developed into a major coaching town on the main London-Liverpool route and not surprisingly still has many former coaching inns. However, it is as the setting for Elizabeth Gaskell's novel 'Cranford' that the town is probably best known. The novel is a chronicle of the daily events and lives of the people of a small Victorian country town, written with a blend of sympathy, sharp observation and gentle humour which still delights readers today.

An interesting feature in the town is **THE HERITAGE CENTRE** in Tatton Street which opened in 1989. This is a reconstruction of a 17th century timber framed building which had been a Smithy in the 19th century.

During the restoration, the old forge and bellows were found in a remarkable state of preservation. It was The Macclesfield and Vale Royal Groundwork Trust who undertook the rebuilding, using original materials wherever possible. The wrought iron gate which leads up into the courtyard in front of the Centre was designed as part of an environmental art project and depicts dancing girls taking part in the local May Day celebrations - another popular tradition that continues today.

The festivities of Royal May Day, which are considered the most impressive of their kind in England, began in 1864 and earned their Royal prefix when the town was visited by the Prince of Wales in 1887. The celebrations consist of Maypole dancing and a large procession headed by Jack in Green and the May Queen in a horse-drawn landeau.

Minshull Street, in the heart of medieval Knutsford, is a busy, thriving thoroughfare of individual and exclusive shops and businesses. Quite fittingly, 1760, a jewellery shop full of surprises is situated here. The jewellery on offer in this delightful shop is colourful, stylish and extremely enjoyable to wear. Seventeensixty have their own work shop and many of the items for sale are made there. Pieces have also been collected from like-minded individual studios and are made using traditional as well as modern materials without compromising quality. The beautiful pieces are created with a stunning effect that will only reflect on the wearer, not on the pocket. Alongside these items is also a vivid array of dazzling hand painted silks and unusual and unique hand made greetings cards. While taking all this in, it is well worth, sitting down and enjoying a cup of coffee and one of the mouth-watering ice creams. The shop is very happy to offer advice on commission pieces and repairs to favoured items of jewellery. This interesting and highly individual shop is well worth browsing around, there is sure to be something to catch your eye.

1760, 15 Minshull Street, Knutsford Tel: 01565 653260

Fryer's Roses

FRYER'S ROSES, situated on the outskirts of Knutsford on the road to Mere, is a world renowned grower of rose trees and shrubs. Over

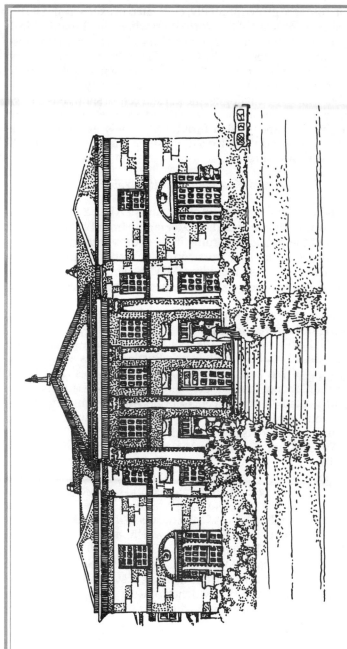

Tatton Hall

half a million roses are grown annually, cultivated in exposed and fertile Cheshire fields. In the heart of the North West where the climate is ideal; sufficiently rigorous for the development of first class, tough, hardy rose trees. Still a family business, run by Gareth Fryer, the nursery was first opened in 1912 by Gareth's grandfather and has grown over the years to now cover some 100 acres. As well as selling a vast variety of roses, from the nursery as well as by catalogue, the garden centre shop sells a large range of plants and goods including dried and artificial flowers, indoor plants, troughs, pots and garden furniture. A new extension to the existing shop, will include a coffee shop just the place to sit down and ponder on your choice of roses.

Fryer's Roses, Knutsford Tel: 01565 755455

Just outside Knutsford on the A5033 stands **TABLEY HOUSE**. The Tabley Estate was the home of the Leicester family from 1272 to 1975 and today is open to the public who come in their droves to see the many treasures it houses. There is an outstanding collection of paintings by numerous well known artists, including JMW Turner, Henry Thompson, Dobson, Lely, Reynold, Cotes and many others besides. These have been rehung in the restored rooms of the main floor and, together with a beautiful collection of Chippendale, Bullock and Gillow of Lancaster furniture, provide an awesome sight.

A visit to the renowned **TATTON PARK**, which lies just outside the centre of Knutsford, heading towards Rostherne, has always been regarded as one of the best days out in the North West and is not surprisingly the National Trust's most visited property. It is the complete historic country estate. A magnificent Georgian Mansion by Wyatt rises from the glorious gardens, widely regarded amongst England's 'Top Ten'. The opulent staterooms contrast with the stark servants' rooms and cellars, working as they did for the Victorian household of the noble Egerton family.

Tatton has a history stretching back to 8000 B.C., when man hunted deer for food and clothing. Eight hundred red and fallow deer still roam the 1,000 acres of parkland and round the two lakes. Tatton's history and variety of historic buildings provide the means to interpret the visitors' day out out as 'A Story for Every Age' which, as you go from one attraction to another, explains by means of boards, leaflets and guides, the relationship of the farm to the mansion, the development of the landscape and so forth. Tatton can be regarded, historically speaking, as a typical country estate, but the evidence of early occupation by man precedes 18th century emparkment which makes Tatton all the more fascinating and exceptional.

The original breeds of animals still live down on the **HOME FARM**, a short walk from the Mansion - working as it did in the 1930's, the farm is the heart of the estate, with its workshops and old estate office. A 'new' steam engine has recently been restored in the engine house.

Old Hall nestles in a wood in the deer park. Visitors are given a guided tour through time from the late Middle Ages up to the 1950's. Flickering light from candles reveals the ancient timber roof of the Great Hall, supported by ornate quatrefoils. Underfoot, the floor is strewn with rushes, providing a warm place for the medieval Lord of the Manor and his servants to sleep. Built around 1520, Old Hall conjures up a hauntingly real image of a journey through history.

To complete the day's enjoyment, visitors can take lunch in the restaurant. Many public events are held indoors and outside in the Park, ranging from a giant classic car show to classical concerts.

Also of interest is the Japanese Koi Carp Show and many craft fairs. The children's adventure playground is specially tailored for pre-school up to twelve year olds and children can happily amuse themselves while parents relax in the picnic area. If you would like to telephone Tatton Park for further information prior to your visit, the 24-hour information line number is 01565 750250.

Tatton Park, Knutsford, Cheshire Tel: 01565 654822

ROSTHERNE, the lovely estate village has cottages that lead up to the church, all named after shrubs and trees - apple, pear, willow, lilac and so on.

At one end of the village a group of 12 house form a square. Built by estate workers in 1909, the cottages bear the crest and initials of Lady Margaret Egerton of Tatton. Lady Margaret was one of few enlightened landowners of the time and provided a bath house and laundry with irons and free soap. Up at the church the lych-gate at the western side of the church yard has an ingenious closing mechanism which uses a heavy wooden weight and pulleys. In the steeply sloping churchyard is a huge gothic-style edifice, a memorial to one Joseph Simpson, probably a rich Manchester merchant who moved out of the rapidly expanding city during the last century.

To the north of the church is ROSTHERNE MERE. At 100 acres in area and 100 feet deep it is the largest and deepest in Cheshire. According to local legend when the church bells were being hung the largest rolled across the churchyard and into the mere, and on Easter mornings a mermaid raises and tolls the bell.

MOBBERLEY. **THE RAILWAY INN** is a lovely old pub in Mobberley run by Lynda and Tony Davies. They are a very friendly couple who made us feel welcome from the moment we arrived. The building is over 200 years old and has lots of atmosphere and charm. It is situated next to Mobberley Station and is signposted from the village. Recently renovated, the Inn has managed to keep its character by retaining its old oak beams, which we are sure could tell a story or two. Whilst Tony is in charge of the bar and cellar, Lynda uses her skills in the kitchen and provides customers with excellent bar snacks, evening meals and also children's portions. All of the food available is very reasonably priced and from what we saw, it is very attractively presented. There is a bowling green outside, and the Railway Inn is a member of the local league. There is also a fully equipped children's are where the youngster can play safely.

The Railway Inn, Station Road, Mobberley Tel: 01565 873155

THE HINTON Guest House is owned and personally run by Joyce and Donald Read and is situated on Town Lane, Mobberley, the main road between Knutsford and Alderley Edge.

The Hinton

Built during the early 1960s, this magnificent detached property

hold a lot more than it would appear at first glance; rather like Doctor Who's tardis!

This really is a wonderful and friendly place that will suite everyone and the Hinton has collected many awards and commendations from travel and tourist organisations. At the rear of the property is a wonderful conservatory that was completed in the Spring of 1995. The decoration, furnishings and facilities here are second to none and, coupled with the warm and relaxing atmosphere, you will have to go a long way to equal the Hinton. The six en suite bedrooms are outstanding; spacious but cosy and warm and with little personal extras. The dining room is very attractive and the rear garden eye-catching and well tendered.

The Hinton, Town Lane, Mobberley Tel: 01565 873484

THE FROZEN MOP is situated in Faulkners Lane, Mobberley just half a mile off the Mobberley to Wilmslow road. A real picture, the building dates back, in parts, to the 18th century though there are plenty of newer extensions. It has a splendid interior, full of character and charm, with wooden and flagstone floors, exposed brickwork and feature fireplaces to admire. Beautifully decorated and furnished, the Frozen Mop is a place for all the family and has the facilities to match. Part of the Brewers Fayre chain of pubs, you can be sure of delicious and mouth-watering food along with excellent, well kept ale. There is also plenty for the children, with a safe play area, family room and the Charlie Chalk children's menu. A smashing place to bring the family.

The Frozen Mop, Faulkners Lane, Mobberley Tel: 01565 873234

THE ROEBUCK INN is a magnificent 17th century former coaching inn standing on what was the Knutsford to Alderley Edge road before the by-pass was built. Signposted from Mobberley, this is a pub not to be missed. Owned and personally run by Lin and David Robinson, the Roebuck is full of character with oak beams, panelled walls in the Library Room and plenty of memorabilia dotted around the place. Popular for both its excellent food and well kept range of beer it is well worth making a detour off the main road to find. Food is available every lunchtime and each evening except Sundays; there is a daily specials board as well as a lovely menu of hot and cold platter dishes that are sure to whet your appetite. The bar serves five real ales include Boddingtons, Hydes Anvil and Speckled Hen. It is advisable to book a table for Saturday evening and Sunday lunchtime.

The Roebuck Inn, Mill Lane, Mobberley Tel: 01565 872757

WILMSLOW, to the east of Knutsford, is a busy, but attractive commuter town situated on the River Bollin.

La Riga

On the main thoroughfare through Wilmslow, and with ample parking close by, is **LA RIGA**, a ladies fashion boutique. This new shop is situated in a recently developed attractive parade. Though it has not been opened for long La Riga is fast establishing a reputation as a boutique offering a wide range of the latest fashions with a close watch on quality.

All the clothes, which include continental fashions as well as British made items, are attractively displayed and separates are imaginatively combined to create a range of moods. The stylish modern interior, decorated in peaceful natural tones and with carefully placed spot lights, gives the shop a calm and relaxed atmosphere. Just right when selecting an outfit for that special occasion. La Riga also stocks a range of stylish and unsual accessories which add to a unique touch to any garment. Owned and run by Marie Musa, you will be sure to find a stylish and sophisticated ensemble for any function.

La Riga, Unit 3, Springfield House, Water Lane, Wilmslow
Tel: 01625 548803

HAMBLETON'S is conveniently situated just a few minutes walk from Wilmslow's main shopping street, set back off Manchester road. Owned and personally run by Maurice Hambleton and his son Gary, this is not just a restaurant but also an excellent café and wine bar. Open all day well into the evenings, this is the place to be seen in Wilmslow and is an ideal place to stop and take a break whilst shopping. The premises used to be an old cycle shop and they have been totally refurbished to create a stylish interior that is provides a comfortable and relaxing atmosphere. On two floors there is plenty of seating and, for fine weather, sitting out on the patio makes a pleasant change. With no fixed menu, the dishes of the day are displayed on boards around the rooms. A delicious mix of English and European dishes, all freshly prepared and beautifully served there is something for everyone and it is obvious why Hambleton's is so popular.

Hambleton's, Warham Street, Wilmslow Tel: 01625 548223

Just off the A34 in the centre of Wilmslow, adjoining the car park between Hooper's and Sainsbury's, is a small memorial garden containing **ROMANY'S CARAVAN**. 'Romany' was a nationally-known journalist, author and broadcaster on BBC Radio's Children's Hour in the 1930s and 40s. An ordained Methodist minister, the Reverend George Bramwell Evens retired from his ministry to Wilmslow in 1939, but continued to broadcast every week during the early war years. 'Out with Romany' became the number one favourite in Request Week and his adventures in the country with his caravan ('vardo' in Romany language), dog 'Raq', horse 'Comma' (- never came to a full stop!) and two companions, Muriel and Doris, sustained the morale not only of children, but adults too. Very much ahead of his time, his interest in nature has had an enormous impact on people of all kinds.

Millions mourned after his early death, in 1943, and over the years his caravan has been a place of pilgrimage not only for those who heard him, and read his books, but later generations who have discovered him either from grandparents or by reading.

Recently restored by Macclesfield Borough Council, and surrounded by Romany's favourite flowers and trees, the caravan has once again become a favourite destination. Many of Romany's personal possessions are on display when the caravan is opened for viewing on the second Saturday in each month from May to September, from 12 - 3 pm. The Romany Society is being revived and can be contacted at Macclesfield Town Hall Tel: 01625 504507

Romany's Caravan, South Drive, Wilmslow Tel: 01625 504507

If you are looking for a readily accessible and centrally situated touring base from which to explore the delights of rural Cheshire, **HEATHERLEE GUEST HOUSE** on Lacey Green is ideal.

Heatherlee Guest House

Friendly host Brian Smidmore provides very comfortable accommodation in five attractively furnished en-suite guest rooms which all have tea and coffee making facilities. For the comfort of other guests smoking is only permitted in the bedrooms. Located just ten minutes drive from Manchester Airport, Brian offers his guests a complimentary courtesy car service, although for those with their own transport, there is ample parking space. In addition to a full English breakfast, Brian will provide an evening meal by arrangement, or if you prefer to eat out, the centre of Wilmslow, with its wide selection of pubs and restaurants, is only ten minutes walk away.

Heatherlea Guest House, 106 Lacey Green, Wilmslow Tel: 01625 522872

THE STANNEYLANDS HOTEL is a handsome country house set in beautiful gardens amid an unusual collection of trees and shrubs, in a tranquil rural setting. It is conveniently located for Manchester International Airport and about ten miles from the M6 and Manchester City Centre. Privately owned and personally run by the Beech family, truly experienced hoteliers, they are totally involved and dedicated to providing the highest standards in this luxurious hotel. The award winning restaurant is renowned in all aspects of the culinary art and has an outstanding menu of English and International dishes. The hotel is most elegantly furnished and the bedrooms reflect this taste with spacious, relaxing, en-suite rooms which are carefully appointed. A superb hotel awarded 5 Crown classification by ETB and 'AA" Rosette. The nearby **BELFRY HOTEL,** a modern hotel par excellence, is also owned by the Beech family.

The Stanneylands Hotel, Stanneylands Road, Wilmslow, Cheshire. Tel: 01625 525225 Fax: 01625 537282

It was just outside the town in an area of peat bog known as **LINDOW MOSS** that the perfectly preserved body of an Iron Age man - the famous 'Lindow Man' - was recovered.

From the centre of Wilmslow you can enjoy a scenic walk through **THE CARRS**, a pleasant riverside park, and follow the Bollin's meandering route the two miles or so to **STYAL COUNTRY PARK**.

Owned by The National Trust, this comprises over 250 acres of woodland and riverside walks surrounding **QUARRY BANK MILL**. The mill was built in 1784 and was one of the first generation of cotton mills. It was powered by a huge iron waterwheel fed by the River Bollin. Also within the park is the delightful STYAL VILLAGE, which was established by the mill's original owner, Samuel Greg, a philanthropist and pioneer of the factory system. He took children from the slums of Manchester to work in his mill and in return for their labour, provided them with food, clothing, housing, education and worship.

Visitors follow the history of the mill through various galleries and displays within the museum, including weaving and spinning demonstrations, and can experience for themselves what life was like for the hundred girls and boys who once lived in the Apprentice House, with guides dressed in period costume.

Styal's only public house, **THE SHIP INN**, is situated in the heart of this picturesque village. Also known as The Old Ship, the inn has been in existence for as long as anyone can remember and it was known to have been a 'watering hole', at the time of Bonnie Prince Charlie's foray into Cheshire in 1745. In past times, when a handful of ale houses dotted the agricultural villages of the area, the Ship Inn survived all competition because, it is thought, of its central location and its source of natural spring water used in making its ale. When Henry Phillips Greg, one of the famous Greg family of Styal mill, inherited the inn in 1894 from his uncle he went about transforming the village pub into a profitable business. Its future was secured.

Today the inn retains all the character and charm of an old village pub, whilst providing the amenities of a modern inn. A warm welcome given to all visitors aided by the roaring fires in winter. A popular meeting place with excellent beer and ale, outstanding food and good company.

The Ship Inn, Styal Tel: 01625 523818

The **STYAL CHOP HOUSE** lies off the main Altrincham to

Wilmslow road, in the old village of Styal. Although Mark Moss and his mother Lynda only took over the business under a year ago, their reputation for excellent, home-cooked food is spreading far and wide in the Cheshire area.

Styal Chop House

The restaurant is small, seating about 40 on two levels, and this provides a wonderful atmosphere, more like Grandma's parlour than a restaurant. The artefacts and memorabilia on the walls and shelves provide interesting talking points, apart from the delicious food that is, and there is a fine collection of old tins. Open for morning coffee, lunch, afternoon tea and dinner it is always best to book a table for the busier times. The menu, supplemented by a daily specials board, is a wealth of tasty, hearty dishes that befit an English chop house. Everything is cooked to order, but the wine list makes the wait easily bearable. Do find room for a pudding, they are all home-made again and just like the ones Mother used to make.

Styal Chop House, Altrincham Road, Styal Tel: 01625 548144

HANDFORTH is not far from Styal and here on the A34 Manchester Road out of Wilmslow, you can't fail to notice **WILMSLOW GARDEN CENTRE** on your left. This beautifully landscaped centre is the largest of the four which make up the group known as 'Garden Centres of Cheshire' and offers visitors the widest selection of plants, shrubs and garden accessories in the most relaxed surroundings.

Christmas is a season which brings it own particular attractions, with a 35 feet tall inflatable Father Christmas proving popular with younger members of the family. However another equally popular and superb feature of the Centre is the extensive pet and aquatic section which specialises in fish and pets with all the associated equipment and foodstuffs. There is even a special cage which houses several chipmunks. The shop has an enormous range of cane, patio and garden furniture, barbecues and there is also a large machinery department. A superb coffee shop/restaurant provides hot and cold food, with a homemade flavour, to round off a visit.

Wilmslow Garden Centre, Manchester Road, Wilmslow Tel: 01625 525700

After twelve years resident at the **RAILWAY HOTEL** in Handforth, Ron and Linda Cook have a well established clientele but are always happy to welcome new customers. Their relaxed and friendly approach makes for the right atmosphere where the best ales such as Robinsons Bitter, Old Tom and Hartleys Fell Runner can be peacefully enjoyed. Food is served at lunchtime which can be taken in the cosy dining room or in the bar area. The choice is varied, the servings plentiful and very reasonably priced. On Sundays there is an excellent two or three course menu (plus children's menu) which includes a selection of sweets from the blackboard. Quiz night each month.

The Railway Hotel, Station Road, Handforth, Wilmslow, Cheshire.
Tel: 01625, 523472

ALDERLEY EDGE to the south of Wilmslow takes its name from a long wooded escarpment, nearly two miles in length and rising 600 feet above sea level, culminating in sandy crags overlooking the Cheshire Plain.

Situated on the main shopping street in Alderley Edge is **No. 15 WINE BAR**. Originally a Victorian town house the owner, John Wheeldon, turned it into a wine bar 21 years ago and what a success it has been. Entering No 15 through a discreet entrance you will be surprised by the grandness and opulence of the Victorian parlour you have just entered. It really is a different world. The unhurried, relaxed service and the tables of happily chatting people make this an ideal place to come and unwind. The peaceful patio garden, accessible from the basement, is a beautiful spot in which to enjoy a glass or two of fine wine. This is the place to be seen in Alderley Edge.

The wine list is vast with a fine selection of Burgundy's, Beaujolais', sparkling wines and champagnes for that special occasion. The more familiar old world labels are perfectly complimented by the list of new world wines. The menu changes monthly and is a mouthwatering list of the very best in home made English cuisine with many Continental dishes. Along with the daily specials board, displayed behind the bar, there is something to tempt everyone.

No 15 Wine Bar is truly a hidden place, but well worth finding. For lovers of fine food and wine, looking for a sophisticated atmosphere with a difference, this is certainly the place to visit.

No 15 Wine Bar, London Road, Alderley Edge Tel: 01625 585548

CLEMENTINES restaurant, situated on the main street in Alderley Edge, was opened in 1994 by John Hough and Mark Zambelli. This experienced restaurant team, they were proprietors of the well known Randalls Restaurant in nearby Bollington before moving to Clementines, have turned the restaurant into one of the finest establishments in the area. With an attractive interior and a smashing atmosphere Clementines is open every day for lunch and for dinner from Monday to Saturday. Due to its popularity it is advisable to book at weekend evenings to avoid disappointment. Mark is the chef and the cuisine is a delightful revival of old English favourites with a different slant. All the dishes are cooked to order and prepared from the very best of local ingredients. Once you have tasted the delicious food it is easy to see why Clementines is so popular.

Clementines, 73 London Road, Alderley Edge Tel: 01625 586560

MOSS ROSE INN is tucked away behind the main shopping centre of Alderley Edge. Once you have found this inn, you will be glad. Originally a row of cottages by 1861 it had become a brewery and was known locally as the Drum and Monkey as an organ grinder and his pet used to entertain people here. Since 1990, Val and Phil Oldham have been running the inn and, though it has been refurbished many times over the years, there is still a great atmosphere. Between Monday and Saturday Moss Rose Inn serves bar snack lunches but it is really the excellent beers and ales that draw people here. That, and the wonderful bowling green. The pub has eight bowling teams but if you would like to have a go do call at lunchtime and Phil will let you borrow a set of bowls.

Moss Rose Inn, Heyes Lane, Alderley Edge Tel: 01625 584747

Alderley Edge itself is a popular area of countryside, rich in history and legend. Walkers will enjoy the network of footpaths through the woods which offer superb views of the surrounding scenery. A short walk takes you to the Wizard's Well, where you will find the following verse: "Drink of this and take thy fill, for the water falls at the Wizard's will." Local legend tells of a farmer who was on his way to Macclesfield market to sell his white horse, when he was stopped by a wizard who wished to buy the horse. The farmer refused, but he failed to sell the horse at market, and on his return was forced to sell it to the wizard. The wizard showed the farmer a cave barred by iron gates, in which a sleeping army of knights and their steeds lay ready to ride out to save the country in its hour of need. The wizard explained to the farmer that he was a horse short and he rewarded the farmer handsomely. Readers of the highly popular novels by local author Alan Garner, will recognise that this story and the setting of Alderley Edge forms the core of his classic children's story 'The Weirdstone of Brisingamen'.

From Alderley Edge a two mile walk along a footpath will take you to **HARE HILL GARDENS**, a little known National Trust property situated close to the pictureque village of Prestbury. The Victorian gardens include fine woodland, rhododendrons, azaleas, a pergola and a walled garden themed in blue, white and yellow flowers. There is access via gravel paths for the less able.

Hare Hill Gardens, Alderley Edge, Cheshire Tel: 01743 709343

CHELFORD. **THE DIXON ARMS** stands on the main A537 in the heart of the picturesque village of Chelford. This magnificent, 17th century former coaching inn, takes its name from the former Lord of the Manor on whose land the Dixon Arms once stood. The inn also has an interesting and varied history; when a farmhouse, it was famous for brewing its own beer and, in the railway age, it was used as a temporary mortuary when there was a terrible railway accident nearby.

The Dixon Arms

Today, managed by Josephine and Geoff Irlam and their daughter Jayne, the Dixon Arms offers the very best in hospitality. There are eleven en suite guest bedrooms and two excellent restaurants. As well as serving a delicious range of tasty dishes from around the world from the menu there is also a daily specials board that is well worth reading. At the rear of the inn is a smashing bowling green, perfect for lazy summer evenings.

The Dixon Arms, Knutsford Road, Chelford Tel: 01625 861313

THE EGERTON ARMS is situated on the A537 Knutsford to Macclesfield Road and is well worth calling in to for refreshment. This is a great 'local' providing outstanding home made food and good service. There's a really good pub menu with lots of selection, choose from the restaurant specials, bar snacks or Sunday Carvery; ample portions and very good value. When you have ordered your meal, enjoy a glass of Real ale and browse at the old memorabilia on display. Children are welcome and have their own room and outdoor play area. Don't pass this by!

The Egerton Arms, Knutsford Road, Chelford, Cheshire. Tel: 01625 861366

NETHER ALDERLEY, which lies on the A34, is where you will find a delightful 15th-century watermill that has been restored by the National Trust. The red sandstone walls are almost hidden under the huge sweep of its stone tiled roof. Inside is the original Elizabethan woodwork and Victorian mill machinery which is still in working order, with two overshot wheels powering the mill. A nearby spring produces mineral water which is bottled and sold locally. If you've time, visit the 14th century church of St Mary with its unusual richly carved pew set up on a wall like an opera box and reached by a flight of steps outside.

Nether Alderley Mill, Nether Alderley, Cheshire Tel: 01625 523012

PRESTBURY, situated between Wilmslow and Macclesfield, is a picturesque village, not surprisingly a regular winner of the Best Kept Village title.

Its attractive tree-lined High Street is flanked by old coaching inns and black and white buildings which mingle with the mellow red brick work of later Georgian houses. **THE CHURCH OF ST. PETER**, which dates from the 13th century, still maintains a tradition which began in

1577. A curfew bell is rung every day at 8pm during the autumn and winter, with the number of strokes corresponding to the date of the month. In the churchyard is a glass case containing pieces of carved sandstone thought to have been part of a cross erected here in the 8th century by early Saxon converts to Christianity. The fragments were discovered embedded in a wall during restoration work, where they had been hidden for 400 years. Close by is a building known as the Norman Chapel, though only the impressive doorway actually dates from Norman times.

Opposite the church is a striking magpie timber-framed building which was once the vicarage. It is said that during the Commonwealth, the rightful incumbent was debarred from preaching in the church by the Puritans, and so the Rector retaliated by addressing his parishoners from the tiny balcony.

PRESTBURY'S Wine Bar and Bistro also stands opposite the old Church and village stocks in the heart of the village. In a former existence the building was a bakers and cafe on the ground floor whilst accommodating a fondly remembered Private Members Club (possibly a bordello!) which boasted the name, The Regency.

Today, Michael Hulme's Prestbury's is certainly popular but for more respectable reasons. During the day, the extensive menu offers anything from warm croissants and continental style breakfast through to a more robust, and equally tasty, lunch. With a wide variety of delicious cakes and patisseries available, afternoon tea is not to be missed. However, come evening, the lights are dimmed and Prestbury's turns into a warm and friendly bistro and wine bar with a selective evening menu. The watchwords here are fabulous food at sensible prices and you will not be disappointed. An excellent place for a relaxed and enjoyable evening out, there is also a sumptuous banqueting suite that can be hired for every type of private celebration.

Prestbury's, The Village, Prestbury Tel: 01625 820320

YE OLDE ADMIRAL RODNEY inn sits on the main street, close to the River Bollin. The building dates back to the late 17th century and before being an inn was part of a row of cottages and then a brewhouse. Full of character and charm that befits of a building of this age, Ye Olde Admiral Rodney is a true old English village inn where good ale and gentle conservation can always be found. Managed by Gail and Peter Brady, the inn serves meals at lunchtime from Monday to Saturday, stays open all day on Fridays and children are welcome to come and eat here. With the well kept ales and smashing atmosphere, Ye Olde Admiral Rodney is sure to become one of your favourite pubs that you will return to time and time again.

Ye Olde Admiral Rodney, Prestbury Tel: 01625 828078

THE BRIDGE HOTEL is situated in the midst of rural Cheshire in the heart of the lovely and unspoilt village of Prestbury. Standing close to the River Bollin, the hotel was once a row of timbered cottages dating back to 1626. In 1745, one of the cottages provided a night's lodging to Bonnie Prince Charlie as he travelled south with his Scottish army. Some 200 years later, in 1952, the entire row of cottages was developed into the hotel by the Grange family. Still in the family today it is run by Elaine and Norman.

The Bridge Hotel

The hotel as 23 en-suite bedrooms, divided between the older, half-

314

timbered part of the hotel and the new wing, which overlooks the river. These rooms, along with the rest of the hotel, have been decorated and furnished to a very high standard to provide comfort in a relaxing atmosphere. The restaurant has made a name for itself for providing fine and hearty English cuisine and is popular for both lunch and dinner. There excellent wine cellar and the cocktail bar is the perfect place to relax both before and after your meal. With a conference centre and a banqueting suite, the Bridge Hotel has a lot to offer whilst it also maintains a warm and friendly atmosphere.

The Bridge Hotel, Prestbury Tel: 01625 829326

Also situated in this prestigious and picturesque village is a charming 300 year old stone fronted, Grade II listed cottage known as **BROOKS COTTAGE**. It has recently been refurbished to a very high standard and is available for short lets. The quality furnishings are delightful and the cottage is fully equipped. The modern kitchen has every convenience and will seat seven people. Upstairs there is a double bedroom with en-suite bathroom, and a twin room with adjacent private power-shower room with all facilities. Very generous fitted cupboards are provided throughout. A comfortable lounge has colour television, a private payphone, and a sofabed gives the cottage accommodation for six adults. A conservatory leads to the pleasant garden and car park. Rates include utilities and provisions for a full English breakfast. Within five minutes on foot there are six restaurants, two pubs and all the services and shops of the village. Ideally situated for Manchester Airport, the City and Motorway network.

No.1 Brook Cottage, Pearl Street, Prestbury, Cheshire. Tel: 01625 828697

MACCLESFIELD, nestling below the adjacent Peak District hills, was once an important silk manufacturing town and a market town with its origins in medieval times. The town's link with silk developed in the 17th century from a cottage industry, expanding in 1743 when Charles Roe built the first silk mill. There then followed a rapid expansion, the industry reaching its peak of activity in the 19th century. Man-made fabrics are still manufactured in the town, but textiles no longer dominate its economy.

Appropriately enough, Macclesfield has the country's only **SILK MUSEUM**, which covers all the aspects of the silk industry, from cocoon to loom. The museum has an award-winning audio-visual presentation of the history of the Macclesfield Silk Industry and there are also fascinating exhibitions on the silk route, silk cultivation, fashion, and other uses of silk. Nearby **PARADISE MILL**, which was built in the 1820s, is now a working museum demonstrating silk weaving on 26 jacquard hand looms. Exhibitions and restored workshops and living rooms capture the working conditions and lives of mill workers in the 1930s. It is also possible to buy locally-made silk products at the museum.

Macclesfield Sunday School was built in 1813 for the education of local working children. It was finally closed in 1970 and as well as housing the Silk Museum, it forms the **HERITAGE CENTRE** with exhibitions on Macclesfield's rich and exciting past and on the story of the Sunday School itself.

On the outskirts of the town is **WEST PARK MUSEUM**, a purpose-built museum founded in 1898 by the Brocklehurst family. The collection includes Egyptian artefacts, fine and decorative arts, and paintings by Charles Tunnicliffe, the well-known artist. The museum itself is set in one of the oldest public parks in England and has reputedly the largest bowling green in the country.

Unfortunately, **MACCLESFIELD 'CASTLE '**has not fared as well over the years as many of the town's other older buildings. It was originally located at the top of Backwallgate and was built in the 14th century for John de Macclesfield, an official at the court of Richard II. An unusual building, it was described in the 16th century as a 'huge place all of stone in a manner of a castle - but now gone much to decay'. By 1932 all that was left standing were the dilapidated remains of the porch, which once led to the great hall and now served as part of an ironmonger's store. During subsequent redevelopment work in the town centre the stones were dismantled, but as part of the new extension to the town hall may be seen in an inner quadrangle.

Modern Macclesfield is an interesting town well worth exploring, with small narrow cobbled streets and alleyways, many lined with black and white timbered houses and old weavers' cottages. There is a fine market square with a market cross and, set on a hill, a handsome church that was originally founded by King Edward and Queen Eleanor. It is probably best viewed from the railway station first, before climbing the 108 steps to view its interior.

The outstanding **OSCAR'S RESTAURANT AND CAFE** is situated in Chestergate in the heart of Macclesfield. Owned and personally run by Judith and Doug Hughes for the past three years, Oscar's is open all day, most days, right through to late evening. During the day, this is very much a cafe, in the continental sense of the word. The menu includes delicious filled sandwiches, hot or cold, filled baked potatoes, salads and light snacks. In the evening the menu changes to provide a tasty selection of dishes from around the world in a pleasant and relaxed atmosphere. Not surprisingly there is a team of chefs, supervised by Judith, who provide this wonderful fayre. A popular eating and meeting place it is a good idea to book a table on Friday and Saturday evenings.

Oscar's Restaurant and Café, 66 Chestergate, Macclesfield
Tel: 01625 611089

THE GEORGE HOTEL stands on the corner of Jordangate in the centre of Macclesfield. Privately owned for the past 6 years, the hotel dates back to the very early days of the 19th century and it was once used as a staging post for the Royal Mail coaches - they used to change their horses here.

The George Hotel

Formerly called the Palace Hotel, this is place full of character, especially downstairs, where the old cellar and drive through passage from the carriages has been turned into a super bar area. Today, The George offers excellent accommodation for the business person and the holiday maker alike in any one of its twelve en-suite bedrooms. Priding itself on its efficient but informal service and friendly atmosphere you will not be disappointed. The restaurant, where all the food is home-cooked, specialises in English and Greek cuisine.

The George Hotel, Jordangate, Macclesfield Tel: 01625 615561

ST MICHAEL AND ALL ANGELS CHURCH was extended at the end of the 19th century, but it retains its 14th century core. Inside is the Legh Chapel, built in 1422 to receive the body of Piers Legh who fought at Agincourt and died at the Siege of Meaux. There is also a tablet to John Brownswood, who was a schoolmaster at Stratford-Upon-Avon, and who is said to have taught Shakespeare before becoming headmaster at the local grammar school. In the Savage Chapel you'll find the famous Legh Pardon Brass, recording the medieval practice of selling forgiveness for sins.

Near the Town Hall, on Chestergate, Macclesfield is **KAMOU**, a shoe shop with a difference. Combining olde worlde charm with the latest in fashion for feet, and with a wide range of associated leather goods, this interesting shop is really more an emporium. Quality is the watch word here, in the standard of articles for sale and also in customer care. Here, you will be treated to a high level personal service that is sadly lacking in many chain shoe shops.

Fashion conscious ladies can expect to choose from a vast range of high fashion shoes from Spain and Italy as well as from home, with up to the minute styles from Red or Dead and other fashion houses. There is a wide range of the latest styles from Caterpillar, Kickers and Dr. Marten's. Kamou is also a major stockist of Churches, Grenson, Loake and Timberland footwear. With an excellent selection of travel bags, handbags and belts, all in fine quality leather, this is a wonderful place to shop.

Kamou, 3 Chestergate, Macclesfield Tel: 01625 421884

The **CHATTERBOX TEA ROOMS** are situated in Sunderland Street, in the older part of Macclesfield. A Victorian building, although the low beamed ceilings and open fires make it look and feel older, Di Chopping and Val Gupta opened it as a tea rooms in October 1995 and have not looked back since. Both excellent cooks, the first thing you notice when stepping inside is the delicious, warm smell of home-baking. Open six days a week, there are tables and chairs both on the ground floor and upstairs and, if the weather is fine, a smart terraced area to the rear of the building. The food is absolutely delicious, mouth-watering and besides the menu there are plenty of daily specials and a fine array of puddings and cakes to tempt you. An outstanding estab-lishment, we wish Di and Val every success.

Chatterbox Tea Rooms, 33 Sunderland Street, Macclesfield
Tel: 01625 618024

To the east of the town centre lies the **MACCLESFIELD CANAL**, one of the highest inland waterways in England, running for much of its length at over 500 feet above sea level. It was surveyed by Thomas Telford and opened in 1831, linking the Peak Forest Canal at Marple with the Trent and Mersey Canal near Kidsgrove, a distance of 26 miles. Between Macclesfield and Congleton, the canal descends over a hundred feet in a spectacular series of 12 locks at Bosley, before crossing the river Dane via Telford's handsome iron aqueduct. Another unusual feature of the canal is its roving bridges which carried the towpath across the canal, thus allowing horses to pass beneath the bridge before crossing it, and therefore making it unnecessary to unhitch the tow line.

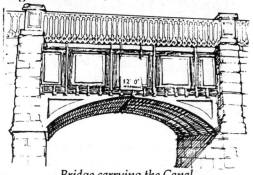

Bridge carrying the Canal

319

The **MACCLESFIELD GARDEN CENTRE** is well signposted from the centre of Macclesfield and lies on the Sutton road which runs from the town. The Lovatt family purchased the land in 1957 when it was derelict allotments and it took them several years before the land was suitably cleared for the growing of top quality trees and shrubs which they are able to offer the public today. Noted for their introduction of new and better varieties of outdoor plants, there is always something new to see at the garden centre. As well as offering a wide range of garden accessories, composts, fertilisers and other bagged products there is also a gift shop stocked to the brim with brassware, pictures, ornaments and silk flowers. Still family run, this is an outstanding garden centre that everyone will enjoy visiting.

Macclesfield Garden Centre, Bullocks Lane, off Byrons Lane, Macclesfield
Tel: 01625 618933

WHITELEY GREEN. THE WINDMILL INN stands one and a half miles off the main A523 in the hamlet of Whiteley Green, midway between Macclesfield and Poynton.

The Windmill Inn

This popular, former 16th century farmhouse is surrounded by the picturesque Cheshire countryside and lies close to the Middlewood Way Walk. Popular with all ages, the Windmill Inn is tastefully furnished with lots of style and character. Outside, there is plenty of room to sit and hanging baskets decorate the front of the Inn in summer. The rear garden also has plenty of room and, in warmer months, there is a bouncy castle to amuse the children. The Windmill Inn is renowned for its delicious food and there is an outstanding menu. It is best to book for the weekends and especially for the Sunday lunchtime carvery. If you enjoy a pint or two of top quality beer this is the place to come with Tetley Pedigree and Kilkenny always on tap.

The Windmill Inn, Holehouse Lane, Whiteley Green, Macclesfield
Tel: 01625 574222

LOWER WITHINGTON. **WELLTROUGH DRIED FLOWERS** is situated in this lovely village. The imaginatively converted farm buildings now house a wealth of dried flowers of every shape, colour and size. There is everything you could possibly want for your arrangements and it is a delight to wander round the displays. Joan Wilkinson, a skilled arranger herself, started the business in 1991 and it really is going well. Apart from the loose dried flowers, there are many silk flowers and arrangements for purchase and Joan also runs a series of workshops and demonstrations which give you all the information you need to create the perfect displays.

Welltrough Dried Flowers, Welltrough Hall Farm, Lower Withington, Near Macclesfield Tel: 01477 571616

BOSLEY. Take time to visit the **HARRINGTON ARMS** at Bosley. Although only recently arrived at the Harrington, Gunther, a top of the range Chef, has been in the trade in one capacity or another for nearly thirty years, most recently as the Catering Manager at the Prestbury Golf Club. He and his wife Heather have wonderful personalities and have already revived the Harrington Arms. Situated on the A523 between Macclesfield and Leek, the inn has outstanding scenic views in all directions over the beautiful Cheshire countryside. The locals are delighted to find such an improvement in their ale and enjoy such good food available every evening. Bookings are now advised at weekends.

Harrington Arms, Leek Road, Bosley, Cheshire. Tel: 01260 223224

ALLGREVE. **THE ROSE AND CROWN** stands high up in the Peak District on the A54 at Allgreve. Surrounded in every direction by spectacular scenery, the pub is a long, low, stone-built building, constructed to withstand the bleak winters of the area. Whatever the weather outside, you can be sure of a warm and friendly welcome from your hosts Sarah and Craig Stevens. With roaring log fires, beamed ceilings and exposed brick walls, this is a traditional pub full of character and charm. This picturesque position draws many visitors and there is plenty on offer at the inn itself. A delicious menu of heart-warming, home-cooked dishes is available at lunchtime and in the evening, with a special children's menu. To wash down you lunch or dinner, or just to quench your thirst, there is an excellent range of ales and beers including Robinson's. With a beer garden, watch out for Robinson, the pot bellied pig, this is a pub well worth visiting.

The Rose and Crown, Allgreve, near Macclesfield Tel: 01260 227232

MARTON. **THE DAVENPORT ARMS** building was originally part of the Capesthorne Estate. Standing in the same spot for over 200

322

years, its original purpose was to serve as a court house. During a later period, the building was used as a collecting house where tenants living on the estate paid their rent. Rumour has it that when the rent was paid, the estate would provide them with a free meal or as much ale as they could drink in return, obviously an incentive for prompt payment! It was during the 1950's that the premises finally became a public house serving the local community.

In recent years, an 80 seater restaurant has been added. Situated inside the inn is an exposed well, which has been in existence since the inn was built and is now a feature of the premises. There is a good selection of traditional ales and non-alcoholic drinks, and a large standard bar snack menu which is served Monday lunchtime through to Saturday evening and Sunday evening. Traditional Roast Luncheon is available every Sunday plus a reduced bar menu; a vegetarian selection is always available. (Food is not available on Monday evenings). Outside is a large, well-equipped play area for children and ample facilities for parking. In addition, Caravan Rallies may be booked on a two and a half acre site.

The Davenport Arms, (Allan & Joan Morris), Marton, Macclesfield, Cheshire. Tel: 01260 224269

For the nature lover **THE MIDDLEWOOD WAY** is a ten-mile, traffic-free country trail which follows a scenic route from Macclesfield to Marple, passing through Bollington. Open to cyclists, walkers and horse riders, this proves highly popular in the summer months and seasonal cycle hire is available, complete with child seats if required.

ADLINGTON. In the village of Adlington is **THE MINERS ARMS**. Originally this was a farmhouse and dates back to the mid-19th century. The darts area is now where the shippen once was. The building has been extended but is still made up of a series of little rooms and always feels intimate. The beer here is excellent and the food is well presented. Recently acquired by Greenalls brewery, the pub also has a Millers Kitchen restaurant and its extensive regular menu is supplemented by a delicious daily specials board. The conservatory-style restaurant area is non-smoking and opens onto the garden. Children will find a play area outside, and the garden is used for barbeques in the summer. As well as standing on the Middlewood Way, the well known scenic walk between Marple and Macclesfield, The Miners Arms is also very close to Lyme View Marina and is a regular stopping off point for canal users. The tranquil location makes this an ideal place to stop when visiting the area.

The Miners Arms, Wood Lane North, Adlington Tel: 01625 872731

Lovers of historic country houses would be well advised to pay a visit to **ADLINGTON HALL**, which lies off the A523 Stockport - Macclesfield road. It has been the home of the Leghs of Adlington since 1315 and is now one of Cheshire's most popular attractions. Quadrangular in shape, this magnificent Manor House has two distinctive styles of architecture, with two sides of the courtyard and the East Wing built in the familiar black and white half-timbered fashion so common in Cheshire, whilst the later additions of the south front and west wing being of red brick. There is much to see as you tour the hall, with beautifully polished wooden floors and lovely antique furnishings enhancing the air of elegance and grandeur and each room has information packs and quiz sheets to challenge the younger visitor.

The Great Hall is a magnificent sight, a vast room of lofty proportions that set off perfectly the exquisitely painted walls and the major feature, a beautifully preserved 17th century organ which was played by no less a fiure than George Frederick Handel when he visited the Hall in the mid-18th century. Outside within the lovely landscaped grounds there are various follies which are being carefully restored.

From around the 12th century, the Legh family of Adlington also had blood ties with the Legh family of nearby Lyme Park, the younger son of Thomas Legh becoming the first Piers Legh of Lyme. However, there was little or no interbreeding and the connection through later centuries was one of friendly neighbours rather than relatives, a relationship that continued even after Lyme Park had been sold to the National Trust.

Adlington Hall, Adlington, Macclesfield Tel: 01625 829206/820201

WOODFORD. BARTON GRANGE GARDEN CENTRE is situated in this picturesque village. Covering some 13 1/2 acres, the centre was newly constructed in September 1995 and it really does have everything for the keen amateur or ardent professional gardener. Well laid out, with plenty of greenhouses to wonder through, you do not have to be a gardener to appreciate the magnificent plants on display. After all that walking about, if you feel a little peckish, the Farmhouse restaurant is the ideal place to revitalise yourself. The restaurant serves a wonderful breakfast, luncheon and afternoon tea menu and caters for all ages. All in all a good day out for all the family, young and old.

Barton Grange Garden Centre, Woodford Tel: 0161 439 0745

POYNTON. AJ's WINE BAR is situated on Park Lane, Poynton, just 250 yards from the junction with the main A523.

AJ's Wine Bar

Owned and personally run by Andrew Jacks, hence the name, the wine bar has quickly established itself as the place to be seen in the area.

Open all day, everyday, you can quench your thirst from an array of wines, draught beers and lagers and bottled beers, the choice is yours. With a pleasant and relaxed atmosphere during the day, at night it can get very busy and the pace hots up. At present, tasty and imaginative snacks are served until 2pm but later this year a fuller menu will be available. Do not be deceived by the small and discreet frontage, this is a wonderful place to enjoy a drink and some excellent company.

AJ's Wine Bar, 42 Park Lane, Poynton Tel: 01625 875350

The attractive **VERNON ARMS** is situated on the main A523 in South Poynton and stands on the site of the original pub of that name. Popular with locals and visitors to the area for its excellent wholesome food and well kept ales. The Vernon Arms caters for everyone; couples, the whole family, the disables and its facilities are second to none. Though the pub's raised restaurant area can seat up to 160 people in comfort, such is the layout that you are not aware of many of your fellow diners. As well as a wonderful and extensive menu, there is a children's menu and a daily specials board. Outside, the safe children's play area is just the thing whilst you sit outside and relax with your drink.

Vernon Arms, South Poynton Tel: 01625 871639

LYME PARK lies half a mile west of DISLEY village on the main A6 Stockport to Buxton road and provides a fun and fascinating day out for the whole family. Set within 1377 acres of deer park, moorland and beautiful formal gardens, this was the country seat of the Legh family for over 600 years until it was donated to the National Trust in 1946 by Richard Legh, 3rd Lord Newton. The imposing Hall is an interesting blend of Georgian, Elizabethan and Regency architecture and contains a wealth of fine period furniture, paintings and tapestries as well as a splendid collection of English clocks; it recently featured as the setting for the popular television dramatisation of *Pride and Prejudice*. Outside you can stroll through the exquisite Victorian Gardens which include an Orangery by Wyatt. With free roaming herds of Red Deer, the unusual landmark known as The Cage and its own Countryside Centre, a trip to Lyme Park will provide you with a day out to remember.

Lyme Park, Disley, Stockport Tel: 01663 762023

HENBURY. THE COCK INN is situated on the main A537 at Henbury village, which is approximately two miles from Macclesfield town centre. Innkeeping has run in the Hallworth family for nearly a hundred years and the Cock Inn was taken over by Ray and Gill Hallworth in 1982. Today is it run by their son, Andy and his wife Sara. Dating from the mid 19th century, the Cock Inn may once have been a farmhouse.

The Cock Inn

The interior of the premises now offers a warm welcome to both locals and visitors and the extra personal care and attention that shows this is still very much a family business. As well as keeping an excellent pint of real ale, including Robinsons Best Bitter, Hatters Mild and Old Tom, the Cock Inn is well known in the area for its delicious food. There is a cosy restaurant where you would be advised to book a table on Friday and Saturday evenings. The special Cockerel's Menu for children makes this an ideal place to bring the whole family. Across the road, the inn has some 15 acres of land and here the Hallworth family have a range of animals such as Shetland ponies, goats and donkeys for you and your children to enjoy.

The Cock Inn, Chelford Road, Henbury, Macclesfield Tel: 01625 425659

FLORA is a wonderful garden centre, flower and gift shop situated on the main A537 road between Macclesfield and Knutsford at the village of Henbury. For many years Dorothy and Les Cornall ran a florists in Macclesfield and, as the shop began to expand, they purchased the land where Flora now stands in 1969. Starting on a small scale the garden centre and gift shop has also grown, latterly with the help of their daughter Carey.

Flora really is a treasure trove. As well as the garden centre the shop has a wealth of magnificent displays and a wide variety of stock. There are artificial, dried and fresh flowers, potters and basket ware, candles and ribbons, shells, pot pourri and a superb display of Christmas decorations towards the end of the year. Flora is always pleased to create a personal floral display and there is also the tea rooms to quench your thirst or fill that empty gap.

Flora, Henbury, Macclesfield Tel: 01625 422428/423957

BOLLINGTON. MAURO'S Italian restaurant, on the main street in the heart of Bollington village, features in many of the good restaurant guides. Well known in the area, this restaurant provides an authentic taste of Italy in the heart of rural England. Owned and personally run by chef Enzo Mauro, this is the place to come for a sophisticated lunch or dinner in intimate and cosy surroundings.

The food, as you would expect, is out of this world. The house specialities include home-made pasta, fish dishes and the wonderful puddings and sweets. As well as the extensive menu there is always a couple of daily specials that make use of the freshest ingredients from the markets. There is also a super wine list with over 60 labels to choose from ranging from the classical to new world vineyards.

Mauro's, 88 Palmerston Street, Bollington, near Macclesfield
Tel: 01625 573898

An interesting feature above Bollington on Kerridge Hill is **WHITE NANCY**, a distincitve bell-shaped structure, erected as a monument and landmark to commemorate the battle of Waterloo in 1815. It's worth climbing up to the top (footpaths lead from the centre of town to the summit) for a magnificent view of the town with its grey mills and the great railway viaduct that cuts across the town and across the Cheshire Plain. You can continue along the ridge that forms Kerridge Hill, itself another spectacular viewpoint.

And so we reach the end of our tour of Lancashire, Cheshire and the Isle of Man, having uncovered just some of the hidden treasures of the region. No doubt you will discover a few of your own, but we feel sure that any places you visit would be pleased to know that you heard about them through Hidden Places.

Tourist Information Centres

ACCRINGTON Town Hall, Blackburn Rd, Lancs BB5 1NT

Tel:01254 386807 fax: 01254 380291

ALTRINCHAM Stamford New Rd, Cheshire WA14 !EJ

Tel: 061 941 7337 fax: 0161 926 8336

BIRKENHEAD Woodside Ferry Terminal, Merseysde L41 6DU

Tel: 0151 647 6780 fax: 0151 6662448

BLACKBURN King George's Hall, Northgate, Lancs BB2 1AA

Tel: 01254 53277 fax: 01254 683536

BLACKPOOL 1 Clifton Street, Blackpool, Lancs FY1 1LY

Tel: 01253 21623 fax: 01253 26368

BLACKPOOL Pleasure Beach, 11 Ocean Boulevard, South Promenade, Lancs FY4 1PL

Tel: 01253 403223 fax: 01253 408718

BOLTON Town Hall, Victoria Square, Lancs BL1 1RU

Tel: 01204 364333 fax: 01204 398101

BURNLEY Burnley Mechanics, Manchester Road, Lancs BB11 1JA

Tel: 01282 455485 fax: 01282 457428

BURY The Met Arts Centre, Market Street, Lancs BL9 0BN

Tel: 0161 7055111 fax: 0161 7055915

CHARNOCK RICHARD M6 Service Area (Northbound), Lancs PR7 5NG

Tel: 01257 793773

CHESTER Town Hall, Northgate Street, Cheshire CH1 2HJ

Tel: 01244 317962 fax: 01244 400420

CHESTER Visitor Centre, Vicars Lane, Cheshire CH1 1QX

Tel: 01244 351609 fax: o1244 319819

CHESTER Railway Station, Station Rd, Cheshire CH1 3NT

Tel: 01244 322220 fax: 01244 322221

CONGLETON Town Hall, High Street, Cheshire CW2 1BN

Tel: 01260 271095 fax: 01260 298243

FLEETWOOD Ferry Dock, The Esplanade, Lancs

Tel: 01253 773953 fax: 01253 899000

FORTON, M6 Services, Bay Horse, Lancaster, Lancs LA2 9DU

Tel: 01524 792181 fax: 01524 792676

GARSTANG, Discovery Centre, High Street, Lancs PR3 1FU

Tel: 01995 602125 fax: 01253 899000

KNUTSFORD Council Offices, Toft Road, Cheshire, WA16 6TA

Tel: 01565 632611

LANCASTER 29 Castle Hill, Lancaster, Lancs LA1 1YN

Tel: 01524 847472 fax: 01524 847 472

LIVERPOOL Merseyside Welcome Centre, Clayton Square , L1 1RQ

Tel: 0151 709 3631

LIVERPOOL Atlantic Pavilion, Albert Dock, Lpool L3 4AA

Tel: 0151 7088854 fax: 0151 7088129

LYTHAM ST. ANNES 290 Clifton Drive South, Lancs FY8 1LH

Tel: 01253 725610

MACCLESFIELD Council Offices, Town Hall, Cheshire, SK10 IDX

Tel: 01625 504114

MANCHESTER TheVisitorCentre, Town Hall Extension, Lloyd Street, M60 2LA

Tel: 0161 234 3157 fax: 0161 2369900

MANCHESTER AIRPORT International Arrivals Area, T1 & T2

Tel: 0161 436 3344

NANTWICH Church Walk, Cheshire, CW5 5RG

Tel: 01270 610983

OLDHAM Central Library, Union Street, Lancs OL1 1DN

Tel: 0161 6271024 fax: 0161 6271025

PRESTON The Guildhall, Lancaster Road, Lancs PR1 1HT

Tel: 01772 253731

RAWTENSTALL 41/45 Kay Street, Rossendale, Lancs BB4 7LS

Tel/fax: 01706 226590

ROCHDALE The Clock Tower, Town Hall Tel: 0706 356592

SADDLEWORTH Museum, High Street, Uppermill, Oldham OL3 6HS

Tel: 01457 870336

SOUTHPORT 112 Lord Street, Merseyside, PR8 1NY

Tel: 01704 533333

STOCKPORT Graylaw House, Chestergate, SK1 1NG

Tel: 0161 474 3320/1

TODMORDEN 15 Burnley Road, Lancs OL14 7BU

Tel: 01706 818181

WARRINGTON 21 Rylands Street, Cheshire WA1 1EJ

Tel: 01925 442180 fax: 01925 442149

WIGAN Trencherfield Mill, Wallgate, WN3 4EL

Tel: 01942 825677 fax: 01942 828540

ISLE OF MAN

BALLASALLA Airport Information Desk, Ronaldsway Airport

Tel: 01624 823311

CASTLETOWN The Old Grammar School, The Car Park

DOUGLAS Harris Promenade

Tel: 01624 686766

LAXEY Old Fire House, nr. Laxey Wheel

Tel: 01624 862007

ONCHAN Village Commisioners Public Library, 10 Elm Tree Road

Tel: 01624 621228

PEEL Town Hall, Derby Road

Tel: 01624 842341

INDEX

THE HIDDEN PLACES

If you would like to have any of the titles currently available in this series, please complete this coupon and send to:

M & M Publishing Ltd
118 Ashley Road,
Hale, Altrincham, Cheshire, WA14 2UN

	Each
Scotland	
Ireland	£ 5.90 ......
Northumberland & Durham	£ 5.90 ......
The Lake District & Cumbria	£ 5.90 ......
Yorkshire and Humberside	£ 5.90 ......
Lancashire & Cheshire	£ 5.90 ......
North Wales	£ 5.90 ......
South Wales	£ 5.90 ......
The Welsh Borders	£ 5.90 ......
Somerset Avon Gloucestershire & Wiltshire	£ 5.90 ......
Thames and Chilterns	£ 5.90 ......
East Anglia (Norfolk & Suffolk)	£ 5.90 ......
The South East (Surrey, Sussex and Kent)	£ 5.90 ......
Dorset, Hampshire and the Isle of Wight	£ 5.90 ......
Heart of England	£ 5.90 ......
Devon and Cornwall	£ 5.90 ......
Set of any Five	£20.00
Total	£

Price includes Postage and Packing

NAME..

ADDRESS...

....

...............................POST CODE.......................................

Please make cheques payable to: M & M Publishing Ltd